AF323731

Understanding
Japan–China Relations

Theories and Issues

Understanding Japan–China Relations

Theories and Issues

Ming Wan

George Mason University , USA

World Scientific

NEW JERSEY · LONDON · SINGAPORE · BEIJING · SHANGHAI · HONG KONG · TAIPEI · CHENNAI · TOKYO

Published by

World Scientific Publishing Co. Pte. Ltd.

5 Toh Tuck Link, Singapore 596224

USA office: 27 Warren Street, Suite 401-402, Hackensack, NJ 07601

UK office: 57 Shelton Street, Covent Garden, London WC2H 9HE

Library of Congress Control Number: 2015021588

British Library Cataloguing-in-Publication Data
A catalogue record for this book is available from the British Library.

UNDERSTANDING JAPAN–CHINA RELATIONS
Theories and Issues

ISBN 978-981-4689-22-9

In-house Editors: Dong Lixi/Prathima

Typeset by Stallion Press
Email: enquires@stallionpress.com

Printed in Singapore

Dedication

This book is dedicated to Anne, Annaliese and Maggie.

Preface

This book follows up on my 2006 book *Sino-Japanese Relations: Interaction, Logic, and Transformation* based on new developments in Sino-Japanese relations and new research conducted in Japan, China and elsewhere since 2006. As a visiting professor at Keio University in Tokyo from August 2010 to August 2012, I had the opportunity to witness several major incidents in Japan's exchange with China up close and gained new insight into the working of the pivotal relationship between the two Asian great powers. The book covers major issues not discussed in the 2006 book, namely the September 2010 Chinese fishing boat collision incident, cross-Strait relations, the Trans-Pacific Partnership (TPP) negotiations, and China's suspension of rare earth exports to Japan. It also revisits the issues of official development assistance and private lawsuits for forced labor during the Sino-Japanese war. But the book is not meant to be a comprehensive survey of Sino-Japanese relations or merely an update to the 2006 volume. Rather, it explores a variety of theoretical understandings of the China–Japan relationship, namely relationship management, domestic politics, national identities, and coevolution. The Sino-Japanese relationship is indeed a complex subject matter and one gains insight by examining the relationship from different analytical angles.

This book uses Japan–China relations for its title because much of the writing in this book is Japan-centered. More of the published works integrated into this book resulted from Japan-related projects rather than China-related ones, and much of the new writing results from insights gained during a 2010–2012 academic leave in Japan.

This book uses the Asian name order of putting the family name first for citations of Japanese and Chinese language writings, but follows the Western practice of listing the family name last for all publications in English.

Ming Wan

Acknowledgments

The book draws from six journal articles and book chapters in print, as listed below. These published works have been revised, updated and fully integrated. I express my gratitude to the publishers for permission for these works to be reproduced in this book.

Chapter 1: Wan, Ming (2011), "Japan–China Relations: Structure or Management?" in Alisa Gaunder, ed., *Routledge Handbook of Japanese Politics*, London: Routledge, 339–349.

Chapter 2: Wan, Ming (2011), "Japan's Party Politics and China Policy: The Chinese Fishing Boat Collision Incident," *The Journal of Social Science* (University of Tokyo) 63 (3–4), 95–110.

Chapter 3: Wan, Ming (2013), "National Identities and Sino-Japanese Relations," in Gilbert Rozman, ed., *National Identities and Bilateral Relations: Widening Gaps in East Asia and Chinese Demonization of the United States*, Washington, D.C. and Stanford: Woodrow Wilson Center Press and Stanford University Press, 65–93.

Chapter 4: Wan, Ming (2013), "The View from Japan," in Gilbert Rozman, ed., *Asia's Uncertain Future: Korea, China's Aggressiveness, and New Leadership*, Washington, D.C.: Korea Economic Institute of America, 83–96.

Chapter 5: Wan, Ming (2014), "Coevolution and Sino-Japanese Tensions," *Asia-Pacific Review* 22 (1), 30–40. Copyright © Institute for International Policy Studies reprinted by permission of (Taylor & Francis Ltd, http://www.tandfonline.com) on behalf of Institute for International Policy Studies.

Chapter 7: Wan, Ming (2007), "Japanese Strategic Thinking toward Taiwan," in Gilbert Rozman, Kazuhiko Togo, and Joseph P. Ferguson, eds., *Japanese Strategic Thought toward Asia*, New York: Palgrave Macmillan, 159–181.

Aspects of this book were presented at workshops and seminars at the following institutions since 2006: American University, the Association of Chinese Professors in Japan, the China Foundation of International and Strategic Studies, the China Institutes of Contemporary International Relations, the Diplomatic Academy of Vietnam, the East–West Center in Washington, the Foreign Service Institute, George Mason University, Keio University, Princeton University, Ritsumeikan Asia Pacific University, Senshu University, the Tokyo Foundation Forum, Ton Duc Thang University, University of California at Berkeley, University of Tokyo, University of Washington, Waseda University, the World Affairs Council Washington, and Yonsei University.

From these academic exchanges, I received extensive feedback and comments as my Sino-Japanese relations project progressed. I benefited from too long a list of organizers and participants to thank individually here, but I do want to give special thanks to Mike Mochizuki and Charles Burress for inviting me to their project "Memory, Reconciliation, Security in the Asia-Pacific Region: Implications for U.S.–Japanese Relations," Quansheng Zhao for his project "Japanese Foreign Policy," Hiwatari Nobuhiro and Jun Saito for their project "Democracy and Diplomacy in Asia," and Gil Rozman for his projects "East Asian National Identities" and "Assessing China's National Identity and Reacting to the Sino-U.S. National Identity Gap." I learned tremendously from participating in those projects, which involved multiple workshops and in-depth discussion by scholars and officials. Chapter 6 of this book is based on a manuscript prepared for the Mochizuki/Burress project.

I have gained much insight into Sino-Japanese relations by talking with countless people who have participated in or observed this important relationship in Japan, China, America and elsewhere. I cannot give their names for confidentiality reasons but would express my deepest appreciation for their trust and friendship, some lasting for over two decades.

I want to thank Professor Kokubun Ryosei for kindly hosting me at Keio University from August 2010 to August 2012. His deep knowledge of China, Japan–China relations and international relations and his dedication to research, teaching and service was truly an inspiration. I learned much from frequent chats with him and from the exciting activities he organized. Keio's China Center and other teaching and research institutions enriched my research and social life. I also enjoyed immensely teaching an undergraduate and a graduate course at Keio.

Last but not the least, I appreciate the encouragement and support from World Scientific Publishing, particularly Lixi Dong and Prathima Venkataraj.

This book is dedicated to my wife and our daughters. We had a wonderful and memorable two-year experience as a family in Tokyo.

Contents

List of Figures

List of Acronyms

AAPC: the American Automotive Policy Council
AIIB: the Asia Infrastructure Investment Bank
ARF: the ASEAN Regional Forum
ASEAN: the Association of Southeast Asian Nations
DAC: Development Co-operation Directorate (of OECD)
DPJ: the Democratic Party of Japan
DPP   the Democratic Progressive Party (of Taiwan)
DSB: the Dispute Settlement Body (of the WTO)
EEZ: exclusive economic zone
EPA: Economic Partnership Agreement
FTA: free trade agreement
FTAAP: the Free Trade Area of the Asia-Pacific
JA: the Central Union of Agricultural Cooperatives
JETRO: the Japan External Trade Organization
JICA: the Japan International Cooperation Agency
JIIA: the Japan Institute of International Affairs
JMA   the Japan Medical Association
JSP: the Japan Socialist Party

KMT: the Kuomintang or the Nationalist Party
(currently of Taiwan)

LDP: The Liberal Democratic Party of Japan

MAFF: Ministry of Agriculture, Forestry and Fisheries (of Japan)

METI: Ministry of Economy, Trade and Industry (of Japan)

MIIT: the Ministry of Industry and Information Technology
(of China)

ODA: Official Development Assistance

OPEC: the Organization of the Petroleum Exporting Countries

PRC: the People's Republic of China

TPP: the Trans-Pacific Partnership Agreement

USTR: U.S. Trade Representative

WTO: the World Trade Organization

About the Author

Ming WAN is Professor of Government and Politics at George Mason University's School of Policy, Government, and International Affairs. His Ph.D. was from the Government Department, Harvard University. He held postdoctoral fellowships at Harvard from the Program on U.S.–Japan Relations, the John M. Olin Institute for Strategic Studies and the Pacific Basin Research Center, and was also a visiting research scholar at Tsukuba University and a George Washington University-Woodrow Wilson International Center for Scholars Luce Fellow in Asian Policy Studies. He was on academic leave in Japan from August 2010 to August 2012, as a visiting professor at Keio University. He has authored *The China Model and Global Political Economy: Comparison, Impact, and Interaction* (Routledge, 2014), *The Political Economy of East Asia: Striving for Wealth and Power* (CQ Press, 2008), *Sino-Japanese Relations: Interaction, Logic, and Transformation* (Woodrow Wilson Center Press/Stanford 2006), *Human Rights in Chinese Foreign Relations: Defining and Defending National Interests* (UPenn, 2001), and *Japan between Asia and the West: Economic Power and Strategic Balance* (M.E. Sharpe, 2001). He has also published in journals such as *Asian Survey, Human Rights Quarterly, Orbis, Pacific Affairs, Pacific Review,*

and *International Studies Quarterly* and in edited volumes. His current research interests include East Asian international relations, international investment protection regimes, and political economy of security.

Part I: Explaining Sino-Japanese Relations

Chapter 1

Structure or Management?

What drives Japan's relations with China? The answers to this question are necessarily complex. A long list of potential causal factors comes to mind readily: Japan's interests and perception, institutions and personalities in Japanese domestic politics, public opinions, the nature of the arenas of interaction, the long shadow of the past, China's approach and actions toward Japan, the U.S. approach and actions toward Asia, and the broader external environment in Asia and the world.

This chapter focuses on one particular dynamic in Japan's relations with China, namely structural constraints and opportunities versus management of the relationship. A bilateral relationship is as much about the world as we make it as the world as is. Accordingly, decision makers need to balance their own responsibilities and the circumstances they encounter. One lesson from examining the ups and downs of the Japan–China relationship in the past two decades is that when the relationship is bad there are things that the governments can do to stabilize the situation and that when the relationship is good we should not forget the underlying causes for concern — real conflictual interests between the two countries.

The first section of the chapter focuses on my structure versus management argument. The next section provides a narrative of Japan–China relations in 2006–2010 to illustrate in greater detail how fluctuations in the relationship may be smoothed out to some extent by careful inter-government management. The third section discusses the current challenges and the last section looks into the future.

Structure versus Management

International politics has been important for Japan–China relations. The strategic realignment among the Soviet Union, China, and the United States allowed Japan and China to normalize diplomatic relations in 1972. That is why despite Japan–China disputes in the 1980s Ezra Vogel, Yuan Ming and Tanaka Akihiko called the period of 1972–1989 the "golden age" among China, Japan, and the United States (Vogel *et al.* 2002). The end of the Cold War removed the anti-Soviet Union strategic basis for a close Japan–China relationship. It also led to a major shift in the Sino-U.S. relationship, which could not but affect the Japan–China relationship. But the end of the Cold War could have led to a different outcome in East Asia. Remember the growing tension between Japan and the United States in the early 1990s? The end of the Cold War also allowed China to improve relations with neighboring countries and elsewhere. Moreover, China had a relationship with the United States markedly better than its relations with Japan in 2002–2006.

Another structural argument frequently heard in both China and Japan is that East Asia has never had two great powers at the same time, which has led to Japan–China tension. This view is based on a false interpretation of both history and the current reality. East Asia has often had several great powers at the same time and currently has more than two. The United States is the dominant player in the region. Energy-rich Russia remains a great power and a rising India wants to be in the thick of things in East Asia. South Korea, North Korea, Taiwan, and Vietnam are armed to the teeth and the Association of Southeast Asian Nations (ASEAN) has played a central role in East Asian regional integration.

Needless to say, the U.S.–Japan alliance has an important impact on the Japan–China relationship. In fact, China's rise and the strengthening or weakening of the U.S.–Japan alliance is arguably the main story of contemporary East Asian international relations (Armitage and Nye 2007). The U.S. factor in Japan–China relations has always been important. In a structural sense, the U.S. factor explains why China and Japan have not been allies and will not be allies in the foreseeable future. The United States is simply more attractive and trustworthy for either Japan or China. The alliance also partly explains why the prospect of direct Japan–China military conflict is limited. The alliance deters China and restrains Japan. At the same time, the alliance has not been a sufficient condition for stability in East Asia. Cooperation with China and economic interdependence are necessary conditions as well.

Some Japanese and Chinese analysts find a ready culprit in the United States for stirring up trouble in Japan–China relations. A view particularly popular in China is that the United States hopes to keep China down by boosting Japan with a stronger alliance. Resentment toward American dominance in East Asia also lingers in Japan. However, this theory works only if the United States acts as an offshore balancer between China and Japan. While some in the United States would like to see the country doing precisely that, a majority in the policy community prefers to see a vibrant American leadership role in East Asia. It is in the U.S. interest to see stability in the region. The United States may benefit to some extent if two major regional powers do not get along; however, it most assuredly does not serve U.S. interests to have China and Japan headed for confrontation. A hegemon wants to have as much control over international events as possible and avoid being dragged into disputes not of its own making.

The United States is involved to some extent over the history dispute. The American policy community was concerned about Japan's worsening relations with China and South Korea over Koizumi's Yasukuni visits. But Koizumi made it clear that he would not listen even if the American government put pressure on him. At the November 16, 2005 summit with President George W. Bush in Kyoto, Koizumi reportedly told Bush that "I will never stop (visiting the shrine), even if asked by the United States not to." He was responding to Bush's question of Koizumi's view of China. Bush did not ask Koizumi about the Yasukuni visit explicitly (*Japan Times* 2006). In the end, the U.S. government was concerned but preferred not to pressure an important ally who supported Bush's Iraq policy and sought to strengthen the alliance with the United States. After Prime Minister Abe Shinzō visited Yasukuni on December 26, 2013, the American government used a much stronger word "disappointment" to express its disapproval, causing a media frenzy in Japan. A wide range of opinions were offered in Japan about the reasons and true meaning of the American statement and about what Japan should do, but Washington had made clear its position on the history issue.

Economic interdependence makes direct conflict less likely. It would be naïve to view economic interdependence as a sufficient condition for peace. But one would also be blind to ignore how close economic ties between Japan and China have served as a positive constraint on their relations. Japan–China trade increased dramatically from $1 billion in 1972 to $312.4 billion in 2014 (State Statistical Bureau of China 1983, 359; China Customs 2015). China is now Japan's largest trading partner and Japan China's third largest trading partner (trailing the European Union, the United States, the Association of Southeast Asia, and Hong Kong). Japan was actually China's largest trading partner in 1994–2003. Japan's "decline" in ranking mainly reflected Japan's stagnant decades since the early 1990s, America's strong economic performance for much of this same period, and the expansion of the European Union to 25 members in May 2004 although the political chill did cool economic ties starting in the late 2000s. Since 2002, China's economic growth has been important for Japan's economic recovery. Thus, Japanese business leaders became more vocal in 2006 to urge the government to improve political relations with China. Conversely, the Japanese government urged Japanese companies to adopt a "China plus one" investment strategy, which essentially meant for Japanese companies to diversify investment away from China since they were already heavily invested in China. Although political tension has cooled economic ties to some extent, the two countries are both World

Trade Organization (WTO) members, which limit their ability to restrict trade flows. With both economies liberalizing, economic agents largely follow market forces in their economic behavior.

Structural constraints are defined broadly here to include those faced by the government at home. Domestic politics in Japan and China have been important. Nationalism is on the rise in both countries. The decline of the progressives in Japanese politics has deprived Beijing of some traditional allies. To make things worse for Beijing, some of the remaining progressive forces are also critical of China's records in human rights and environmental protection. The presidentialization of the Japanese prime minister that began with Koizumi makes it necessary for Japanese political leaders to make a direct appeal to the public rather than making backroom deals only (Kabashima and Steel 2007). As Figure 1.1 shows, the Japanese public's view of China has deteriorated drastically since

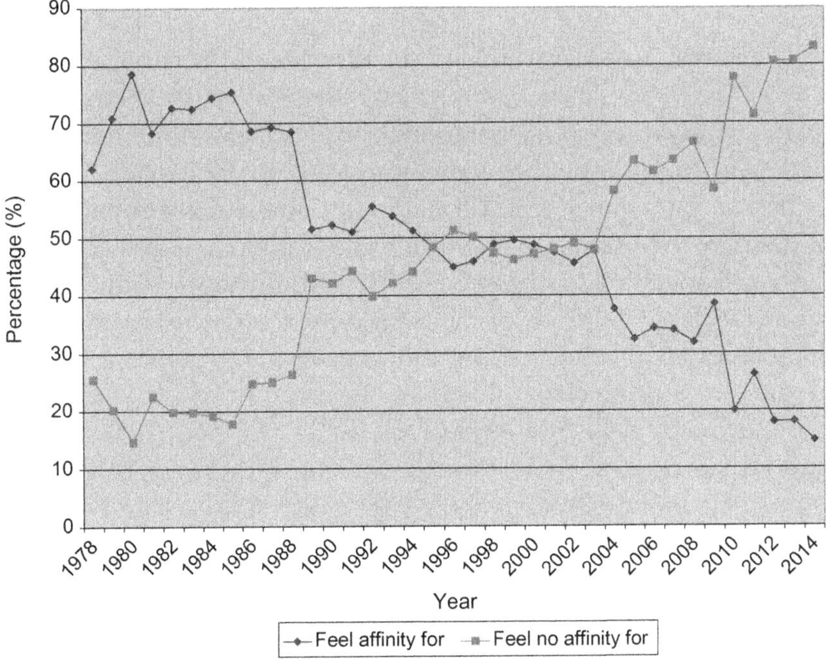

Figure 1.1   Japanese Affinity for China.

Source: Japan Prime Minister's Cabinet Office 2014.

1989. Thus, management of China policy has become more difficult than previously. A majority of Japanese do not want to yield to Chinese pressure even if many want to improve relations with Japan's neighbors.

On the Chinese side, although we do not have reliable tracking polls, various polls show strongly negative Chinese views of Japan (Wan 2006, 69–71; Genron NPO 2014a).[1] The anti-Japan mass demonstrations in April 2005 and August–September 2012 revealed the depth of Chinese anger at Japan. Activists have also utilized the Internet to rally support for anti-Japan activities. All this tie to some extent the government's hand in managing relations with Japan.

Structural explanations offer valuable insights but are often indeterminate. And they do not leave much room for diplomacy. The danger of attributing growing Japan–China tension only to structural problems is to shift responsibility from human agency to the external environment; bad things happen and nobody is responsible for it.

The 2006 upswing, which will be discussed in detail in the chapter, allows us to sharpen our causal analysis of the Japan–China relationship. Whereas, international structure and domestic politics remained important, they were too constant to explain why the swings were so sharp. The Chinese and Japanese governments are not merely responding to domestic and international developments. Rather, leaders made choices and should also be accountable for their policies. There was of course a dramatic downswing after the September 2010 Chinese fishing boat collision incident, which will be discussed in the next chapter.

Tokyo and Beijing should blame their own poor management rather than external factors for the tensions prior to October 2006. By management, I mean choice of strategic goals and ways to

---

[1] As a recent example, a Xinhua News agency poll conducted on November 15, 2014 showed that 83 percent of the surveyed had a negative view of Japan and less than 3 percent had a positive view (*Yomiuri shimbun* online November 16, 2014). While it is difficult to verify the validity of such polls and use those to track changes, but they generally point at a widely shared negative view of Japan in China, no surprise to anyone who studies Sino-Japanese relations.

achieve them in the context of their relations with each other. The root cause of Japan–China tension is the incompatibility of their strategic goals and of the manners by which the two governments chose to play the game. Through the late 1980s, China and Japan had different goals that allowed a balance between them. In the 1970s, China engaged in a strategic game of balancing the Soviet Union. By contrast, Japan focused on economic development, economic statecraft, and reconciliation with its neighbors. China sought economic reform in the 1980s, which Japan welcomed and could take pride in serving as a teacher. Both China and Japan were principled and flexible. China emphasized political principles such as history and Taiwan. Japan focused on legal or international principles when negotiating over end of war or over China's cancellation of commercial contracts in the early 1980s. But Japan and China are now pursuing similar objectives to become great powers (Rozman 1999 and 2002; Pyle 2007; Deng 2008). Japan is no longer satisfied with being just an economic power. China has acted like a great political power for some time now but increasingly has the economic might to back its claim. Two great powers do not have to clash, particularly in a world of globalization and American dominance. But China and Japan have chosen to view each other's rise with suspicion and to compete and undercut each other for regional leadership, energy supplies, and global influence. Rising nationalist sentiments in China and Japan are largely incompatible. Chinese nationalism is heavily defined in terms of anger at Japan. Thus, Chinese nationalists want to see Japan apologize for the past. Japan's nationalism, as defined now, is about feeling good and proud about Japan, which apologies to foreigners would undermine.

Prior to 2006 both the Chinese and Japanese governments wanted to improve their relationship since the mid-1990s and they adopted policy accordingly. But Japan–China relations continued to deteriorate due to two major management problems. First, both countries focused on persuading or forcing the other side to change views while making little adjustment to their own strategic goals. Second, the positive gestures from the two governments did not coincide. Japan reached out to China in the early 1990s and some

Japanese urged their country to "re-enter Asia", partly due to resentment over American trade pressure during the first term of the Clinton administration. But China took a tough stand on Japan as soon as it re-emerged from the international isolation around 1994. After President Jiang Zemin's visit to Japan in 1998, which was widely viewed as having worsened the relationship with Japan, the Chinese government took measures to improve relations with Tokyo. But that gesture was not sufficiently reciprocated since many in Japan viewed Japan's tougher stance as making Beijing shift its position in the first place. Why change if you think your approach is working?

A Sharp Turn for Better in Late 2006

The dynamic between structure and management in Japan–China relations was vividly revealed in late 2006. What a difference a few months made in Japan's relations with China! After Prime Minister Koizumi Junichirō and the Chinese leaders did not visit each other's nation for over four years and did not meet even when they attended multilateral summits for almost two years, his successor Abe Shinzō met Chinese President Hu Jintao twice and Premier Wen Jiabao twice within a 100 days after early October 2006. The fact that the Japanese and Chinese leaders were talking again made it possible to discuss more seriously the sensitive issues in the relationship.

This turn of events raises two questions. First, why did we see such a dramatic upswing in the bilateral relationship? Second, would this improvement last?

The drama in the Japan–China relationship in 2006–2010 highlights the fact that although the international system and domestic politics have set the parameters for the interaction between the two countries and have been decisive at times, this relationship has always been highly personal and emotional. The relationship during the five plus years of the Koizumi administration was worse than it should have been judging by the structural imperative and domestic politics. A correction from that low was natural but efforts by the Abe administration and the Hu government made the rebound bigger than warranted given the underlying sources of tension.

Abe became prime minister on September 26, 2006 and selected China as his first stop for overseas visits. In the several rounds of discussions prior to his visit, the two sides talked about the thorny issue of prime ministerial visits to Yasukuni Shinto Shrine, which was at the core of bilateral tension during the Koizumi administration. The Chinese government had first rejected mutual visits and then meetings in third countries due to Koizumi's annual visits to the shrine. The Chinese officials wanted to make sure that Abe had decided not to visit the shrine. But Abe was decisively vague about his intention, which was apparently sufficient in the end for Beijing to shift position. Abe did express his desire to adhere to Prime Minister Murayama Tomiichi's 1995 speech that acknowledged Japan's war responsibilities more explicitly than previously. Abe met Hu, Speaker Wu Bangguo, and Wen, the top three leaders in China busy with the annual meeting of the Chinese Communist Party Central Committee at the time.

The Beijing summit set in motion a series of positive events. Abe and Hu met at the Asia–Pacific Economic Cooperation (APEC) meeting in Hanoi in November 2006. Abe and Wen met at the ASEAN Plus Three summit and the East Asian summit in Cebu, the Philippines on January 14, 2007. At the Cebu meeting, Wen accepted Abe's invitation to visit Japan. During his April 11–13, 2009 visit to Japan, Wen spoke at the Japanese Diet, a first for a Chinese Premier.

Most sensitive issues on the bilateral agenda were discussed in a better political atmosphere. At his meeting with Hu in October 2006, Abe proposed a bilateral joint history project, which would hold its first meeting by end of the year. At the APEC meeting in November 2006, the Japanese and Chinese foreign ministers created the framework for the project. In a lightening speed, the ten-member teams on both sides were assembled and the first meeting was held in Beijing on December 26–27, 2006. The Japanese and Chinese governments agreed to speed up the pace of disposal of chemical weapons left in China. Japan has legal obligations but this announcement of a faster pace added another positive note.

In the security realm, the legal experts from Japan and China met in early January 2007 to discuss the overlapping claims of exclusive economic zones (EEZs) in the East China Sea. After a suspension of almost two years, the Japan–China Defense talks resumed. As a symbol of improved relations, the two sides agreed on navy mutual visits. The Chinese and Japanese governments first talked about such an exchange in 2000 but the planned visits were repeatedly suspended due to China's protests over Koizumi's Yasukuni visits.

In the economic arena, the Japanese and Chinese governments agreed to create a ministerial level economic affairs meeting between the two countries to discuss issues such as renewable energy resources and intellectual property rights (IPR). The new mechanism was modeled after the China–U.S. strategic economic dialogue held for the first time in December 2006. The Japanese and Chinese officials also began a joint study of a free trade agreement (FTA) among China, Japan, and South Korea. In December 2006, Japan's Mizuho Corporate Bank and Bank of Tokyo-Mitsubishi were among the nine foreign banks, the Chinese government allowed to convert their branches in China to corporations.

Taking a cue from the improved state-to-state relations, the Japanese public's image of China saw a modest rebound. According to an annual survey conducted by the Prime Minister's Office in October 2006, about the time Abe visited China, the percentage of the surveyed who felt a sense of affinity for China was 34.3 percent, an increase of 1.9 percent from the previous year and the percentage of those who felt no affinity for China was 61.6 percent, a decrease of 1.8 percent from 2005, as shown in Figure 1.1. As a visible sign of improvement, the more serious repair work began in December 2006 on the building of the Japanese Consulate General in Shanghai, which had been damaged during the anti-Japan demonstrations in April 2005.

This positive swing looked particularly large if we look at the history of Japan–China relations since 1972.[2] The bilateral relationship

---

[2]For some studies of Japan–China relations in English, see Iriye 1992; Soeya 1998; Rose 2004; Lam 2006; Wan 2006; Mochizuki 2007; He 2009; Sun 2012; Yahuda 2013; Lai 2013; Manicom 2014.

exhibits a cyclical pattern trending downward. After a honeymoon period in the 1970s, the relationship began to experience problems after 1982 but those disputes were always followed by significant rebounds. The relationship was good in the early 1990s when China was isolated due to the 1989 Tiananmen Incident. Japan was also positioning itself as a bridge between China and the West. But tension between Beijing and Tokyo began to rise after 1994. There were serious disputes but also serious efforts to patch things up until 2002. With the five plus years of Koizumi as prime minister, we see the worst and sustained tension in the bilateral relationship since 1972. One should be somewhat surprised about the sharp turn for the better in the relationship starting in October 2006. After all, the relationship was deteriorating for more than four years. It would be harder to reverse the trend the longer the tension escalated. Yet here we were, observing a mini-honeymoon.

Despite his achievement in improving relations with China and South Korea, Abe stepped down abruptly on September 26, 2007 due to domestic problems. Under Prime Minister Fukuda Yasuo, the arrangements made during the Abe administration were carried out without incident. Most noticeably, a Chinese naval ship visited Japan in November 2007 and a Japanese naval ship paid a return visit to China in June 2008. Considered a good friend of China, Fukuda had the warmest relationship with China among prime ministers for the past few years prior to the current Hatoyama Yukio administration. Unlike Abe, Fukuda made it clear that he would not visit Yasukuni, which was welcomed in China. Fukuda made a trip to China on December 27–30, 2007, described as the "welcome spring trip" in the Chinese media, a step up from the "ice-breaking trip" made by Abe on October 8–9, 2006.

Chinese President Hu Jintao made a lengthy and successful visit to Japan on May 6–10, 2008. The length of Hu's visit was meant to send a signal that the Chinese government respected its Japanese hosts. Economic and political equality were emphasized on this trip, as shown in Hu's interaction with Japanese leaders and public and in the joint statement. The Japanese side achieved its goal for a future-oriented approach to the relationship. The joint statement did not talk that much about history. Immediately after Hu returned to Beijing, a massive earthquake occurred in Sichuan province. Japan's outpouring of sympathy for the earthquake victims and its sending of rescue and medical teams to the disaster areas were well received by the Chinese government and public.

In a major breakthrough, on June 18, 2008 the two governments reached consensus in principle on joint development of the petroleum and natural gas fields in the disputed areas in the East China Sea. Both governments took political risk at home. In fact, the two governments delayed announcement of the consensus reached during the Hu visit to avoid domestic criticism of the visit itself, at Beijing's suggestion. Fukuda was criticized at home, particularly after Chinese Vice Foreign Minister Wu Dawei's interpretation of the consensus at a press conference the very next day. Wu stated that the consensus would not compromise China's sovereignty and administration of the East China Sea, that China did not recognize Japan's "middle line" position, and that Japan had agreed to participate in Chunxiao gas field (Shirakaba by Japanese) according to the Chinese law. The Japanese government was fully aware of the domestic pressure on Hu and understood Wu's remarks as reflecting that pressure. Ironically, that strong domestic criticism was also interpreted as indicating the concessions by the Chinese side.

After barely a year as prime minister, Fukuda resigned on September 24, 2008, also because of domestic problems. Asō Tarō who replaced Fukuda did not want to say that he would not visit Yasukuni. But Asō largely maintained the momentum in improvement in Japan's relations with China. The tone of the governments remained positive. Compared to the Koizumi years, history and Taiwan were not that contentious. But looking back, the mini-honeymoon peaked in May–June 2008. There were signs of trouble in the relationship. The joint history project discussed previously had dragged on, despite the Japanese side's wish for publication of some of the results, which they saw correctly as reflecting the Chinese worry about public backlash.

A far thornier issue was the territorial dispute in the East China Sea and Diaoyudao/Senkaku. The territorial dispute became somewhat tense in the open again although the two governments had managed it so far. On December 8, 2008, the Chinese government sent survey ships to the disputed area around Diaoyudao to challenge Japan's control of the islands. In response, the Japan coast guard reportedly deployed a patrol vessel equipped with two helicopters in the Senkaku area on a regular basis on February 1, 2009. This move was interpreted as Japan's attempt to enhance its actual control of the island. Beijing warned Japan not to escalate over Diaoyudao. Later in February 2009, Asō announced that Senkaku is Japan's territory protected by the Japan–U.S. alliance, the first such assessment from a Japanese prime minister. In early January 2009, the Japanese government protested that China had broken the agreement and continued the development of Kashi gas field (called Tianwaitian by the Chinese side) unilaterally. The Japanese argued that although Shirakaba, Kashi, and another field Kusunoki (Duanqiao by the Chinese) are on the Chinese side of the median line Tokyo claims, they are connected to the fields on the Japanese side. The Chinese maintained that the agreement does not cover fields like Tianwaitian which are not in any disputed areas even judging by the median line, which Beijing does not recognize.

The Japanese government wanted to reach an agreement with China to formalize the June 2008 consensus because the joint development requires adjusting Japanese laws regarding the borders. However, from the Japanese perspective the Chinese government did not show much willingness to finalize the compromise mainly because of strong domestic pressure. That assessment was basically correct. The Chinese government was under pressure concerning the East China Sea. Critics argued strongly that China should not share the fruits of the fields it had already developed on its undisputed territories. In early July, the Japanese government became alarmed by the Chinese transport of equipment to Chunxiao field and warned that a unilateral operation would violate the June 2008 agreement. It was reported in Japanese media that the Chinese ships had left the field on July 15, without engaging in digging operation.

Despite warm government-to-government relations, the Japanese public view of China remained largely negative. As shown in

Figure 1.1, according to the annual polls by the Japanese prime minister's office, the percentage of the surveyed who felt a sense of affinity for China decreased from 34.3 percent in October 2006 to 34.0 percent in October 2007 and 31.8 percent in October 2008, and the percentage of those who felt no affinity for China increased from 61.6 percent to 63.5 percent and 66.6 percent. But Japanese public opinion improved in 2009, seeing the percentage of those who felt affinitive for China increased to 38.5 percent and those who did not decreased to 58.5 percent. Japanese opinion of China began to decrease after the 1989 Tiananmen incident and continuously due to a series of events such as the Chinese nuclear tests in 1995, the Chinese missile tests aimed at Taiwan in 1996, negative publicity surrounding Jiang Zemin's visit to Japan in 1998, and particularly anti-Japan demonstrations in 2005. Despite warming government relationships, the "poison dumpling incident" starting in January 2008 cast some shadow on Hu's visit to Japan. Critics of Fukuda thought he was soft on China. In March the Olympic torch relay in Japan and the unrest in Tibet also had a negative impact on the Japanese view of China.

After a major defeat in the Tokyo metropolitan election on July 10, 2009, Asō announced that he would dissolve the parliament on July 21 and hold the general election on August 30. As expected, the Democratic Party of Japan (DPJ) routed the LDP in the election. This election was mainly about Japan's domestic problems and seemed unlikely to have a significant impact on Japan's foreign policy in general and its China policy in particular. But DPJ's victory initially brought some benefit to Japan–China relations from Beijing's perspective because the party made it clear that a DPJ prime minister would not visit Yasukuni.

President Hu Jintao met with Prime Minister Hatoyama on September 21, 2009. Hatoyama discussed the issues that had been important for the Japanese government, namely signing a formal treaty over the East China Sea, climate change, and North Korea. Most importantly, Hatoyama pushed his idea of the East Asian Community modeled after the European Union. As was often the case, Hu emphasized broad principles and the issues important for

China, namely history and Taiwan. He reportedly also mentioned the Tibetan issue as China's internal affair and failed to respond directly to the East China Sea Treaty and the East Asian Community proposal. Although Hu had met Hatoyama several times before, this was the first meeting between the Chinese leaders and Hatoyama as prime minister. The Chinese government needed to take measure of the new Japanese leader. The Chinese responded positively in later meetings — the foreign minister meeting between China, Japan, and South Korea in Shanghai on September 28 and the summit of China–Japan–South Korea in Beijing on October 10 — to Hatoyama's regional cooperation initiative although they clearly did not see an EU-type regional organization emerging in East Asia any time soon. China had been actively promoting regional cooperation in recent years. But Hatoyama brought new dynamism in Japan's policy toward China and Asia, showing a willingness to set the agenda for Asian affairs. Japan might also expect some cooperation from Beijing over climate change and North Korea. But Beijing was not ready for an East China Sea joint development treaty even though such a treaty would be a major step toward solving Japan–China territorial disputes and laying a strong foundation for future cooperation.

The Challenges

Would the post-2006 warm relationship hold? There was suggestion at the time that Japan–China relations had entered a third stage of strategic accommodation, a theme emphasized during Abe's visit to China in October 2006. Then Chinese ambassador to Japan Wang Yi told Chinese media in December 2006 that, both the Chinese and Japanese governments were studying the substance of a "mutually beneficial strategic relationship" (China News Agency online December 11, 2006). Some Japanese analysts concurred. Both sides had realized that they could not afford to miss another opportunity and made some strategic adjustments to accommodate each other. This shared realization and a shared fear of a freefall in the relationship made the 2006–2010 rebound possible. But real differences in national interests between Japan and China persisted. The Japanese officials and China specialists I talked with, in Tokyo, in June–July 2009 all considered Japan–China relations stable and agreed that all efforts should be made to keep a stable relationship. At the same time, they recognized the serious underlying sources of tension. In particular, most were concerned about China's intention in its military modernization. The Chinese experts I talked with, in Beijing, in August 2009 largely concurred about the state of affairs between China and Japan.

The post 2006 stable Japan–China relationship lasted for about four years. But one should be realistic enough to see the fragile foundation of the current improvement. The honeymoon this time around had a far weaker foundation than the first in the 1970s. For one thing, the generation of senior Chinese and Japanese leaders who actively promoted Japan–China friendship had passed away. The older generation had extensive Japan–China networks of friends and acquaintances and many had years of experience living in each other's country. And they observed the destruction of war between the two countries. Thus, they demonstrated a great capacity to empathize with each other and they had the political clout to get things done. By contrast, the current Japanese and Chinese leaders have limited knowledge of each other and have diverged greatly in historical views.

Furthermore, none of the underlying issues between the two countries had been truly resolved, particularly the East Asia China Sea and Diaoyudao/Senkaku. History had not gone away either. China's relative silence on the issue was contingent upon improvements in the overall relationship. If the relationship goes down again, there would be no reason for them not to raise the issue. Whereas, the Chinese government had toned down the emphasis of history as the political foundation of Sino-Japanese relations, its actions suggested that history still shaped Chinese thinking about Japan. The government's patriotic education campaign since the early 1990s has contributed to this rising anti-Japan nationalism but there is a ready audience for anti-Japan rhetoric. Otherwise, how would one explain the fact that Chinese propaganda has fallen on deaf ears in so many other issues? Concern for public criticism was an important reason that the Chinese side delayed twice publication of the joint history project. On the other side, Japanese politicians increasingly profess a distinct view of history. Take Yasukuni for example, Abe and Asō clearly did not see anything wrong to visit the shrine and refrained from doing so for diplomatic reasons. The air self-defense force chief of staff Tamogami Toshio defended Japan's attack on Pearl Harbor and its colonial actions in China and Korea and viewed Japan as the victim of war in a winning essay in a public essay contest organized by a private firm. He was sacked by Asō on October 30, 2008. But he became a champion of the right, giving public speeches and writing books (e.g. Watanabe and Tamogami 2008). On April 9, 2009, the Japanese Ministry of Education approved a history textbook for middle school by the same group of rightwing historians who had produced a controversial history book. The Chinese government did not protest but they were watching all this closely.

Japan was continuing down the path of becoming a more asser-tive "normal state," driven partly by their concerns about China and partly by North Korea's nuclear and missile programs. The Japanese government criticized China for a lack of transparency in its double-digit annual growth in military spending and for its military modernization drive. The Japanese government also continued to protest the Chinese research and naval vessels in the disputed areas. The news of China building air carriers caused a stir in Japan. The Chinese Defense Ministry formally announced its intention to build carrier for the first time in December 2008 and the Chinese Defense Minister expressed a strong desire for carriers in a meeting with the Japanese Defense Minister on March 30, 2009. The Japanese defense thinking was increasingly about how to deal with China. The Japanese government continued to be openly opposed to Europe's lifting of its arms embargo on China.

Taiwan emerged as a major wedge issue between China and Japan (Takagi 2006; Wan 2007). Taiwan's own diplomatic efforts apart, Japan was increasingly involved in Taiwan. The strengthening of the alliance meant a greater degree of security cooperation between Japan and the United States over Taiwan in the face of a rising China. Taiwan became a common strategic goal for Japan and the United States in the meeting between the Japanese and American foreign ministers and defense ministers in February 2005, publicly so far for the first time. Japanese and American strategic planners now shared a basic assessment that the military balance in the Taiwan Strait was tilting in favor of the mainland. It follows then that the United States and Japan would have to do more. But that might also lead to a moral hazard problem in which Taiwan does less while pushing the envelope.[3] Independent of the alliance, Japan also had its own interest in Taiwan's destiny because of its crucial shipping lanes connected to Southeast Asia and the Middle East and its fear that it might be marginalized with a potential ally taken over by Beijing. With Ma Ying-jeou as president, the cross-straits relationship improved. Ma did not show any hostility toward Japan, but he moved closer to the mainland, which the Japanese government was watching closely. The Taiwan factor will be discussed in great detail in Chapter 7 of this book.

The U.S. factor also reflected in Japan's anxiety over "Japan passing," as will be discussed in Chapter 4 in this book. The Japanese became particularly concerned that China is now rising and there is much support from the United States to form a closer tie with China, particularly to deal with the global financial crisis. The discussion of "G-2" between the United States and China was not amusing to the Japanese. With the new Obama administration, the Japanese were concerned. Hillary Clinton who became Obama's secretary of state had written an article in *Foreign Affairs* magazine that emphasized China's importance and barely mentioned Japan. To alleviate Japanese concern, Clinton picked Japan as her first stop as secretary of state, before visiting China. Similarly, President

---

[3]That is why Armitage and Nye (2007) argued that the U.S. and Japan will inevitably join the defense of Taiwan but they have to re-evaluate their interests if Taiwan no longer supports a vision similar to those of the U.S. and Japan in preventing use of force in the Taiwan Strait and also Taiwanese moves toward independence.

Barack Obama visited Japan first for his first presidential visit to Asia in November 2009.

Conclusion

Management of Japan–China relations is now important because whether the governments choose to emphasize the negatives or the positives in the relationship makes a large difference. There are plenty positives that, Beijing and Tokyo can draw from. To start with, economic ties between the two countries continue to strengthen. The 2008 Global Recession has increased incentives for regional cooperation. Although the crisis started in the United States, East Asian economies suffered as well. Unlike the United States, Japan can borrow from home as a saver's country to stimulate its economy. China thus has no influence over Japan in this regard. However, in the long run Japan continues to count on China's transition to a consumer economy to provide opportunities for its aging population. On August 17, 2009, the Japanese government announced that Japan's economy grew from April to June, recovering from the sharpest decline among developed countries in the current crisis, thanks to a government stimulus package and a rebound in exports to China. China replaced the United States as Japan's largest export market in 2009, a first since World War II.

Needless to say, the economic relationship between China and Japan is not all rosy. No bilateral economic relationship is. In particular, one area of potential rivalry is Beijing's attempt to internationalize the yuan during and after the Great Recession. But positives clearly outweigh negatives in this arena.

Second, although Chinese and Japanese opinion of each other has worsened sharply, greater societal contacts may come to play a positive role in the long run. Chinese tourists to Japan surpassed one million in 2008. The Japanese government was hoping to increase Chinese tourists, by making visa easier for the affluent Chinese citizens. There have been a growing number of students exchange. China constitutes the largest foreign student body in

Japan and Japan is one of the largest senders of foreign students to China. While it has mainly been Chinese students who seek degrees in Japan, there are also an increasing number of Japanese students pursuing academic degrees in China. While interested in the tourist income, the Japanese government also hopes to expose everyday Japanese life to Chinese citizens. Those who have visited their neighboring country for studies or sightseeing do not have to be pro-Japan or pro-China. Their necessarily more nuanced understanding of each other should be a welcome correction to the prevailing negative stereotypes.

Chapter 2

Japan's Party Politics and China Policy

The September 2010 Chinese fishing boat collision incident was a serious dispute in Japan–China relations. Like all international disputes, a whole range of causal factors were involved in this incident and one could identify problems in all directions. But this chapter examines mainly how Japanese party politics contributed to the start, the middle, and the end of the collision dispute, with how China conducted itself kept in the background.

Japanese Party Politics and Diplomacy

Japanese party politics was important for post-war Japanese diplomacy and arguably more important than for most major advanced democracies. It is often said that for the United States politics stopped at the water's edge, which means that partisanship should not be reflected in American foreign policy. There were ideological fights in the United States, particularly between the Republican Party and the Democratic Party. The Republicans consistently view competition as the defining feature of international politics and the United States should therefore take a hardline position, including use of military force to destroy enemies or to deter aggression. The Democrats generally prefer international cooperation by accommodating other countries. But the Republican presidents define what Republic foreign policy is (Dueck 2010). So do the Democrat presidents. Thus, party politics was important for selecting a president but not as much the conduct of diplomacy. There was general consensus on foreign policy for the United States for a long time and one can still see much bipartisanship in American diplomacy now, fierce rhetoric aside. One may suggest that it is unfair to compare Japan to a hegemon. But Japanese party politics was more constraining on Japanese diplomacy than most major Western European powers such as France, Britain, and Germany.[1]

Important though it was, the role of Japanese party politics in Japanese diplomacy was well-understood, which explains partly why scholars did not write that much about this topic.[2] Similar to other parliamentary systems, the Japanese Diet often simply ratified the decision by the prime ministers who by definition had a majority at least in the lower house. But unlike most other parliamentary systems, the Liberal Democratic Party (LDP) enjoyed single-party domination, which helped explain the fundamental stability in post-war Japanese political system (Curtis 1988, 1–2. Also, Thayer 1969; Satō and Matsuzaki 1986). The Japanese Diet did offer a public forum for discussing national policies and most post-war controversies in the parliament involved foreign policy issues (Baerwald 1977). Japanese party politics was reflected in the intraparty politics of the LDP, dominated with the Yoshida line and the Hatoyama line. Both were conservative but differed over defense policy and alliance with the United States. The Japanese Foreign Ministry bureaucrats typically handled routine business while political leaders focused on sensitive and controversial diplomatic issues (Fukui 1977). Major foreign policy decisions such as normalizing relations with the Soviet Union, renegotiating the revision of the Japan–U.S. Security

---

[1]For example, Guibourg Delamotte (2011, 28), "A French specialist on Japan, judges Japan as different from France that has much diplomatic consistency despite power transitions between political parties."

[2]For important exceptions, see Scalapino 1977; Hellmann 1969.

Treaty, and normalizing relations with China all came from LDP leaders rather than bureaucrats (Curtis 1988, 106–107). The differences among various decision makers were managed by the Policy Affairs Research Council and various committees within the LDP (Reischauer 1977, xiv). There was also inter-party politics between the LDP and main opposition parties such as the Japan Socialist Party. Again, the difference mainly lay in the defense policy and the Constitution. While the LDP could ignore the opposition parties in most cases, the opposition parties could make things difficult for the LDP through obstruction techniques, as vividly shown in the case of the revision of the security treaty with the United States. Thus, there was much restriction on Japanese diplomacy. With its focus on economic development and aversion to conflicts and use of military force, Japan had a distinct style of diplomacy, which was highly predictable even though Japanese policy over a specific issue was complex.

Japanese party politics began to change significantly with the end of the Cold War (Curtis 1999; Krauss and Pekkanen 2011). Powerful global and domestic forces affected the Japanese political regime. As a result, there are more policy debates and the political parties have to explain their positions better to win votes. Thus, Japanese party politics should have a greater direct impact on Japanese foreign policy than before.

This chapter contributes to our understanding of Japanese party politics and diplomacy by examining how Japanese party politics affected the Chinese fishing boat collision incident as one of numerous causal factors. As of now, we do not have sufficient theoretical analysis of the incident, which came to be overshadowed as should be by the mega disasters on March 11, 2011. But there was also reluctance in both Japan and China to think about the collision incident theoretically. While there have been some casual references to Japanese domestic politics, Japanese commentators have focused on the Chinese problems. If it was China's fault, how Japan handled this, including the role of its domestic politics, is largely irrelevant. Moreover, since many Japanese felt humiliated, it seemed inappropriate to engage in self-reflection. In addition, when some Japanese wanted to blame the Democratic Party of Japan (DPJ) government they focused on what they viewed as its ineptness and mostly attacked the government on a personal level. The Chinese analysts blamed Japan and therefore thought that Japan's behavior had domestic sources but they tended to write about the supposedly conspiracies by some Japanese politicians viewed as hawkish. Departing from how they dealt with the previous disputes, the Chinese showed little interest in figuring out what was going on inside "the Japanese black box" this time around and focused instead on the policy output.

Thus, I will use the collision incident case against the following broad theoretical arguments people have advanced to explain how Japanese electoral politics has affected Japanese diplomacy in general or toward other countries such as the United States.

1. High turnover of prime ministers: With frequent change of prime ministers, it is difficult to maintain any continuity in foreign policy, as recognized inside and outside Japan. As a case in point, as observed by Japanese media and lamented by Japanese diplomats, for four years in a row in 2006–2009, there was a new prime minister in that position for less than a month before they needed to speak at the UN General Assembly in September (*Asahi shimbun* September 8, 2010, 4). Kan Naoto had been on the job for three months before the UN General Assembly in 2010. But there would be a new prime minister again in early September in 2011 (*Asahi shimbun* August 20, 2011, 4). In fact, Japanese media observed that only Japan had a different prime minister speaking at the UN General Assembly every year in the past three years (*Asahi shimbun* September 2, 2011, 4).

In terms of Japan–China relations, five Chinese leaders interacted with 23 Japanese prime ministers starting with Prime Minister Tanaka Kakuei in 1972–2010. As a contrast, there were eight American presidents in the same period, which was a contributing factor for the two countries to be able to manage their often testy relations.[3] The Chinese and American leaders often have tension

---

[3] As Henry Kissinger (2011, xvi) noted, "Eight American presidents and four generations of Chinese leaders have managed this delicate relationship in an astonishingly consistent manner, considering the differences in starting points."

at start but they serve long enough to adapt and mend the relationship. With a parliamentary system, Great Britain has also had eight prime ministers in this period. But frequency of leadership turnover is an insufficient causal argument to explain the ebb and flow of Japan–China relations. After all, the longest tension in the bilateral relationship occurred during the term of Prime Minister Koizumi Junichirō, a long-serving popular leader (April 26, 2001–September 26, 2006). We may well see another period of sustained tension under Prime Minister Abe Shinzō (December 26, 2012–present) who has already served for more than two years and is well positioned after his major electoral victory in December 2014 to become another long-serving prime minister.

2. Transitional challenge from shift to a two-party system: This was indeed a major reason why the collision incident became such a crisis because such transition affected long-term foreign policy commitment. All regime transition would cause some diplomatic problems. By definition, a new ruling party comes to power partly based on its different policy programs from the previous government. But regime change does not have to cause problems for all foreign partners, potential gains for some and losses for others. Specific to Japan–China relations, a prevalent view in the West was that the DPJ government would significantly reorient Japan's diplomacy to a pro-China stance and move away from the United States. The DPJ wanted to differentiate itself from the LDP and said so in its manifesto and various documents (Easley, Kotani, and Mori 2010; Harris 2010). But it was incorrect to view the DPJ as pro-China. As the Chinese understood it, while there was potential gain from a DPJ government, there was inherent danger for Beijing with this regime transition. Despite high tension during the Koizumi years, Koizumi's successors Abe Shinzō, Fukuda Yasuo and Asō Tarō maintained decent relations with China. The three prime ministers had different ideological orientations but behaved consistently. There was thus a sentiment that there was now some consensus in Japan about how to deal with China. That is why although people knew that there were structural problems troubling Japan–China relations, analysts including myself were cautiously optimistic that both

the Japanese government and the Chinese government would value their hard-learned lessons and tread carefully over sensitive issues.

There was some hope on the Chinese side that the DPJ government would continue the LDP government's China policy under Abe, Fukuda and Asō and possibly do more. But they also knew that the DPJ took what Beijing viewed as hardline positions on a number of foreign policy issues such as territory, human rights, Chinese military spending, and Taiwan even though they were more careful than the LDP regarding controversial prime ministerial visits to Yasukuni Shrine. Indeed, the DPJ cabinet avoided Yasukuni on August 15 twice in a row.[4] While the Chinese like to emphasize certain "principles" to guide their relationship with a foreign country, they are also driven by the imperative of a particular diplomatic issue. Principles affect how those issues are framed and handled, but those issues that have their own history and dynamic often take on a life of their own. So the Chinese would go over the list of issues to see how a new Japanese government might affect them. It is not regime transition *per se* but what the new government brings to the table that ultimately matters.

The Japanese political system as a whole was inexperienced with regime transition, which complicated Japan's foreign policy. Since the LDP had stayed in power for such a long time, Japan had an inadequate system of power transition unlike countries with more established practice of power shift. The DPJ was inexperienced as a ruling party even though some DPJ leaders served in the ruling

---

[4]But right before the August 29, 2011 DPJ presidential election, Noda Yoshihiko caused a controversy with his comment that Class-A war criminals were really not war criminals and that there is no reason asking a prime minister not to visit Yasukuni during a press conference on August 15, 2011 (Martin and Johnston 2011). Once a prime minister, Noda stated at his first prime ministerial press conference that he and his cabinet would continue the policy of the previous cabinets and would not visit Yasukuni (*Asahi shimbun* September 3, 2011, 1). In fact, the DPJ leadership continues to hold a different position on history from the LDP. Okada Katsuya, elected the party president on January 18, 2015, made it clear that he differs from Abe in that Japan's past mistake must be acknowledge and that he does support Abe's notion of collective self-defense (*Asahi shimbun* online January 18, 2015).

party or government before. But the LDP also had no experience being a responsible opposition party. This problem should be temporary however. By definition, the Japanese political parties will become more experienced over time. But one wishes for a shorter and smoother transition period.

3. Politics in command versus bureaucracy in command: Since the DPJ government was inept to some extent, the fact that bureaucrats were pushed down added to the difficulties in Japanese diplomacy. The dynamic between politicians and diplomats was different from the dynamic between politicians and domestic ministries. Major post-war diplomatic initiatives came from the prime ministers and required cooperation between politicians and bureaucrats. But the DPJ initially took a populist, harsh position on the bureaucracy, which affected negatively the morale and way of doing things for elite bureaucrats and prevented effective information sharing.

4. Democratic accountability for diplomacy: It is important in the long run to have transparency and accountability in diplomacy. But if one believes that diplomacy is preferable to non-diplomatic measures, one has to give political leaders and diplomats some space to operate. The U.S. government certainly has much autonomy in conducting American foreign policy. Fundamentally, voters should also be held accountable because they have voted those leaders in. And public opinion partially shaped by big media (major print papers and TV stations) influences foreign policy, for better or for worse.

This chapter seeks to contribute to our understanding of Japanese party politics and foreign policy by being more precise about how the arguments discussed above apply in different stages of the incident. While the DPJ's inexperience was a common factor in all stages, Japanese party politics played out differently in different stages. The DPJ was preoccupied with intraparty politics driven by personality clashes and policy differences before the crisis. Its hardline positions combined with insufficient understanding of how the previous Japanese governments had handled some diplomatic issues. Its lack of foreign policy expertise combined with intimidated bureaucracy made the crisis management difficult. The post-crisis finger-pointing was more typical of party politics in Japan and elsewhere. The analysis in this chapter is based on observation, interviews, reading of Japanese newspapers and magazines and watching of Japanese television programs based in Tokyo at the time of the crisis.

Before the Crisis

The fishing boat collision incident took place in an improved atmosphere between Japan and China, continuing the general trend since late 2006 after Prime Minister Abe mended ties with Beijing. There were underlying structural problems between the two countries such as China's rise and difference in political systems, but the two governments managed the relationship without major incidents, as discussed in the previous chapter of this book. In fact, the existence of structural reasons for tension makes skilled management of disputes more important.

The regime transition from the LDP to the DPJ in August 2009 did not have an immediate negative impact on Japan–China relations. There was actually much expectation that the DPJ would lean to China and away from the United States. However, while it is true that Hatoyama managed to worsen relations with the United States over the Futenma issue that does not necessarily prove that the DPJ was pro-China. As discussed previously, the DPJ was a mixed bag for Beijing. The Chinese assessment of the DPJ's China policy was basically right. While Japan's strained relationship with the United States was necessarily in China's interest, Beijing was cautious reflecting its understanding of the DPJ. This was an untested government and nobody was certain how it would handle crises. And it was well understood that the DPJ took hardline positions on territorial disputes, Taiwan and human rights while being "correct" over prime ministerial visits to Yasukuni Shrine. By contrast, the post-Koizumi LDP leaders seemed to have formed a realistic understanding of Japan's relations with China and followed a cautious policy line.

Beijing's underlying uneasiness with the DPJ does not mean that it created a crisis to test the DPJ government or to take advantage of

Tokyo's strained relations with Washington. Fundamentally, the Chinese government would react the same way if a LDP government behaved like the Kan government. But in retrospect, while the LDP feels equally strongly about Senkaku being Japanese territory it is likely that we would have an ugly incident but not a crisis. The DPJ dropped the ball.

The DPJ's intra-party politics was the principal factor explaining how the incident was handled on the Japanese side. This is not because some DPJ politicians created an incident involving China to advance their domestic agenda against political rivals such as Ozawa Ichirō or to create a crisis situation to justify better relations with the United States. Politicians seek to advance their political agenda, which means that they make choices accordingly when facing an evolving situation. Some politicians may indeed have thought about how tension with China might help improve relations with the United States by providing a stronger rationale to the public about the importance of the alliance and may even claim credit for such moves years later. But I at least did not observe any conspiracy. To have a conspiracy, one has to be well organized and think through multiple steps.

Rather, the DPJ was preoccupied with intra-party politics. The incident occurred in the middle of a highly contentious DPJ presidential election between the pro- and anti-Ozawa camps. China was not mentioned that much in the scheme of things in this period. Domestic issues dominated in the debate as it is normally the case for democratic elections. When it comes to foreign policy, Futenma was the single most important issue. China factored in over that issue because Futenma became almost a test whether Japan was leaning to China and moving away from the United States. To further discredit a conspiracy theory, it is difficult to see how creating an incident would advance anyone's political interest. To utilize a crisis, one needs to work through media to influence public opinion. Since Ozawa was viewed as pro-China, he did not have incentives to talk about China that much. Kan did not need an incident because he already had overwhelming public support in his fight with Ozawa. Japanese big media followed mainly domestic political drama. They did not like Ozawa. But on the whole they did not link Ozawa to China as a way to attack him. Rather, they focused on Ozawa's money politics. Moreover, Japanese big media generally toned down the incident before the presidential election ended on September 14.

One could be cautiously optimistic about the Japan–China relationship through August 2010. It was apparent that the most serious issue between the two countries was territorial dispute. There were increased Chinese activities and Japan was also moving to strengthen its position. But the two sides discussed restarting negotiations over the East China Sea natural gas field again for May 2011. The two countries reached an agreement in 2008, but that needs to be legalized into a binding arrangement. The negotiations would not be easy, but the two governments were talking, which was a good sign.

During the Crisis

The fishing boat collision incident was serious but it did not have to turn into a crisis. The problem resulted partly from the tension between the DPJ commitment to voters and Japan's past diplomatic practices and partly from Beijing's harsh reaction. Crisis is defined here as an emotionally charged stage of event in which high instability may lead to a decisive negative turn for the relationship. The crisis over the fishing boat collision incident lasted for two weeks from September 10 to September 24. The collision took place in the morning of September 7. The Japanese officers boarded the Chinese ship early that afternoon and took the Chinese captain and his crew to a Japanese port. The captain was formally arrested that night. But what triggered strong Chinese reaction was the Japanese government's decision on September 10 to detain the captain for ten days. That decision was important because the incident now largely became a zero-sum game. Someone now had to "lose" in the immediate sense. The Japanese government decided in the afternoon of September 19 to extend the detention of the captain. The crisis escalated with China's increasingly tougher retaliatory measures. In the end, the Japanese government released the captain, announced in the afternoon of September 24, and the Chinese government took him back with a charter plane that night. The crisis was over with the release of the Chinese captain but tension between the two nations continued.[5]

Given the growing tension in the disputed area and moves taken by both sides, the fishing boat collision was an accident waiting to happen. This was a worse incident than previous ones and things could be ugly. But one could imagine how the two governments would somehow muddle through as they had done before to avoid a major confrontation. But it became clear within two days that the Japanese side was not going to play by the old rule book, which the Chinese side viewed as unilateral and thus unacceptable. Since the Japanese had the Chinese captain in captivity, the only way now for the Chinese government to get him back would be to apply pressure. China's rise added to Beijing's determination and leverage but China would have done the same even if it were in decline. One may argue that the Japanese government was perfectly justified to do what it did given the nature of the incident (ramming of a Japanese law-enforcing ship in what the Japanese side considers to be its territorial water) or Japan should have done so before, but the fact of matter is that the Japanese government's decision to try the Chinese captain according to Japanese domestic law was a departure from past Japanese practice.

Japanese party politics was indeed the principal driver for the crucial decision to try the Chinese fishing boat captain. The DPJ government treated the incident as a domestic law and order issue, which should be dealt with within the Japanese judicial system. However, they had to frame the issue first, which was political in nature.

---

[5] The Japanese government has not dropped the legal case against the Chinese captain. On February 12, 2014, the Japanese prosecutors brought a civilian case against him in a Naha court for compensation for the damage to the Japanese patrol boat. The Chinese foreign ministry spokeswoman responded that Japan had violated China's sovereign rights and the rights of the Chinese captain and should apologize and compensate (*Yomiuri shimbun* online February 12, 2015). The Chinese captain remains in China, outside Japan's jurisdiction.

The DPJ departed from Japan's past practice, namely shelving the territorial dispute over Senkaku/Diaoyudao. To complicate things, we need to discuss whether Japan had indeed agreed to "shelve" the Senkaku issue. Some leading DPJ politicians now stated that Japan never accepted that position.[6] That was a surprise since it was widely assumed that such a fundamental mutual understanding between the two sides existed even though it did not ever appear in any public official agreements.

Like in some other countries, the political leaders in Japan, including those in the LDP, often avoid explaining and informing their successors and the public what kind of commitments they have made and why it is so important for the country. They often promise to get out of a tough spot and then backtrack, particularly under public scrutiny. A prominent example is the U.S.–Japan textile dispute during the Nixon administration, worsened because Nixon thought Prime Minister Satō Eisaku had promised to reduce Japanese textile exports to the United States but Satō denied making such a promise. In a recently revealed case, when the Japanese and Americans negotiated over right of jurisdiction over crimes committed by American soldiers in Japan in 1953, a Japanese justice ministry official stated that Japan would not exercise such rights unless the criminal cases are important. The Japanese negotiators faced domestic criticism of inequality and the resistance in the U.S. Congress to passing the right to Japan. The record was kept from the Japanese public. The Japanese government had denied the existence of such a secret agreement. But after the U.S. documents were opened, Foreign Minister Okada Katsuya requested an investigation. Foreign Minister Matsumoto Takeaki announced on August 26, 2011 that the Japanese document reflected a unilateral policy statement rather than a bilateral agreement and it was difficult to confirm whether there was a secret agreement (*Asahi shimbun* evening August 26, 2011, 1 and August 27, 2011, 5; Martin 2011).

---

[6]For example, Foreign Minister Maehara Seiji said at a Diet committee meeting on October 20, 2010 that shelving the Senkaku issue was Deng's own remark and that the Japanese side did not agree (*Asahi shimbun* evening October 21, 2010, 10).

By that standard, the Japanese government would find it easier to deny an informal agreement believed to be operating for so many years with a country not as important as the United States.

This commitment problem happens in the domestic context as well. For example, did Prime Minister Kan commit to stepping down in a short time period or not? The Kan exit episode shows that this is not simply a lost-in-translation issue because Kan made that promise to his fellow Japanese political leaders and the Japanese public.

Both the Japanese and Chinese governments made important compromises as they should, but they chose not to inform and let alone explain to their public. As a non-democracy, the Chinese government is worse in this regard. But they do on the whole keep their promise precisely because they do not have to tell the public what they are doing although it is getting more difficult for Beijing due to the Chinese citizens' greater ability to access alternative sources of information.

The DPJ government behaved the way most Japanese thought reasonable and the Japanese public was disappointed only because the DPJ government did not get the job done. The Japanese public basically shared the view that the Chinese captain should be tried according to Japanese domestic law. Senkaku is Japanese territory. The Chinese captain violated Japanese law in the Japanese territory and should be punished. Japan is a country of law, unlike China. Japanese big media has been part of that commonsense consensus forming process. Japan is not unique because all countries have their own consensus or commonsense about certain issues and build opinion bubbles around them.

Similar to other countries, Japan's opinion bubbles cause problems. This is the case when it comes to Japan's territorial disputes with all its neighbors, including totalitarian North Korea, authoritarian China, basically authoritarian Russia, and democratic South Korea and Taiwan. Some of Japan's neighbors such as Taiwan like Japan and others do not. With such a huge variation, commonsense should be that the problems cannot be all on Japan's neighbors. Thus, there should be greater recognition of other countries' viewpoints, some of which have merit.

We should also know about the fundamental beliefs of some DPJ leaders. As discussed before, the DPJ took hardline positions on a number of issues including territorial disputes. The DPJ politicians in charge did not believe that Senkaku was a diplomatic issue. Since the Japanese side had already defined the issue as domestic, if China protests, it was by definition unreasonable. Japan therefore should act sternly or *kizen* as a favorite Japanese expression used at the time to indicate how Tokyo should act towards Beijing. However, the fact that the DPJ seemed to be completely convinced about Senkaku being a non-issue diplomatically rather than being rhetorical made a major difference. From Beijing's perspective, that very denial was an emotional trigger for its tough reactions. As one seasoned China thinker put it to me, since Japan unilaterally refuses to recognize the dispute, it has left no room for the Chinese but to react strongly to force recognition of the dispute despite obvious costs to Beijing.

Furthermore, the DPJ did not know what they were doing. The DPJ actually had people familiar with foreign policy, people like Ozawa who had spent years cultivating relations with China. He took over 140 parliamentarians to China in December 2009. But the Kan camp did not want to use the Ozawa people due to an ugly intra-party fight. Kan and his supporters seemed determined to end Ozawa's influence once for all. This internal fight affected the Japanese handling of the incident. Kan was not that familiar with foreign policy and if his key supporters in the intra-party fight made policy suggestions, he went along. But this incident would cost him politically. He was reportedly angry at what he viewed as Chinese arrogance. But he most probably would have done things differently if he could do this again.[7]

---

[7]The Kan people seemed to have learned the lesson, as revealed in their more cautious reaction to the two Chinese fishing patrol ships operating in the Senkaku area and reportedly briefly entering what the Japanese side considers to be the Japanese territorial water to avoid a repeat of the incident right before another DPJ presidential election (*Asahi shimbun* August 25, 2011, 4). As a principal player in the 2010 incident, Maehara was not in the government this time around, but the other key players remained in the cabinet.

The DPJ did not appear to have a good institutional memory, which resulted from regime transition and its efforts to push the bureaucracy down. In a democracy, elected politicians should ultimately be in charge, but the Japanese Foreign Ministry was somewhat different from more domestic ministries. Virtually all big post-war foreign policy decisions were decided by political leaders and supported by diplomats. When Japan was successful, it was typically when a political leader made a reasonable choice and then let able bureaucrats do their job. The DPJ seemed to think that bureaucrats were above politicians, but instead of elevating the politicians to a higher level, it managed to push down the bureaucracy, resulting in an overall lowering of Japanese diplomacy.

Messy party politics complicates foreign policy in any democracy. A non-democracy may be more consistent with its foreign policy but often suffers greater disasters in the absence of healthy domestic checks on the government. A democracy can sometimes use its party politics to its advantage in diplomatic negotiations. When you have power transition or intra-party difficulties, a foreign government might give you a temporary pass, but it still fundamentally wants to see you keep your commitment.

In the collision case, the Chinese side did not act that tough initially by its standard because they wanted a low-key solution and because they recognized that Kan could not look weak in his fight with Ozawa. The Chinese did not want themselves to be the main issue of Japanese party politics, which could only be negative for Beijing given Japan's current political atmosphere.

The DPJ government adopted what it viewed as a calm and reasonable approach by denying the existence of any diplomatic dispute. Japanese media played along. Both the government and big media thought that talking too much about the dispute would play into China's hand. That would backfire. In any dispute, one of the worst things one can do to the other side is to dismiss their grievance. It did not help when some key Japanese politicians took Beijing's relative calm as vindication of their own approach and publicly praised the Chinese government for doing so, which embarrassed it in front of the Chinese public and providing weapon for hardliners. The Chinese were angry at the DPJ for unilaterally destroying the mutual understanding and humiliating the Chinese government in front of Chinese people and the international community. That is why the Chinese government urged the Japanese side to recognize the severity of the incident and to not misread the situation.

When the DPJ presidential election was over, the Chinese government promptly urged Prime Minister Kan to make a "political decision" to release the Chinese captain.[8] Kan and his key supporters were preoccupied with forming a new cabinet while keeping Ozawa and his supporters from any posts of importance. China was not mentioned that much.[9] Coming out of a convincing victory over powerful Ozawa, the Kan government appeared confident. The day after a new cabinet was announced, there were two prominent stories on the front page of the *Asahi shimbun* (September 18, 2011, 1), one to the right about the new cabinet and the other to the left about Chinese activities at their East China Sea natural gas field. That was a clear case of the government using media to shape a narrative. The details about what was going on in the natural gas field had to come from government sources released strategically to put a check on China.[10] But that story would not stick. The eyes were focused on the Chinese captain.

Beijing began to take much harsher measures. The DPJ government began to feel the heat. Kan himself became more involved.

---

[8] Reflecting the government's view, an editorial at *Huanqiu shibao* [Global Times] (online September 15, 2010) the day after the DPJ presidential election said specifically that now with electoral pressure gone Kan should be resolute and release the Chinese captain immediately.

[9] For example, there were some stories on pages 4, 9 and 11 in *Asahi shimbun* on September 15, 2010. But the dominant story was the presidential election.

[10] In a role reversal, immediately after the Noda cabinet was announced, *Asahi shimbun* carried a substantive story about "new waves in the South China Sea" on Page 4 on September 4, 2011. It was actually one month old news, without commenting on recent developments such as the Philippine president's visit to China. The news story linked the South China Sea to Senkaku and the Japan–U.S. alliance. This was big media reminding the Noda government and the public of the China threat.

In particular, if the Chinese president decided to boycott the APEC summit to be held in Yokohama, that would be a serious blow to his image. Since Kan had to attend the UN General Assembly in New York City, Chief Cabinet Secretary Sengoku Yoshito was in charge. He made the right and courageous decision to let the Chinese captain go to defuse a crisis. Diplomacy is different from domestic politics, in that, compromises have to be made between countries with different political systems and values in the absence of an overarching authority. Much of the criticism of him over his ending of the crisis was not particularly fair. If politicians are always criticized by media if they seek some compromise with foreign countries and they become too afraid as a result, what would happen to Japan's foreign relations? If one cannot do diplomacy, which by definition involves compromises, one would probably end up with less desirable non-diplomatic solutions.

Having said that, Sengoku's decision looked sudden and the rationale for the decision was convoluted. It would have been better to explain why the Japanese government needed to end the crisis or at least to spin the outcome as strengthening the Japanese territorial claim. Instead, the government shifted the burden to a district prosecutor's office. The Japanese government of course had its calculations for releasing the captain. They may not be the best arguments but should be shared publicly with the nation. Not saying them served to erode the legitimacy of those arguments. As a case in point, a senior official at the prime minister's office reportedly refuted the critics of the decision to release the Chinese captain by asking what else Japan should do and whether people want to go to war like in the past (*Asahi shimbun* September 26, 2010, 2). That was a legitimate argument to make for any international disputes. In fact, Japan–China relations have deteriorated so much that people need to recall that avoiding another war was a fundamental motivation for the early Japanese and Chinese leaders to make compromise to make this relationship work. Shelving of territorial disputes was essentially a delay strategy to avoid conflicts now. China had just had a border clash with the Soviet Union over territorial disputes in 1969, merely three years before Premier Zhou Enlai wanted to push the Diaoyudao/Senkaku issue to the side, essentially shelving the issue without using that expression. By saying that the Japanese government made its decision to prevent conflict, the Japanese government would take some criticism, but it was criticized anyway. Moreover, taking some domestic heat would also help improve relations with the Chinese government, which felt that by forgoing previous commitment, the Japanese government had unfairly exposed the Chinese government to domestic criticism.

The DPJ government was severely criticized by the media, the public, the opposition and from within the DPJ. In some way, the treatment of the DPJ government is typical in a democracy when the government is perceived to have failed in a major foreign policy issue and to have embarrassed the nation. But in the Japanese case, all these attacks were mainly personal in nature and there was not much serious debate over policy. In particular, even though the LDP might have done better if they had been in charge but viewing their attack on the DPJ without any clear policy alternative makes you wonder whether that would necessarily be the case. The simple fact is that Japanese party politics was not functioning well at this juncture of Japanese political history.

Regional Comparisons

If we put the collision incident in the context of China's interaction with the Northeast Asian democracies, a few observations stand out about Japanese diplomacy. Comparing the three democracies, Taiwan should be most concerned and vulnerable vis-à-vis China. China claims Taiwan, which would be an ultimate threat if one considers Taiwan not to be part of China. China supports half of Korea while maintaining a good relationship with the other half. From an international law perspective, both Koreas are sovereign states. But from a historical cultural perspective, the Korean nation is divided. By contrast, China and Japan have territorial disputes over a few rocks at their peripheries. But they managed to turn the dispute into a major fight. What does this say about Taiwanese diplomacy, Korean diplomacy or Japanese diplomacy?

One may argue that precisely when China affects a country's basic national security interest that country has to be more careful. By contrast, because Japan is in the same power league as China and has a formal alliance with the United States, it may feel more confident facing China. One may also argue that this is more about China's growing ambition, capability and domestic vulnerabilities than about the three democracies. But focusing on the Japanese side of the story in this chapter, I view a key reason for the differences between the three democracies in their relations with China in the fact that transition in Japan has been particularly detrimental to its diplomacy. The DPJ government managed to have problems with most of its neighbors and for a time with the United States over Futenma. Japan also did not help itself in the multilateral forums such as the Trans-Pacific Partnership Agreement or climate change.

When Taiwan went through transition in the mid 1990s, it experienced far worse security tension with China. Then both the Kuomintang (KMT) and the Democratic Progressive Party (DPP) adapted. President Ma Ying-jeou has demonstrated impressive diplomatic skills by maintaining a good relationship with Beijing without compromising Taiwan's autonomy. Taiwan also has a good relationship with Japan. The transition in the Republic of Korea actually helped to improve relations with China. President Kim Daejong adopted a sunshine policy towards North Korea. In the end, what matters is what policy a new government adopts rather than power transition itself. The DPJ government was not that flexible over a number of issues. When it came to tough issues, the government either dragged things out until circumstances change, as in the case of Futenma, or made it appear that Japan had no choice, thus shifting responsibility to foreign pressure. Both approaches created their own problems.

Japan's diplomatic problems resulted from dysfunctional party politics and lack of effective leadership, which refers to the ability to set a clear and reasonable objective, be decisive, have courage to tell the public what he or she is really doing and why that is important, formulate a plan, and follow through. To do that, one has to have a system to choose the most capable leader and then give that leader a reasonable length of time to accomplish policy goals for the country.

The Aftermath

The collision incident was a pivotal event that cast a long shadow over the Japan–China relationship, partly through its impact on Japanese domestic politics. As always, the bilateral relationship has experienced some twists and turns. The March 11 disasters helped to improve the Japan–China relationship for a while. While feeling compassionate based on their own experience with mega natural disasters, the Chinese also saw March 11 as creating an opportunity to improve relations with Japan, allowing them to do things that could not yet be done prior to March 11.[11] The Kan government was also seeking to repair the relationship with China. But despite better atmosphere in Japan–China relations, all the existing issues remained.

China's rise has shaken up East Asian international relations and there is much uncertainty about its intention and ability. Specific to Japan–China relations, the old structure and commitment are breaking down but we are yet to see a new structure for the relationship. Strategic partnership sounds good but it is too broad and vague for operational impact. What the two countries need are practical, middle-range mechanisms to manage existing and emerging disputes while allowing the deep and extensive economic and cultural ties built over the past four decades to finally have a chance to play a greater moderating effect on the relationship. I myself thought in late 2011 that it was doubtful that the two countries could manage another collision incident without a serious breach in their relationship. The best they could do at the time was to avoid disputes. The Chinese government was going through its own power transition and facing severe domestic challenges despite its relatively stronger performance in the Great Recession. And Japan needed to put its house in order. I was right that the two governments would

---

[11] Author's discussion with Chinese analysts, Beijing, June 9–11, 2011.

not be able to handle another crisis and the only difference was that it was not another collision incident but the Noda government's "nationalization" of the disputed islands that would send the relationship to brink of military conflict.

Japanese party politics was adrift, a principal reason that Japanese diplomacy was also adrift. The DPJ would have its general party election in September 2012, which meant that Noda Yoshihiko, who became Japan's new prime minister on August 30, 2011, would have to face possible contenders within a year if not being challenged before. Like the September 2010 election, the August 2011 election was also defined by the pro- and anti-Ozawa tension. Noda's cabinet lineup announced on September 2 reflected these intra-party concerns, balancing different factions to achieve intra-party harmony and including few big names seemingly with a one-year term in mind. Thus, the Noda government was not ambitious. While Noda wanted to improve cooperation with the opposition parties, they continued to criticize the DPJ. In particular, the LDP was determined to force an election in which the DPJ would surely lose seats if not power altogether. With all these party politics intrigues and given that Japan should indeed focus on reconstruction and bringing the Fukushima nuclear accident to a closure, it was difficult to see how Japan would be able to punch at its weight in the world.

To make things worse for Japanese diplomacy, some foreign countries essentially stopped considering the nuance of Japanese party politics and simply moved forward with their agenda following their own timetable and bureaucratic routine. As a case in point, two Chinese fishing patrol ships operated in the area close to Senkaku and briefly breached the area considered by Japan to be its territorial water in the morning of August 24, 2011. This Chinese move did not appear to be a test of Japanese resolve during another DPJ presidential election. Rather, the Chinese were trying to regularize their claim to Diaoyudao without much concern about Japanese domestic politics. An accident would be far more serious this time around, than in September 2010 because it would now involve Chinese government ships rather than a private fishing boat.

Tokyo Mayor Ishihara Shintarō provoked another crisis between the two countries. Ishihara was widely recognized as a rightwing politician who despised China. Angered by what he viewed as aggressive Chinese actions and weak DPJ response, Ishihara announced during a visit to the United States in April 2012 that the Tokyo Metropolitan Government would purchase the Senkakus from a private owner. He subsequently planned survey missions to the islands, hoping to shore up Japan's sovereign claim and knowing well that the Chinese government would react, which would suit him just fine. The Chinese government indeed reacted with a series of warning about grave consequences if Ishihara's plan would materialize.

The Noda government now faced a serious headache. Noda eventually decided to "nationalize" the islands rather than letting the Tokyo metro government buy them. He apparently believed that his action would maintain the *status quo*. He also indicated that the Chinese government had understood his intention, a claim that the Chinese government strongly rejected. Noda announced his decision on September 11, 2012, a week before the anniversary of Japan's seizure of Manchuria. The Chinese government reacted with unprecedented protests. The official channels froze. The Chinese government boats began regular patrol near Diaoyudao. A wave of anti-Japan demonstrations broke out. Sino-Japanese relations were now at their lowest since before 1972. Observers were now openly concerned that the two countries might have a military skirmish, which would be highly dangerous.

The LDP led by Abe Shinzō won a landslide electoral victory against the DPJ in December 2012. Departing from his conciliatory approach toward China during his short stint as prime minister in 2006–2007, Abe now took a hardline position on the Senkakus and also indicated his desire to visit Yasukuni as prime minister during the election campaign. The LDP now posed both a territorial dispute and history problems for Beijing. The LDP might be better organized than the DPJ government but now organized in a way that would be worse for China than the DPJ government.

China was also going through power transition. Xi Jinping assumed the party secretary general position on November 15, 2012, as expected. Two weeks later, Xi led the other six members of the standing committee of the politburo to the national museum for an exhibit on national revival. He announced his "China Dream" slogan (Wan 2013a). Xi was ambitious and determined from start, which would affect how he would deal with the tension with Japan. He had reportedly taken a hardline position over territorial issues as vice president.

Tensions between Abe's Japan and Xi's China continued to rise in 2013–2014, with close encounters by the patrol boats, navy ships, and fighter jets. The two governments also openly fought in public relations around the world. The multilateralization of the dispute had seriously begun after the collision incident. A military skirmish is no longer unfathomable.

Partly to appear reasonable and responsible for the Japanese audience and the international community, Abe and his advisors actively sought to arrange a meeting with Xi. With some general understanding about the territorial dispute and history, considered as concessions by the Chinese and later denied as such by the Japanese side, Abe and Xi met briefly on the occasion of the APEC summit in Beijing in November 2014. Despite the fact that the meeting was not particularly warmly, official dialogues gradually unfroze, allowing the two sides to discuss some concrete issues in a better atmosphere.

Abe called a general election shortly after his meeting with Xi Jinping in Beijing. It was surprising because Abe did not need another mandate to justify his decision to delay the second stage of a previously decided consumption tax raise from eight to ten percent given the worsening economic situation in Japan. Most observers argued that Abe was seeking an election for four years of LDP dominance before his popularity sank further. Abe seemed to believe that the LDP might lose some seats but could maintain its majority, reflected in his effort to lower expectations. However, the polls came to show that the LDP would possibly gain seats and might even win a two third majority on its own, thanks to the disarray of the opposition parties. In the end, the LDP lost four seats (from 295 to 291) while its junior partner New Komeito gained four (from 31 to 35).

Thus, the ruling coalition maintained its 326 seat absolute majority. Since the new lower house had been reduced by five seats, the coalition now has a higher percentage at 68.4 percent, a historical record (*Yomiuri shimbun* online December 15, 2014).

It was well understood that the economy was the top concern for this election and China was not mentioned that much. At the same time, the China factor was clearly in the background.[12] To some extent, one can take it for granted that the China concern is already understood. One damning criticism of the DPJ was its lack of decisiveness, with its handling of the fishing boat incident as a prominent exhibit. Abe and the LDP came to power based on the public's disillusion with the DPJ and the belief that the LDP would be a better leading force. It is unfortunate that the public had come to think that any decision would be better than no decisions. Furthermore, a rising nationalist sentiment means that Abe's appeal for a prominent Japan resonates with the public, particularly the young. The adjustment has been made about China.[13] To drive this point home, the U.S. factor was not discussed that much either in the December election, except in Okinawa. What is there to debate about when people share a strong consensus on a strong U.S. alliance?

Did Abe win a public mandate? On the one hand, he won a major electoral victory, which was a fact. At the same time, this election had the lowest voter turnout rate since the end of World War II, around 52 percent. Abe's electoral victory came about mainly because the opposition parties were in disarray. The polls showed clearly that the voters did not trust the opposition parties and preferred to give Abe's LDP more time and they wanted a leader that could make decisions in a stable political situation (*Yomiuri shimbun* online December 16, 2014; *Asahi shimbun* online December 18, 2014). Abe has clearly wanted to revise the Constitution. But the

---

[12] Some conservative media commentators actually attributed the LDP victory to the China factor (e.g. *Sankei shimbun* online December 15, 2014).

[13] The Japanese public does not trust China. A joint poll by *Yomiuri shimbun* and Gallop shows that 91 percent of the Japanese polled do not trust China, the highest level since the poll began in 2004. And the poll was conducted after the Abe–Xi meeting in Beijing (*Yomiuri shimbun* online December 23, 2014).

election did not suggest that a majority of voters wanted a revisionist, right-wing policy.[14] After all, the more rightist party for future generations led by an ultra-conservative political Ishihara Shintarō was virtually wiped out. The Komeito Party that supports pacifism gained 4 seats and now had 35 seats. The Japan Communist Party had more than doubled their seats. At the same time, the Japanese voters prefer a LDP government at helm, partly dealing with an assertive rising China in mind, which gives the Abe government much policy room.[15]

Despite resumption of diplomatic exchange, the larger trend of Sino-Japanese tensions continues. On the Japanese side, the Abe government continues to strengthen the U.S. alliance, to allow the Japanese military to operate outside Japan, to seek allies to counter China, to adapt domestic laws to relax regulations on arms export and international collaboration in defense research and production. His governance approach has so far worked well for him and for the LDP. Abe started the new year of 2015 with strong measures with China in mind. He increased defense budget, the third such increase in row since he took power. The new defense budget includes purchase of Osprey aircraft, amphibious vehicles, F35 fighters and other weapon systems to shore up defense of the Senkakus and other islands facing China. The LDP held a meeting on January 14, 2015 to consider creating a new international broadcasting agency to spread the Japanese government positions and counter what it views as Chinese and Korean propaganda over the history issue and territorial disputes. In that context, the Abe government has decided to increase diplomacy budget and slightly ODA budget (*Sankei shimbun* online January 14, 2015). Thus, Abe's

---

[14] In fact, a Kyodo News agency poll (2014) showed that 55.1 percent of respondents do not support Abe's defense and security policies against 33.6 percent said they do.

[15] A *Yomiuri shimbun* poll (online January 11, 2015) conducted in January 9–11, 2015 shows that support for the Abe cabinet increased from 49 percent in late December 2014 to 53 percent. While a slight majority did not think highly of Abe's economic performance, 64 percent of the polled had a high opinion of Abe's "active pacifism" while 27 percent said no.

Japan is now a normal state, utilizing all the normal instruments of state, military preparedness, diplomacy, economic statecraft and propaganda, to advance its national interests, which are heavily defined as competition with China.

On the Chinese side, Xi Jinping has consolidated his power and is apparently focused on advancing his domestic and foreign policy agenda in the coming year. His "China Dream" theme continues to be important and is tied with a "strong army dream" (Wan 2015). Thus, one should expect him to continue an assertive foreign policy. And he emphasizes China's past humiliation at the hands of Japanese. He has invited Russian President Putin to commemorate the 70th anniversary of victory over Japan in early September. The Chinese government has decided to stage a military parade then, an unprecedented event for such occasions, which is interpreted in Japan and elsewhere as a transparent move to intimidate Japan.

Put simply, we now have two strong leaders who are determined to defend their countries' national interests and honor, which are now viewed as in conflict with each other. While we may not see the type of diplomatic conflict resulting from ineptitude in the case of the Chinese fishing boat collision incident, we should be concerned about tensions and conflicts resulting from determined and coordinated strategic moves from the two governments. What makes management of Sino-Japanese relations so difficult now is a clash of national identities, as will be discussed in the next chapter.

Chapter 3

National Identities in Sino-Japanese Relations

National identities often take precedence over national interests in Sino-Japanese relations, and, in turn, these identities are influenced by the two countries' interactions. These identities explain why the ties between China and Japan seem peculiarly emotional relative to their relations with other countries. Affinity or arrogance resulting from a long history of cultural exchange, contempt, and victimization from wars or aggression since the 1890s and confidence in superior modernization, shape how the Chinese and Japanese view each other. In particular, both China and Japan have acquired a great power identity that is partially contingent on exclusivity with each other, which underlies their current tensions.

Three features of national identity deserve to be emphasized for influencing the Sino-Japanese relationship. First, once formed, they have a degree of stickiness even if the relationship has moved in a different direction. For example, the ugly mood that in the years 2002–2006 reinforced mutually negative identities continued to limit relations, despite official warmth in the following years. Second, identities evolve, particularly in relative saliency in the overall identity complex. Third, with relations compartmentalized from each state's overall foreign policy, such porousness damages bilateral ties when the two countries exhibit their worst tendencies toward each other, despite a calmer orientation overall.

This chapter examines the post-Cold War period in Sino-Japanese relations after reviewing the pre-1945 and Cold War periods for insights on how the bilateral identity gap took shape. I need to provide substantive discussion of the pre-war and post-war periods because what happened in the past has a crucial impact on relations today. I have previously discussed how Chinese and Japanese national identities, particularly how they played out in interactions, have affected the bilateral relationship and have been shaped by it (Wan 2006, 158–165). Here I deepen the analysis with specific attention to how these identities have been transformed through recent interactions and are complicating the cooperation that is understood to be in each country's national interest as China's rise reverberates in Japan's identity debate and, at the same time, fuels a more assertive outlook toward Japan as part of China's evolving national identity.

National identity is a complex and contested concept.[1] It is often reinvented to serve specific purposes (Befu 1993). In this chapter, I am concerned with how national identity relates closely to interaction, which involves watching with strong interest developments in the other country, particularly the attitudes of the other toward one's own country.[2] Samuel Huntington (2004, 23) noted in his study of American national identity that "identities are defined by the self, but they are the product of the interaction between the self and others. How others perceive an individual or group affects the self-definition of that individual or group." National identity has a strong component of exclusivity. Interaction often reinforces or creates perceptions that one side is indeed different. Familiarity can breed contempt. Identities are typically sticky; once they are formed, it takes time to change. This emerges clearly over the long history of Sino-Japanese interactions and mutual perceptions.

---

[1] On the complexity of identities in China, see Dittmer and Kim (1993).

[2] The national identity framework used in this chapter is influenced by Gilbert Rozman's analysis of national identities (Rozman 2012a).

Pre-1945 Interactions

Historically, China had a strong cultural influence on Japan, as seen in the conscious and organized cultural borrowing from China at the turn of the seventh century, which lasted for the next two centuries. Chinese culture affected mainly Japanese ruling elites and scholars at this early stage. The China factor is also reflected in the narrow world horizon for Japan at this time, which was largely limited to China, Korea, and India, with China being particularly important. This history shaped a strong Japanese sense of cultural affinity with China, which was based more on reading Chinese classics than on actual human interaction. The Japanese absorbed Chinese culture and developed their own distinct culture. A millennium after the massive wave of borrowing, Japanese officials again turned to Confucianism, as they strove to legitimize their political dominance, often by combining Neo-Confucianism with Shintoism. They differentiated cultural China from political China, which was made easier by the fact that there was no state-to-state relationship. More broadly, the Japanese sought to define Japaneseness against what they imagined to be Chineseness, as revealed in their literature starting in the tenth century (Sakaki 2006), while remaining within the Chinese world order by sharing the values and expectations that made East Asia different from the Western international system, whose impact was drawing closer (Suzuki 2009, 46–55). In the late Tokugawa period, a school of national learning emerged to emphasize Japan's unique imperial institution and values as superior to Chinese culture. With China's defeat in the Opium War and inability to resist the West, this contrast became increasingly appealing.

The Chinese were aware of Japan's presence and provided the earliest written records of the ancestors of the modern Japanese (Fogel 2009, 7–13). The first Chinese studies of Japan began in the fourteenth century due to the threat of "Japanese pirates" with blurred national origins. However, the Chinese did not conduct research in Japan (Yū 1998), and they were largely ignorant of what the Japanese wrote about China without concern for possible counterarguments from the Chinese (Sakaki 2006, 21). In an asymmetrical relationship, Japan was less central for China, which had established a sense of itself as the center of the world and largely focused on its relations with steppe peoples to the northwest and north (Perdue 2005). The Chinese Middle Kingdom mentality is now one of the analytical lenses used for studying Sino-Japanese tensions. Some say that cultural arrogance and contempt of Japan provoked resentment that such attitudes revealed a Chinese intention to dominate the country, which endures. Although such a psychological dynamic does exist, one needs to scrutinize the validity of such claims. Cultural arrogance *per se* does not necessarily lead to political efforts to dominate and subjugate. It is often the consequence rather than the root cause of political domination, although it may be a powerful enabling factor. The Chinese sense of cultural superiority, which does exist, was arguably superficial when it comes to Japan due to limited direct contact before the mid-nineteenth century.

In the Sino-Japanese War of 1894–1895, the Chinese and Japanese threw racist insults at each other with abandon, with the Chinese digging up ancient derogative terms for the Japanese and the Japanese creating their own insulting epithets (Paine 2003, 136–138). But one does not need centuries of interaction to exhibit cultural hatred in a time of war, as seen in the Pacific front of World War II between Japan and the United States in 1941–1945 (Dower 1986). Japan's delegation to the Chinese capital in AD 702 requested that their country be called Nihon (*Riben* in Chinese) instead of Wa (*Wo* in Chinese), which the Chinese had used for their country until then. The Chinese accepted this request and have used *Riben* ever since (Fogel 2009, 19). There has been a controversy over whether the term "*Wo*" was derogatory. Similarly, early Chinese rulers called agricultural peoples Koreans, Japanese, and Vietnamese "Eastern Barbarians" and "Southern Barbarians," but they subsequently called these countries as they preferred to be called and did not treat them as barbarians throughout history. Yet this does not mean that the Chinese came to appreciate Japanese culture or even to show much awareness of it.

Having had little exposure to Japanese culture before the late nineteenth century, the Chinese have needed to overcome a strong negative association of Japanese culture with the militaristic Japanese state. The import of Japanese culture coincided with, first, a clear sense of Japanese superiority, and then with outright aggression against China. If, at times, leaders appealed to cultural similarities in an effort to improve relations, resting their case on firm historical grounds, this message was repeatedly overwhelmed by the populist preoccupation with Japanese culture serving as the source of jingoism.

In the 1860s, China and Japan began to perceive each other in the context of the Western international system. By 1862, the Chinese had basically accepted this system after the British and French sacked Beijing for violating the treaties imposed after the Opium War. The Japanese no longer treated China as the Middle Kingdom. They were cordial and deferential because they wanted the right to trade and to have a consulate in Shanghai. During the next several decades, Japanese confidence grew as the gap between the two countries' reforms and modernization widened. In the midst of fervent Westernization, Japan began to reject Asia, culturally sharpening differences with it while drawing closer to the West. Fukuzawa Yukichi famously called for Japan to leave Asia and join the West and seek civilization, pointing to a divide between enlightened Japan and unenlightened China. He made it clear that China was a negative "other" to be rejected, whereas the West was a positive "other" to be emulated. Along with Nishi Amane, he had a tremendous impact in contrasting the Enlightenment and progress to Neo-Confucianism and stagnation (Najita 1974, 86–101). By contrast, China initially sought in vain to maintain the traditional East Asian international system (Suzuki 2009), incurring Japanese contempt and laying the basis for its adventurism in Asia.

Japan's psychological attempt to break from China and to adopt a Western lens to the world was reflected in its use of the name "Shina" rather than "Chūgoku" (the Middle Kingdom) for China after the Meiji Restoration (Tanaka 1993). This departed from the past practice of using the same characters, even though they were pronounced differently in China, Japan, and Korea, such as in the case of China accepting the characters for Nihon, pronounced

Riben. Because "Shina" consists of two Chinese characters that capture the Western pronunciation of China but otherwise have no intrinsic meaning and was imposed by Japan for discourse between the two countries, it conveyed Japan's superiority over China and was seen as derogatory. This is the reason that it was no longer used after Japan lost the war, and its revival by a few right-wing Japanese politicians would be reported resentfully in China.

Japan regained confidence in the late 1880s and the 1890s, particularly after winning the war with China. Chinese learning was part of Japanese tradition, which now drew more support. This would be the first period of a well-articulated identity of Japan as the most civilized country in Asia and the tutor for others. But the Western influence was felt in this process. Leading Asianists such as Okakura Tenshin framed their discussion based on an imported European discourse about Asia (Zachmann 2007). Japanese thinkers talked about pan-Asianism as a way to fend off Western pressure and viewed Japan's progress as tied to Asia's progress (Hotta 2007). This was based on an identity of superiority in Asia while keeping a distance from the West. The Sino-Japanese War of 1894–1895 partly resulted from clashing national identities, as recalled by Mutsu Munemitsu (1982), the Japanese foreign minister at the time. The war put Japan on the world map and won the country a large indemnity from China that helped stabilize its finance and monetary system. Its decisive victory had a great impact on its self-image. Equally important, the West came to view Japan as a modern power and China as a backward country, an easy target for imperialist powers (Paine 2003). Such perceptions led to different attitudes and policy toward the two, which contributed to self-images. Increased pressure from Japan focused China's emerging nationalism on it.

In the 1920s, the Japanese government turned to cultural diplomacy toward China. This was due to a confluence of factors. Japan's own internationalists were responding to democracy, disarmament, and peace. They were also concerned about increasing Chinese nationalism and Chinese's negative image of Japan, amid cultural rivalry with the United States and Europe. Some Japanese were asking questions one would hear today, namely, why students who have studied in Japan seem to dislike Japan while students who have studied in the United States seem pro-American. This awareness did not lead to any soul-searching about Japanese identity, although it did bring more money and better treatment of Chinese students. The Japanese government took the center stage, and took an approach that was different from the American one but similar to those of some European countries. It wanted to shape Chinese thinking. Some may see this as a case of cultural imperialism, but there was a degree of idealism and internationalism for many who were enthusiastic about this endeavor, and there was an attempt to elicit Chinese participation in some of the cultural projects (Teow 1999).

In the 1930s, some Japanese thinkers, particularly military officers, wanted Japan to unify Asia under its leadership in an epic battle against the Western powers (Peattie 1975). Japan descended into a period of heightened racist identity and military conquests, which ended in its own destruction. This period of militarized interaction, with the large presence of the Japanese military and the Japanese nationals in China who counted on the military for protection, furthered the Chinese association of the Japanese with the Japanese military (Fogel 2009, 3–4).

The Japanese national identity of superiority and contempt for the Chinese contributed to the start of the Second Sino-Japanese War of 1937–1945. As later research shows, the hawks within the Japanese army for expanding the war in 1937 were centered in the China Section of the General Staff Intelligence Division. Though they were considered second rate in the army because more promising officers developed expertise on Europe and the United States, the division's old China hands had acquired their expertise through service with the field units and special service organs in China, focusing on espionage and subversion to keep China weak and divided. Not surprisingly, they did not acquire a deep knowledge of China, particularly the meaning of rising Chinese nationalism. Their contempt for Chinese military capabilities, shared by the army and the country, resulted in their limited knowledge of China and Japan's sinking ever deeper into a prolonged war on the continent (Peattie 1975, 286–289).

Japan's invasion and atrocities, particularly the Nanjing Massacre, have defined contemporary Chinese nationalism. The personal suffering and humiliation experienced by many Chinese were passed down from generation to generation, forming a societal basis for anger toward Japan. However, there were some "good Japanese" from the Chinese perspective. Some worked for the Nationalists as well as the Communist government or armies during the war. Communist Party cadres working with them during the war became key players dealing with Japan affairs for the People's Republic of China. And the large number of Japanese who had China experience and felt guilty or affection for China formed the social basis for "friendship" with China in later years (Mizutani 2006). In contrast, the far more "good Chinese" for imperial Japan,[3] as collaborators with a defeated country, played no visible role in post-war "friendship."

At least four arguments have been raised to showcase the powerful legacy of historical memories left for China as it reasserted itself under Communist leadership and Japan as it found a new direction through democracy dominated by one party. First, the long delay in normalization without Japan making genuine efforts toward reconciliation permitted the gap in national identities to harden. In modern times, failure to bridge differences from a war of such magnitude is a recipe for prolonged enmity, primarily from the victim's side. Second, a cause of this legacy can be traced to the abnormal national identity in post-war Japan, where refutations of the revisionist thinking of right-wing figures resonate weakly in a population distracted by other identity themes while the political system gives veto power to those with the strongest national identity consciousness. Illusions about China, such as that growing dependency on Japan would diminish historical resentments or that propaganda was solely responsible for enduring resentment, misled many Japanese. Third, exceptional features of Chinese national identity nurtured by Communist leaders also bear responsibility for

---

[3]We are beginning to see in-depth studies of Chinese collaborators based on archives in China. See Pan (2006); Wang (2008).

this gap. If the Maoist approach to national identity spared the Japanese nation as a whole from blame, it also distorted history and international relations to such a degree that a balanced perspective on postwar Japan was unrealizable, even after the two countries normalized relations, leading to "friendship" ties. Starting in the mid-1980s, Chinese leaders had decided to oppose on moral ground Japan's revival as both a political and military great power, and then, as revealed in the brief effort at "new thinking" in 2003, various one-sided interpretations of Japan were reinforced as part of China's identity. Fourth and finally, a failure to narrow the gap over pre-1945 history is rooted in competition for leadership in East Asia, in which China is driven to reassert its superiority and Japan is anxious to avoid any reinforcement of the opprobrium of its past immorality.

Cold War Interactions

China and Japan ended up in different places in post-war East Asian international relations defined by the Cold War. China was pulled toward world revolution, at first in the camp led by the Soviet Union, and Japan was directed toward pacifism and identity with the West rather than Asia. Thus the interactions between China and Japan in the years before their 1972 normalization were shaped in important ways by their evolving national identity complexes.

Japan could not establish diplomatic relations with China, even though many Japanese wanted to do so. The United States left some room for economic and cultural exchanges, being aware of China's prior economic importance for Japan and the consensus in Japan, not only for economic reasons, of the need to expand contacts with the Asian continent (Schaller 1997, 77–95). Japan's relationship with China was noticeably different from that between the United States and China (Ogata 1988). Because of the Korean War, the United States had virtually no ties with China. By contrast, Japan's unofficial economic, cultural, and political contacts with China were upgraded over time to semiofficial status and increasingly served different national identity goals.

A combination of war guilt and revived appreciation of Chinese cultural influence on Japan helped the Japanese form a favorable view of China. Japan's progressive forces identified, to some extent, with a socialist China, while also finding it useful in their opposition to the U.S. alliance and American military bases in Japan. If conservatives stressed the value of the alliance and friendship toward Taiwan, many welcomed diversification through Asian networks in order to avoid subversion from a United States-centered national identity. However, they rejected the progressive tendency to use the China factor to bolster identity as a victimizer of Asia, fearing that Japanese youth would become masochistic in lieu of a positive understanding of Japanese history. On the basis of cultural affinities and experience in China, the Japanese tended to view the members of the Chinese Communist Party as nationalists who were bound to clash with the Soviet Union. Yoshida Shigeru predicted that China would eventually split from the Soviet Union, pointing to the "extremely proud" Chinese character (Chin 2000, 9–18). The Japanese also felt that as fellow Asians, they understood China better than the Americans.

The Chinese government understood and took advantage of Japan's divisions over China and sense of war guilt and culture debt. Officials such as Zhou Enlai appealed to Japanese identity as a teacher and early modernizer and a shared sense of Asian destiny.

From 1952 to 1972, China juggled several identities shaping its foreign policy: Socialist identity, third world identity, victimization-based identity, and Asian identity. Due to its victimization identity, China criticized Prime ministers Kishi Nobosuke and Satō Eisaku for reviving militarism, but Japan was a low priority compared with the Soviet Union and United States. Given frequent visits by Japan's progressive leaders, China had reason to emphasize Asian identity too.

Apart from its national interest in neutralizing Japan from a hostile encirclement of China in the 1950s and in seeking trade and technology in the 1960s, China's policy toward Japan was also shaped by its class-based ideology that the majority of Japanese people were victims of Japanese militarism and only a minority of Japanese militarists was responsible for a common disaster for the Chinese and

Japanese peoples. Such an assessment played a central role in Mao Zedong's decision not to seek reparations from Japan out of concern that it would put too much of a burden on innocent Japanese. Given Mao's status and the authoritarian nature of Chinese politics, strong resentment against Japan among ordinary people was suppressed. China was preoccupied with frequent domestic strife, and thus it had plenty of "villains" at home for both its class struggle and demonization of first the United States as the capitalist/imperialist enemy and then the Soviet Union as the revisionist betrayer of socialist identity. This left Japan as mostly an afterthought.

Normalization of China–Japan relations led to the "1972 system," a carefully constructed framework for the bilateral relationship (Kokubun 2001). National interests were crucial, but national identities also played a role. In the 1970s, China tried to get Japan to play a more strategic role against the Soviet Union, but this did not have a visible effect on Japan's well-entrenched identity as a peaceful country not involved in international conflict, even though the country was allied with the United States and hosted American bases. Starting reform in 1978, China publicly sought out Japan's assistance, which reinforced Japan's identity as the most advanced country in Asia and alleviated its sense of guilt because it was helping the country it had victimized. In a dramatic shift, the Chinese government sought official development assistance, direct investment, and policy advice for economic activities (Lee 1984). This approach worked to a large extent because Japan's wartime generation largely felt guilty and expected resentment from the Chinese. The fact that the Chinese government seemed forward looking and sincere in forging a relationship fit with the Japanese desire to pay in some way for the past and then move on and be proud of themselves again. The Japanese were rightly proud of their post-war economic miracle, and by sharing their economic model with the Chinese, they expected to transform Chinese national identity away from socialism and victimization and toward shared modernization and Asian identity. Japan's large program of official development assistance was meant as compensation for past aggression, even if China barely publicized it.

In the 1980s, there were some incidents involving history textbooks and a prime ministerial visit to Yasukuni Shrine. China's pressure played into Japan's divided politics and achieved some results but could not solve the problem to its ultimate satisfaction because Japan had divided identities. This was still manageable because Japan could balance it psychologically as a teacher and by thinking that this phase would pass as China became more moderate as it developed. On the Chinese side, there was a division between the state and the society not far below the surface. The government handled Japan-related issues politically, often not to the satisfaction of much of the citizenry.

Post-war interaction between China and Japan was largely asymmetrical. Before 1972, the Japanese could deal with China only on a societal level, but Japanese officials and politicians also had ways to participate. On the Chinese side, it was a state-controlled process, consistent with overall foreign relations at the time. Private Chinese citizens could not take the initiative in engaging the Japanese. Such a pattern continued on the Chinese side in the 1970s. Japan's aggression was not studied, and scholars were urged to emphasize friendship, but history and victimization-based national identity loomed large in the background. On the Japanese side, the government took center stage after diplomatic relations were established, as the public gradually grew more enthusiastic.

With the economic reform in 1978, social restrictions in China began to relax, which led to greater direct interaction between Chinese and Japanese citizens. A new wave of Chinese students and trainees came to Japan, often funded by the Japanese government, foundations, companies, or universities. Japanese businessmen, scholars, and tourists became part of the Chinese scene. The drastic expansion of trade and investment during those years was also a powerful engine for the two countries. The two governments adopted policies to promote bilateral exchanges to lay a foundation for further friendship. As a dramatic example, Hu Yaobang, arguably the most pro-Japan Chinese politician since 1949, invited 3,000 Japanese youth to China in the mid-1980s. However, these intensified interactions did not prevent the relationship from deteriorating, and the interactions even had some negative short-term effects. With better access to China, the Japanese came to have a more realistic assessment of the situation in the country, adjusting overly rosy assessments of views of their country. On the Chinese side, those who came to Japan or interacted with Japanese tended to reject the excessively negative views of Japan ingrained in the Chinese public, but their new understanding was overwhelmed by the public's negativity.

If there had not been state-led bilateral interactions, the honeymoon would not have happened. Despite the sense of guilt, it would be hard to imagine that the Japanese elites would have felt as willing to cooperate if they had confronted the Chinese public's long-held anger at Japan. Indeed, as they acquired a better understanding, they could have responded with contempt for China. At the same time, it would have been better if the two countries had more genuine interactions starting in 1972. Suppression of some emotions might have been expedient, but it pushed the problem toward the future. In fact, when the Chinese government's position changed and unleashed societal anger, the relationship was prone to suffer a greater shock. An accurate understanding of Chinese sentiment could have led the Japanese to view history differently and recognize the need for greater urgency. The older generations of elites arguably could have better handled a confrontation over the national identity gap. After all, they had seen the war, the worst kind of bilateral interactions, and had the credentials and experience to manage a public confrontation, which could have served as a kind of immunization for constructing a long-term, healthy relationship.

In the 1980s, conditions were more favorable for facing the emotions of clashing historical memories. Japan had an opportunity to proceed from confidence, while China was striving for inclusion in the regional and global community with no foundation for arrogance. Japan would have had to take the initiative to win the trust of the Chinese as well as convince the leadership, as Nakasone Yasuhiro tried with a flawed strategy in his dealings with Hu Yaobang. Not only did overconfidence expose Japan's lack of foresight, but the response in China as Hu was ousted revealed China's reluctance to narrow this identity gap. National interests were quite well aligned, but the national identity gap widened.

The Sino-Japanese relationship remained largely unchanged in its basic 1972 framework, which appeared special compared with their relationships with other countries, except for Japan's more special relationship with the United States. Ties were inconsistent with their national interests, and national identities were lurking in the background and even surfaced from time to time, because some Japanese leaders could not wait to press a revisionist agenda as they warned that China was intervening in Japan's internal affairs and hurting its prestige, while some Chinese leaders called the Chinese approach toward Japan too soft and insisted that Japan could not be trusted without confronting its history.

Post-Cold War Interactions

The end of the Cold War did not predetermine the nature of the Sino-Japanese bilateral relationship. Both sides had been struggling with their national identities as perceptions of how the other thinks fed into this process. In the first half of the 1990s, the focus in each state was on the United States. With it leading in isolating and sanctioning China, Beijing saw Japan as the weakest link, and thus made extra efforts to cultivate relations with Japanese visitors. The Japanese also had their own reasons to maintain good relations with China, sensing an opportunity to act as a bridge between China and the West, which could allow them to leverage better relations with both sides to their advantage. The Chinese felt Japan owed China a historical debt not to pressure it for human rights. The Japanese understood that in light of their troubled modern history in China and a stronger Asian identity after the Cold War, they had to keep a low profile. Many were concerned about China's collapse rather than its rise, renewing Japan's identity as a teacher that could lend a helping hand to a China in trouble. Soon, when Japan was challenging the Washington consensus, they also saw China's economic growth as confirming Japan's development model. If Japan had to do something in line with the West because it did not want to look too different, knowing well that much had been said about such differences in the heat of trade wars, China understood Japan's dilemma and wisely did not overreact.

New developments taking place at this time would have a greater impact in later years. The Japanese government openly talked about putting its relationship with China in a global context, which reflected its desire to end the special relationship as its status in the world was rising rapidly. A globalized Japan–China relationship would work to its advantage by moving beyond the 1972 system in which Japan seemed to be bowing to its neighbors over history. The Japanese were also reacting to criticism of checkbook diplomacy during the Persian Gulf War. Many felt that Japan needed to make political and military contributions to acquire an international status consistent with its economic power. Given trade tension with the Bill Clinton administration, the United States rather than China was at the center of Japanese identity consciousness.

In the early 1990s, a debate ensued about how to better assert Japan's identity, which had ramifications for the identity gap with China. One focus was internationalism and international contributions. Ozawa Ichirō and Hashimoto Ryūtarō stressed political and military contributions. Ozawa felt that Japan had to seek international cooperation to ensure its security, which economic power alone could not. Hashimoto talked more about Japan's unique traditions. By contrast, Takemura Masayoshi and Kaifu Toshiki focused on pacifist contributions, as the latter highlighted Japan's harmonious relations with the environment. All these politicians wanted Japan to emphasize greater contributions to the international community in exchange for higher standing (Nakano 1998), presenting as a responsible member of the existing legitimate international society. In the mid-1990s, Japan moved gradually toward greater security responsibilities, a shift mainly meant to shore up its alliance with the United States and for it to become a normal, great power respected in the world.

Japan tried to reconcile internationalism and Asianism at a time when there was much discussion of Japan "re-entering Asia." This failed because of contradictions in the way Japan approached these identity issues and also because of China's new assertiveness rather than Japan's seizing the opportunity. To make Japan a normal state, some conservatives felt that they had to go back to the root of what they viewed as its abnormal status, which would reignite disputes with its Asian neighbors over history (Hasegawa and Togo 2008). After the U.S. government adjusted its policy to strengthen the alliance, Japan continued to pursue Asianism in a cautious manner while testing China amid recurrent uncertainties in bilateral relations.

Japan's shift toward greater security cooperation in about 1994 was largely read as threatening in China, compounding the reaction to its growing revisionist views in Japan. The Chinese government turned to patriotic education as a way to shore up its legitimacy after the Tiananmen massacre in 1989, recalling its status as a great power for two millennia and as a victim in modern history (Swaine 1995, 83–84; Kirby 1994). This move was triggered mainly by China's negative reaction to the West; but once the patriotic campaign began, it could not help but focus on Japan, which did the most damage to China and gave the Chinese Communist Party legitimacy in the resistance struggle (Hughes 2008). Japan remained the crucial "other" in China's victimization-based national identity (Suzuki 2007). One often hears people argue whether negative views of Japan come from the top or the bottom. Both are important. If resentment against the United States is often offset by admiration, the case of Japan aroused a more unambiguous reaction.

China took the first move, leading to a downward spiral. When Western pressure began to ease in 1994, the Chinese government became more critical of Japan, which in turn fueled Japanese resentment. The Taiwan Strait crisis began as a triangular dynamic involving Beijing, Taipei, and Washington but spilled over to Sino-Japanese relations when the issue arose of whether the United States–Japan alliance covers Taiwan, and Japanese saw it as added reason for strengthening the alliance. Feeling that only Chinese and Koreans were so critical when their country was respected in the rest of the world, the Japanese were alienated, and this was compounded by generational change. From 1981 to 2005, those who had experienced World War II had decreased from 46.2 to 16.0 percent, as younger generation preferred to focus instead on Japan's positive contributions in the post-war era (*Yomiuri shimbun* War Responsibilities Examining Committee 2009, 222–224). One senior Japanese diplomat explained to me that he felt that his grandfather's generation did bad things in Asia and was wrong, his father's generation tried very hard to be good, and now his generation is not denying history but does want to move forward.

Japan's identity as a democratic country also mattered. The difference in political regimes had become an important factor to explain why the two countries diverge, why the Chinese side behaves as it does, which should not be taken seriously, and why Japan cannot ultimately trust China. The Tiananmen massacre seriously damaged China's image, even though the Japanese government took a low posture, and its effect intensified with the widening identity gap in the second half of the 1990s. One way to reconcile internationalism and Asianism is to see Japan as a voice of human rights and democracy in the international community and in Asia. When Abe Shinzō and Asō Tarō toned down their insistence on Japanese uniqueness in favor of claims to be pursuing value-based internationalism, they were in obvious tension with a non-democratic China.[4] Although neither explicitly criticized China's non-democratic values and systems while in office, both emphasized Japan's shared democratic values with the United States, India, and Australia, and this explains a policy to improve strategic cooperation with major democracies as a check on China, which is increasingly viewed as a threat.

With Jiang Zemin's visit to the United States and Clinton's visit to China, the Chinese government grew more confident in dealing with Japan. Jiang's 1998 visit to Japan revealed his personal sentiments, but also his underestimation of Japan in contrast to the United States, which he saw as central to China's domestic reform and foreign relations. The ill will generated by this visit triggered

---

[4]For their political views, see Abe (2006); Asō (2007a); Asō (2007b).

popular reactions on both sides. With cyber-nationalism on the rise, Japan was a tempting target. In the years 2003–2006, the absence of summits blamed on Koizumi Junichiro's Yasukuni Shrine visits further fueled these emotions (Wu 2007). A vicious cycle unfolded. The national identities of both sides clashed with each other. Both sought great power identities (Rozman 1999 and 2002), but they viewed each other as a main obstacle to that ambition. The compromise reached in October 2006 involved virtually no change of mind on either side. The Chinese and Japanese think less and less of each other because they think the other thinks less and less of them. In a speech on October 24, 2008, before Hu Jintao, Asō explained low mutual positive views despite strong economic interdependence by saying, "In both Japan and China, the percentage of people holding at least some degree of positive feelings towards the other country does not even reach 30." He then noted that "even if we hold different views, at a minimum, we should always have a correct understanding of what the other is thinking." He advocated youth exchanges as a way to show that what they have heard is not true. A Chinese youth may find out that Japan is not becoming militaristic and a Japanese youth may realize that "I had heard that in China there is strong anti-Japan sentiment, but in fact everyone I met was very kind."[5]

One important issue is where the Japanese or Chinese consider their country to be relative to each other. China has been gaining rapidly on Japan, which is affecting its identity. The Ministry of Economy, Trade, and Industry (METI) issued a report in the summer of 2009 that China would surpass Japan in gross domestic product by the end of year. Most elites with whom I talked in Tokyo at the time expressed sadness as Japanese. As one put it, "Number 3 is not Number 2. Who cares about Number 3?" The fact that there was much discussion of the "Group of Two" between the United

---

[5] Asō Tarō, "My Personal Conviction Regarding Japan–China Relations," talk given at the Reception to Commemorate the Thirtieth Anniversary of the Conclusion of the Treaty of Peace and Friendship between Japan and China, October 24, 2008, Great Hall of the People, Beijing. Press Release, Embassy of Japan, Washington, October 24, 2008.

States and China for dealing with the 2008 global financial crisis adds to this anxiety about Japan's place in the world. The fact that the crisis started in the United States while China continues to grow is a serious worry for many Japanese commentators (Moriki 2009). But more serious scholars and officials also see a sea change in world politics, in which China is rising, to which Japan has to adapt (e.g. Sakakibara 2007). There is a broad concern over China's military modernization (e.g. Kayahara 2008), which is accompanied by reluctant acceptance of Japan's declining power position in the world.

To be sure, the Japanese are aware of the severe challenges that China is facing. A quick glance at the Yaesu Book Center near Tokyo Station will give one a strong impression of "negative" stories about income disparities, corruption, crimes, and so on, with new titles added frequently. However, such negative stories, which are often accurate portrayals of the situation in China, are nothing new. The dominant view among Japanese policy elites has recently tilted to the China rising theme rather than the China collapsing theme.[6] As a senior METI official explained to me in July 2009, whereas, he had told people not to worry about China a number of years ago, now he wondered how much longer Beijing would maintain such a rapid pace of growth. He judged the Chinese government "wise enough" to continue China's economic success. Although he continued to view China as an opportunity for Japanese companies, he was not alone in being clearly concerned.

Partly because of a stronger yen, Japan barely maintained its position in 2009. But in mid-August 2010, news broke that China had surpassed Japan as the world's second-largest economy. The Japanese media did not play up the story. For example, *Yomiuri shimbun* reported on this on page 3 on August 17, 2010. The lead economic story on the front page was how to stimulate the economy. Even related to China, there was a much longer story on the front

---

[6]There are, of course, views by some leading thinkers that China's rise is not as impressive as it appears. E.g. Watanabe and Miwara (2009) view China's growth as merely based on processing.

page about how China is expanding its English-language media presence in the United States. Given a lengthy heat wave in the hottest month since 1946, the strongest yen for the past 15 years, a sharp decline in the stock market, and a high drama of political fights within the ruling Democratic Party of Japan, the Japanese public did not react to Japan's loss in status. Some commentators suggested that many Japanese had already been resigned to a declining Japan.[7]

Japanese resignation about their declining power does not mean that the Japanese are now ready to embrace China or that the government is no longer hedging against China's perceived expansion. According to a poll released by the *China Daily* of China and Genron NPO of Japan on August 14, 2010, 72.0 percent of Japanese said in interviews done in June and July that they had an unfavorable impression of China, citing poisoned food and China's pursuit of energy and natural resources. This was only slightly better than the 73.2 percent reported in 2009. By contrast, the Chinese view of Japan had improved more, with negative feelings declining from 65.2 percent in 2009 to 55.9 percent in 2010. The Japanese media believed that was mainly due to the more positive media coverage of Japan in China. The Japanese fear of China is based on current events, whereas the Chinese think mainly about the past (*Japan Times* 2010a). The Japanese government is becoming more concerned about China's military modernization and its intention in the world. The Council on Security and Defense Capabilities in New Era, a private advisory board, submitted its final report to Prime Minister Kan Naoto on August 27, 2010, prepared for a planned revision of the defense program outline for the country. The council study reportedly called for a more proactive defense and cited China's military buildup and naval activities (*Japan Times* 2010b). The Democratic Party of Japan government's view was reflected in the Defense Ministry's annual defense white paper issued on September 10, 2010.

---

[7]According to an earlier poll, the Japanese public was divided over whether it would be a problem to lose the number two position to China. And more than half those polled did not want Japan to be a great power. (*Japan Times* 2010c).

This white paper used more space to express concern about China's rapidly increasing defense budgets and lack of transparency in its intention, detailing the Chinese navy activities close to Japan (*Asahi shimbun evening* September 10, 2010, 2). The Democratic Party of Japan did not differ that much from the Liberal Democratic Party in this regard (*Asahi shimbun* September 11, 2010, 4).

There is virtually no Japanese acceptance of a scenario in which China would dominate in Asia, given Japanese identity. As one China school diplomat who favors good relations with China explained to me, Japanese are OK if the United States or France does better than Japan, but not China. Yet there is a sense of resignation to the fact that Japan may not be able to compete with China over gross domestic product, given the country's demographic decline and unstable politics. There is a shifting focus on Japan's comparative advantage and options in a world of a relatively declining America and a rising China. Opinions vary, but a common theme is to subtly downplay hard material power resources and to favor Japan's soft power or unique contributions, such as "Cool Japan," which attracts the youth of the world. An illustration of this is Nakanishi Terumasa's view that Japan's real strength lies in its "solid" nature and that it is more important to be solid than strong. Japan also draws strength from its traditional values and the emperor system, its autonomy, its people, and its entrepreneurship (Nakanishi 2009).[8] This quest for pride in a unique identity is unlikely to produce any consensus, given the vagueness of any comparative advantage with China, whose national identity looms in the shadows of such claims.

The Taiwan issue was part of a broader Japanese tendency to view China as an empire with distinct ethnic groups. Such a tendency was used before the war to carve out the Japanese sphere of influence from China by defining certain regions as distinct from "China proper." A good example is an artificial Japanese definition of "Manchurians" as different from Han Chinese. In post-war

---

[8] He also doubts the reliability of the United States, which necessarily pursues its own national interests.

periods, the Japanese continue to view China as a conglomeration of different nationalities, albeit not from an imperialist intent to divide and conquer. In recent years, there has been much interest in Tibetans and Uighurs and other minority issues. The current Japanese way of thinking is actually consistent with much of Western scholarship on China, but it nevertheless conflicts with Beijing's views. Japan's official position has been cautious, but underlying views of China guide some policy choices that have an impact on the bilateral relationship.

The United States continues to heavily factor in Chinese and Japanese thinking. On some level, a rising China means that the Chinese have gained more confidence and worry less whether the United States will lean toward Japan. As a matter of fact, from the Chinese perspective, the United States has always leaned toward Japan on issues that truly matter in the post-war decades. The Japanese have been more sensitive about the United States treating China as more important while relegating Japan to a position of irrelevance. As a recent example, the Japanese media's initial reaction to Barack Obama's victory in the 2008 U.S. presidential election was that he would stress China's importance at Japan's expense (Doi 2008).[9] This, of course, shows that the U.S. factor makes Japan view China as a competitor for America's attention, whether or not the Chinese are actually trying to be so.

Both Japan and China have been eager for some sort of Asianism to take root that would limit U.S. dominance in the region. Both have questioned U.S. values and looked for partners in Asia to gain leverage in asserting their own approach to values. After the Cold War, there was an upsurge in Japanese interest in Asianism (Rozman 2008). Indeed, in the 1990s one may argue that China's economic success contributed to this rediscovered regional identity (Nakano 1998, 506). However, the window of opportunity for China and Japan to narrow their identity gap following this pathway after fluctuating over a decade has been closing. By the time China became serious about pursuing regionalism, Japan had

---

[9] My reading of selected Japanese newspapers confirmed her observation.

grown more suspicious of China's intention to marginalize it. Starting in the early 2000s, it grew nervous about China's ambitions to gain dominance over Asia. In 2010, this turned into alarm. A decidedly more confident China was no longer reassuring Japan, as it had once done. With growing doubts about China's intentions vis-à-vis the East China Sea, the South China Sea, Taiwan, and the Korean Peninsula, the Japanese are in the midst of redefining China more negatively and reconstructing their own national identity in opposition to China's.

The Chinese and Japanese have studied each other extensively in recent years. The Japanese scholars have had the advantage of being in a more open society and freer academic environment. But studies of Japan in China have also improved. Some Japan-trained Chinese scholars are actively teaching and writing about Japan. A large number of Chinese citizens or China-born naturalized Japanese citizens teach and do research in Japan, and they have published a large number of books on various aspects of China and Japan, past and present, in Japan and China (e.g. Zhu 2009; Li 2010; Wu 2010). In recent years, Japanese students have also been studying for degrees in Chinese universities, and it is just a matter of time before some will publish books in Chinese.[10]

There is a positive trend of joint research projects that attempt to go beyond national borders (e.g. Ryū and Kawashima 2009; Kishi 2009; Mitani and Kimu 2007; Ryū, Mitani and Yang 2006). The process of these projects and outputs can only deepen mutual understanding, if not friendship, in all cases. Even if scholars do not physically participate in collaborations, they are increasingly aware of academic writings from the other country, as shown in the reference lists in their works. Put simply, the Chinese and Japanese now have to imagine their national identities partly defined in relations to each other under the gaze of the other. But despite a better

---

[10] Even for those without Chinese degrees, we begin to see publications or blogging in Chinese. E.g. Fujiwara Daisuke (2008), who was a correspondent for Japan's TBS, wrote in Chinese for Chinese audience about some very sensitive topics voicing Japanese perspective.

mutual understanding among some scholars, the identity gap between the two countries has not narrowed, as shown in opinion polls and in comments by observers on both sides.

For decades, it was assumed that the Sino-Japanese identity gap was largely about history — since the end of the Cold War, issues linked to history have been conspicuous in arousing national identity consciousness toward the other country — and it would gradually diminish as the two countries interacted more closely and became more interdependent. The two countries have become highly interdependent economically, and person-to-person interaction has also expanded dramatically with an ever-increasing number of Chinese tourists going to Japan due to rising Chinese incomes and a corresponding relaxation of visa requirements by the Japanese government and a greater number of Japanese nationals studying and working in China.[11] Then why has the national identity gap not narrowed?

One immediate reason is that much of this interaction is driven by pragmatic economic motives. The Japanese welcome Chinese tourists as a source of income, which has been the case for China's view of Japanese tourists for a much longer period, and the increasing number of Japanese learn Chinese and go to China in order to advance their careers, similar to their Chinese counterparts in an earlier period. In fact, a persistently negative Japanese view of China results from a new source: Ordinary Japanese being more exposed to Chinese nationals in Japan, who are often portrayed as not that well mannered.

A more fundamental reason for the persistent gap is divergence in recent aspects of worldview. For instance, despite Prime Minister Hatoyama Yukio's enthusiasm for cooperating with China in forging an East Asian community, there was no progress in narrowing differences in visions of what such a community signifies. The two states disagree on how to manage climate change, how to advance toward

---

[11] Although Japan was viewed as a land of opportunity for young Chinese for a long time, China, particularly Shanghai, has become attractive in recent years for some young Japanese, particularly women, who find work more challenging and promotion more likely working in Japanese or foreign firms or starting their own business. For recent Japanese media coverage, see *Asahi shimbun* September 6, 2010, 3.

denuclearization, and how to combine market forces with state guidance of the economy — to mention three recent themes highlighted at global summits. Japan has drifted closer to the United States in advocacy of universal values at the very time China has become more assertive in challenging some of these values and pressing for a different regional and global order. Although clashing national interests are evident, the growing hiatus in foreign policy choices is couched in national identity thinking.

As a case in point, it is recognized by some of the most experienced observers of Sino-Japanese relations that the single most important bilateral issue now is the territorial dispute in the East China Sea, which starts with and feeds back into the identity gap. This was confirmed when a Chinese boat and two Japanese Coast Guard ships had a collision incident near the Senkaku/Diaoyudao Islands on September 7, 2010, an accident waiting to happen. The Japanese government decided to try the Chinese captain in the Japanese court according to Japanese law while calling on the Chinese side to be calm. Predictably, however, the Chinese government took a strong stance, calling for the immediate release of the captain and then suspending the scheduled talks on the East China Sea and canceling a senior Chinese legislator's planned visit to Japan. The Chinese government was responding to public pressure for tough actions against Japan and was also clearly angered by Tokyo's initial downplaying of the seriousness of the incident, which fits their perception of an arrogant country wantonly disregarding the sentiment of its neighbors.[12] On the Japanese side, a question was raised in the media of why China was acting so tough, with one reason cited as China's stronger big power mentality (*Asahi shimbun* September 14, 2010, 3). The national identity gap thus contributed to the escalation of the incident.

The fishing boat collision incident also further enlarged the identity gap between China and Japan. Similar to the Americans and

---

[12]Chinese state councilor Dai Bingguo called in the Japanese ambassador at midnight, urging the Japanese government not to "misjudge the situation" and to make "a wise political decision" (China News Agency online September 12, 2010).

some of China's Asian neighbors, the Japanese view China as too aggressive since around early 2009. With China's protection of North Korea despite the sinking of the South Korean warship Cheonan in March 2010 and the North Korean shelling of Yeonpyeong Island in October 2010 as well as Chinese tension with Vietnam and the Philippines in the South China Sea, the Japanese policy elites now feel strongly that China is an outlier in Asia and Japan needs to cooperate more actively with the United States and other countries to force China to play by the international rules. Beijing's support for Kim Jong-un after his father Kim Jong-Il died in December 2011 further damaged its reputation in the eyes of the Japanese even though Tokyo wanted to utilize Beijing's perceived leverage over Pyongyang to advance its own policy objectives. Conversely, for many Chinese, Japan's tougher stance proves their suspicion that Japan always wants to keep China divided and weak.

Conclusion

The relationship between China and Japan seems to have a clear trajectory looking back, with good reasons why it makes a turn here or there. However, this relationship has never been predetermined, similar to all other bilateral relationships. Different historical outcomes could have been imagined and were imagined at different times. National identities have been important but have had a complex causal impact on the bilateral relationship and have in turn been informed by it. There are layers of national identities, and how important they are is partially contingent upon the distribution of national interests at a given time and the internal dynamic of national identities enhanced by generational changes.

The national identity gap between China and Japan is now deeply ingrained, centered initially on an inability to achieve reconciliation over Japan's aggressive conduct up to 1945. Various attempts to narrow this divide over history have not succeeded (He 2009). The friendship mode of relations offered only a superficial approach to reducing tensions over history. Efforts to draw attention to other periods of history and patterns of mutual benefit failed to elicit public support, remaining peripheral to national identity. When circumstances were most favorable for reducing differences over history, the visit by Nakasone to the Yasukuni Shrine and the purge of Hu Yaobang with criticisms of his overfriendliness to Japan were symptomatic of the lack of receptivity in both countries. After nearly 40 years of normalized relations, there is no sign that the tremendous benefits both sides have gained are being appreciated at the level of national identity. Instead, the divide over Japanese aggression is being compounded by a widening divergence in outlooks vital to national identity.

Looking into the future, there are strong uncertainties about how the Sino-Japanese relationship and the national identity gap will evolve. In the end, the Sino-Japanese relationship will largely be what the two countries will make of it. The national identities that may be positive or negative for the bilateral relationship are both present. Despite real underlying challenges to the relationship, what identities the Chinese and Japanese will seize upon will have a large impact on their future relations, which will in turn help shape their identities.

As for the identity gap, the past experience shows that the official relationship does affect the underlying perception and identity, but not in an immediate or one-to-one fashion. On the Chinese side, a positive tone set by the government may mean room for a more complex discourse about Japan or past interactions with the Japanese, which may contribute to a narrower identity gap between the two nations. But the uncertainty lies in whether the periodic official warmth will last pending domestic and international developments.

Will greater economic and cultural interaction improve the two countries' mutual images? Such interaction has so far failed to close the identity gap, and some of the harshest critics of China studied in China. At the same time, it is likely that the interaction in recent years will come to play a bigger, positive role in the next round. After all, the promoters of Sino-Japanese interaction are mostly driven by a desire for the Chinese and Japanese to know each other more realistically with their own eyes, rather than viewing each other based on mere imagination or fed information. Logically, close interaction should help narrow the identity gap in the long run because much of the gap has been based on wild imagination, such as "Japan wants to revive militarism," even though one should not anticipate quick results.

Chapter 4

Japan Views the Sino-U.S. National Identity Gap

The United States has been the most important factor in Sino-Japanese relations since before the start of the Pacific War. The United States emerged as the world superpower after the war and dominated over Japan as a protector and an ally. The Cold War constrained the ability of the Japanese government to develop a diplomatic relationship with China against its own identities and interests. Throughout its post-war history, the Japanese government has sought at times to enlarge its autonomy from the United States but has ended up depending even more on the United States facing a rising China. This chapter focuses on only part of that U.S.–Japan–China triangular dynamic, namely how the Japanese view the U.S.–China national identity gap.

The Japanese views of the Sino-U.S. national identity gap are naturally informed by their own national identities and their national identity gaps with China and the United States, while also viewing the Sino-U.S. relationship through the lens of Japan's perceived national interests. They long regarded Japan as a natural bridge between the two countries, briefly feared that the two would have found an affinity at Japan's expense, and recently have found consolation in the notion that irreconcilable differences are driving

China and the United States far apart. This progression is traced below before this chapter concentrates on the recent Sino-U.S. gap, noting Japan's overlap with its ally, but also observing Japan's loss of interest in learning from the United States.

After the end of World War II, the Japanese imagined their country to be a natural bridge between China and the United States, a clear reflection of their national identity as a country both in Asia and the West. Yes, Japanese also took pride as an Asian country that modernized first and, by the 1970s, as the leader in bringing development to Asian countries, giving it a solid basis to think from both perspectives. But in assuming it is entitled to be a bridge between China and the United States, Japan necessarily regards its national identity gap with either China or the United States as much narrower than that between China and the United States. Thus, the Japanese often suggested, explicitly or subtly, that they could help the Americans understand China because they connect with fellow Asians in a deeper and more nuanced fashion that the latter. The Japanese also often lectured the Chinese, not always subtly, about the modern international rules, which they thought they understood better than late-modernizing, non-Japanese Asians.

Apart from that primary identity, there was also growing concern among some Japanese elites since around the 1990s that the Chinese and Americans might be similar to each other in personality traits, communications styles, and a habit for strategic thinking, leaving Japan as the odd man out. This identity anxiety coincided with a fear of "Japan passing" from the United States. But it went deeper to the Japanese insecurity about their place in the world or, more exactly, about Japan as a border culture caught between two universal civilizations that differ in substance but connect in universality.

Japan's relationship with China has worsened sharply since the Chinese fishing boat collision incident in September 2010. The relationship between the United States and China also became tenser around the same time. Not surprisingly, the Japanese closely follow the relationship between China and the United States, the two major "others" for Japan. Much of the Japanese analysis in this regard is based on geopolitical calculations (e.g. Yamaguchi 2013), but national identity has been an important part of the Japanese thought process. There is now a strong Japanese wish to see irreconcilable differences between China and the United States, focusing on political values and political regimes, the *status quo* power versus the challenger, and international rules and responsibilities.

Underlying that dominant trend in the Japanese view of China as a rising threat and of an enlarging Sino-U.S. national identity gap, there is also a less visible, basically unconscious, undercurrent of Japan adapting to the Chinese system (not as a conscious model to learn from), combining political control and market competition, decisive decision making and social mobility, which is drawn from long intertwined Japan–China exchanges entrenched in Japanese traditions. While Japan has moved closer to the United States strategically, it has ceased to learn consciously from the United States. Japan's subconscious adaption to the Chinese system does not indicate China's growing influence in world affairs. In the short run at least, it results from competition with China and will lead to greater tensions with Beijing.

It is challenging methodologically to pinpoint the Japanese views of the Sino-U.S. national identity gap. The Japanese do not normally frame their analysis from the angle of national identity gaps. It is harder still to find the Japanese analysis of the Sino-U.S. national identity gap. Even if we find "perfect quotes" of some Japanese using that framework, it does not necessarily mean that mainstream Japanese see things that way. There is not much secondary academic analysis in Japan analyzing this issue. But this chapter builds on my previous research on the national identities in Sino-Japanese relations, particularly as a participant in several related research projects led by Gilbert Rozman (e.g. 2013), which has produced some of the best theoretical and empirical research in this research area. Furthermore, based on observation and research conducted as a visiting professor in Japan from August 2010 to August 2012, I discerned that national identities matter even more now than before in Japan. I have continued my research since then. More than casual observation, I anchor my analysis in empirical research, drawing from reading newspapers and weeklies, viewing television programs, analyzing Japanese books and opinion polls, and partaking of conversations and interviews. The Internet is, arguably, the most fertile ground for an identity-based assessment of growing Japanese tensions with China. While I do think that the extreme views often found there are partly shared and largely tolerated by mainstream thinkers, this chapter does not focus on them. The aim is a more mainstream perspective.

This chapter follows in chronological order: (1) The Japanese view of the Sino-U.S. national identity gaps through the 2000s; (2) diverse current Japanese views of the Sino-U.S. national identity gap; and (3) a deeper look at Japanese national identity and its historical trajectory, showing tension with conscious thinking about relations with the United States vis-à-vis China. A fourth section presents the conclusions from this analysis.

The Japanese View of the Sino-U.S. Identity Gap through the 2000s

To gauge the Japanese views of the Sino-U.S. national identity gap, one wishes for tracking polls with questions such as: "Do you think China and the United States are similar or different and why?". One can also include control questions to ask about views of the degree of similarity of the Japanese to the Chinese or the Americans. No such data exist, as far as I know. However, we can make some inferences from existing polls. Since 1978, the prime minister's office has asked the public about its sense of affinity with some countries viewed as important for Japan. Figure 4.1 shows that the Japanese now feel much closer to the United States than to China, with 82.6 percent feeling close to the former and 14.8 percent to the latter in 2014.

One way to interpret the trends depicted is that the wider "sensitive difference" perceived with the Chinese indicates a growing national identity gap. Sensitive difference is not substantive difference. The Japanese assessment of China was simply too rosy in the late 1970s when that country had just emerged from the disastrous Cultural Revolution. It is actually striking that the Japanese felt the same way about China and the United States in the 1980s, leaving other countries in the dust. The Japanese perception of the sensitive

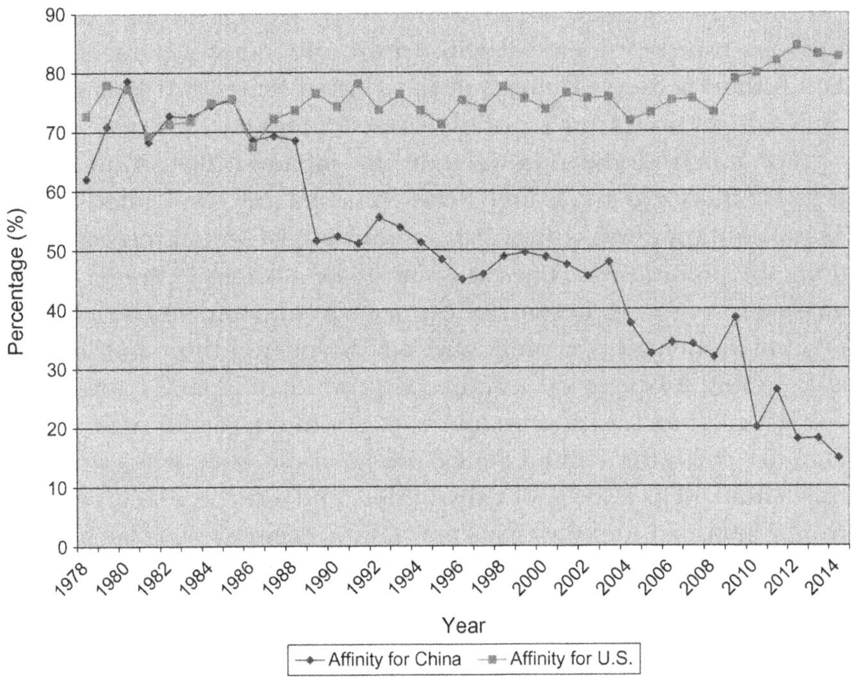

Figure 4.1   Prime Minister's Office Polls: China versus the U.S.
Source: Japan Prime Minister's Cabinet Office 2014.

difference with the Chinese adjusted to the substantive difference in the 1990s, but it is, arguably, overshooting in the negative direction at present. It is not clear whether the Japanese affinity results from a sense of similarity with the Americans or a sense of finding the United States trustworthy even if it is different culturally. But we readily observe how conservatives (dominating in the Japanese system) and progressive forces (weakening in their appeal) both have something to like about the United States and plenty of things to dislike about China, national security for the former and human rights and democracy for the latter.

The prime minister's office polls do not ask the Japanese about their view of the Sino-U.S. national identity gap. National identities are deeper than simply a sense of like or dislike. One may dislike one's twin brother too. The Japanese national identities are complex, conflicting with each other and evolving due to the internal logic of these identities and to changes in the external environment

(Rozman 2012b; Togo 2012; Hosoya 2012). To see through the fog, I discuss two prominent identity-driven orientations, namely Japan as a bridge between China and the United States and Japan as an outlier from both China and the United States.

For much of the post-war era, the Japanese felt strongly that Japan could serve as a bridge between China and the United States. This orientation was convenient in both international relations and domestic politics. Who does not want to be a bridge? Using network analysis in vogue at present, we can see why one wants to be a bridge or a hub, which gives a competitive advantage over those not situated as favorably. A bridge was a good compromise in Japan's contentious domestic context, with everyone seeing some merits in such an orientation. With the United States, the Japanese often suggested that they could help the Americans understand China, which resulted from a national identity that knew fellow Asians better. Such sentiment was ever present in the Japanese analysis of American policies in Asia. Sometimes, it came up in intergovernmental talks with U.S. officials. Citing just one example, at a bilateral trade and economic cooperation talk held in Kyoto in July 1966, Fujiyama Aiichirō, the director general of the Economic Planning Agency, criticized America's Vietnam policy, reasoning that political instability results from thinking only about democratic ideals and suggesting that Asian history is different from that of the United States and Europe. U.S. Secretary of State Dean Rusk responded sarcastically that he could not understand why only Asians can understand Asians.[1]

The Americans rightly assumed that they could understand China on their own. In fact, the experience of World War II and what happened before shows that the Japanese understanding of China was seriously deficient while many Americans, at least, had a better grasp. The same may be true today. The Americans have extensive direct exchange with the Chinese leaders. There are also deep people-to-people exchanges. As an immigrant country, the United States has an expanding Asian American community that

---

[1] The episode was discussed in the Japanese Foreign Ministry archives declassified on July 31, 2012 (*Asahi shimbun* August 1, 2012, 4).

contributes to American understanding. When it comes to China, the United States has educated excellent China experts with language proficiency and extensive experience on the ground. And a large community of China-born scholars in the United States also contributes to the English language knowledge pool about China.

Another challenge for Japan to serve as a bridge was that Japan was not located in a "neutral" location in East Asian international relations. Japan was a close ally of the United States, the superpower that has military bases in Japan, and was used as a crucial location for supporting the American war efforts in Korea and Vietnam. Thus, there was much illusion in thinking of Japan as serving as a bridge. In foreign policy practice, other Asian countries and the United States did not use Japan as a bridge. The United States and China maintained some contact in Warsaw, and Rumania and Pakistan served as the messengers to 1972. Vietnam negotiated with the United States in Paris, not Tokyo. That Japan sustained a myth about its special role should not be seen as unusual, but it serves as a vital clue about how national identity has shaped Japan's foreign policy orientation.

Imagining Japan serving as a bridge is a well-intentioned ideal for connecting the other two countries in a positive fashion. This national identity-driven orientation matters in diplomatic practice as well. While Japan's opinion of China began to decline sharply after June 4, 1989, its self-consciousness about becoming a bridge between China and the United States reached a peak in the early 1990s (Wan 2001a, 87–91). Whether China was violating human rights was not a serious concern for many Japanese as long as China was viewed as on good terms with their country. In this period, awareness of a widening Sino-U.S. identity gap amid troubled relations also emboldened Japanese to foresee a rare opportunity.

With difficulties in their relationship with China and realization of the degree of economic problems the country faced, the Japanese felt increasingly insecure, which was reflected in a new assessment of the relationship between China and the United States. In the 1990s, there was overwhelming concern expressed in public or private conversations that the United States now viewed China as more important than Japan, thus bypassing Tokyo. Japan, in stages, became far more concerned about making sure the United States was on its side than about bridging the gap between China and the United States.

One Japanese concern that came up often, particularly in private conversations, was the observation that the Chinese are more similar to the Westerners in some key personality traits such as direct, forceful expression of opinions and a natural habit for thinking strategically. The Japanese were also concerned that the Chinese government was manipulating the Americans to marginalize Japan. The fact that Chinese President Jiang Zemin paid tribute to the United States at Pearl Harbor during his state visit in October 1997 convinced many Japanese of the Chinese plot, which partly explained the difficulties Jiang would face during his later visit to Japan.[2] Yet, as the visit showed, China bears some responsibility for shifting away from reassuring Japan to the sort of posture Jiang displayed in his 1998 visit, which served to reduce Japanese trust.

The Japanese sense of insecurity partly resulted from a period of intense American criticism of Japan as different from the Western democracies. That experience helps to explain why Japanese views of some Sino-U.S. disputes were not unsympathetic to China as late as the 2000s. For example, Japanese analysts often saw the U.S. critique of unfair Chinese trading practices as rejection of *"ishitsusei"* [heterogeneity], similar to American arguments against Japan in earlier years. Unlike the United States, Japan had mostly enjoyed trade surpluses with China if one views Japan's exports to Hong Kong as largely transit trade to China. Japan's trade surpluses

---

[2] More recently, Japanese media (e.g. *Yomiuri shimbun* online February 11, 2015; *Asahi shimbun* online February 12, 2015) took notice of Chinese President Xi Jinping's scheduled official visit to the United States in September and viewed him as seeking to make an international appeal to the international community as a "victory state" along with the United States and Russia against Japan even though the United States appears unwilling to go along. One should expect Japanese to follow this story closely. The year of 2015 is the seventieth year anniversary of the end of World War II and founding of the United Nations.

against the United States decreased through its investment in China and the formation of East Asian production networks.

Current Japanese Views of the Sino-U.S. Identity Gap

Sino-Japanese relations experienced a sharp decline in late 2010, crucially due to aftermath of the September fishing boat collision, reflected in the opinion polls in Figure 4.1. With another round of heightened tension after the Noda government purchased three disputed Senkaku islands (Diaoyudao for China or Tiaoyutai for Taiwan) from a Japanese landowner in early September 2012, Japanese views of China worsened still. Increasingly aware of the Chinese discourse on Japan with a widening identity gap, the Japanese public feels more and more alienated from China. By contrast, views of the United States improved further with America's quick and massive disaster relief efforts in Operation Tomodachi. Figure 4.2 below shows that contrast more clearly.

The Genron/*China Daily* polls, which started only in 2005, offer a more direct comparison of Japanese views toward China versus the United States than the prime minister's office polls used in Figure 4.1. They asked how close Japanese and Chinese feel toward the other country versus the United States for the first time in 2012, revealing that the Japanese overwhelmingly feel closer to the United States (51 percent) than to China (7 percent). By contrast, the Chinese polled also feel closer to the United States (26 percent) than to Japan (6 percent), but a larger share likes neither (38 percent) (Genron NPO 2012). The United States is in a favorable position since both the Japanese and Chinese like it better than their neighbor. As Figure 4.2 shows, that tendency has become stronger still in the 2014 poll.

The Genron/*China Daily* polls do not ask the Japanese about their assessment of how close the Chinese and Americans feel toward each other relative to Japan. But they contain some interesting information to help us understand the Japanese view of the Sino-U.S. national identity gap. In particular, the polls ask why the polled feel close or not close to China. Not surprisingly, a main

Japan's Views (2014)

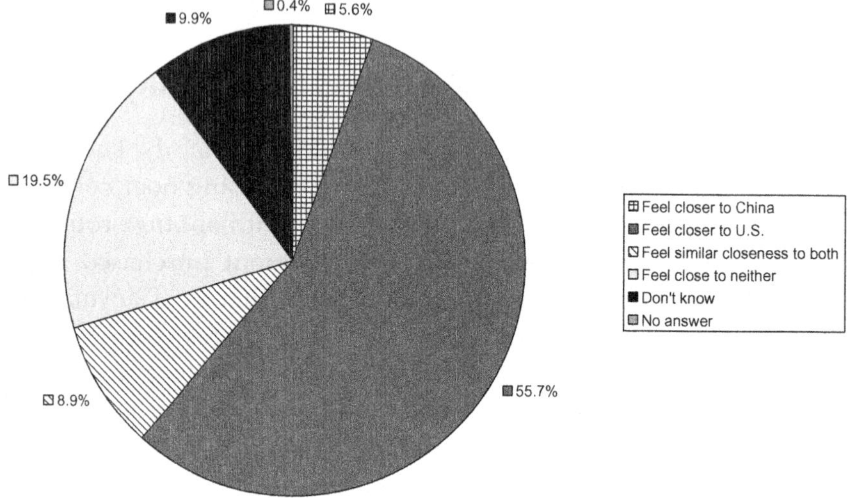

China's Views (2014)

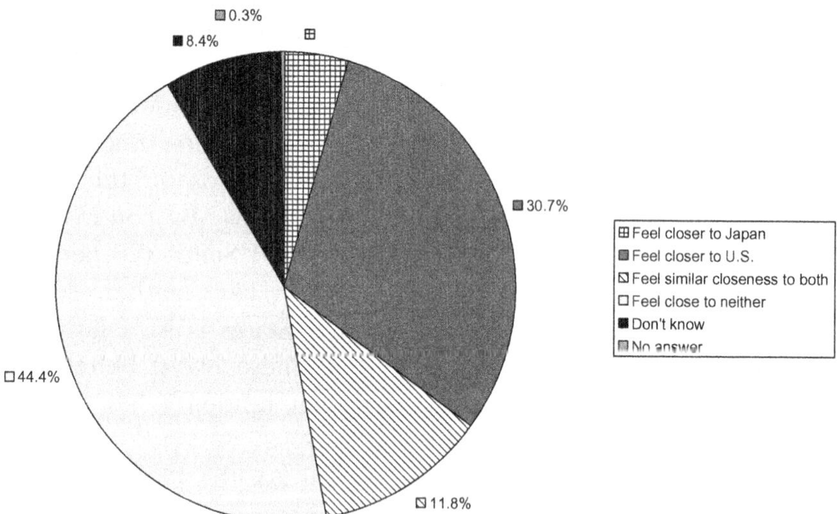

Figure 4.2   Genron Polls 2014.

Source: Genron NPO 2014b.

reason for the Japanese not to like China relates to the territorial dispute, which a majority of Japanese acknowledge exists, in contrast to the government position. The Japanese are also concerned about China competing for natural resources in a self-centered fashion and about China's rising military power. These geopolitical and geo-economic calculations are not divorced from national identity tension. In particular, as Japan's recent territorial tension with all its neighbors' shows, how one understands the past has much to do with geopolitics in East Asia. The Genron/*China Daily* polls show that 44 percent of the polled in 2012 and 52.2 percent in 2014 view Chinese criticism of Japan's past as a key reason for not liking China while only 4.9 percent in 2012 and 3.3 percent in 2014 cites the past war itself as the reason. By contrast, the Chinese polled overwhelmingly (78.6 percent) in 2012 cites Japan's past aggression as the main reason for not liking Japan, decreasing to 59.6 percent in 2014. Thus, the Chinese view the dispute over Diaoyudao as a continuation of Japan's past aggression against China while the Japanese view China as showing interest in the Senkakus only with the news of rich oil deposits in the region in the 1970s. More directly, a significant portion of the polled cite more explicit identity reasons for disliking China, with 48.3 percent in 2012 and 55.1 percent in 2014 seeing China as not following the international rules and 26.5 percent and 25.7 percent citing China's different political system. To add to the identity gap with the political system at issue, 67.9 percent of the Japanese in 2012 and 69 percent in 2014 view China as a socialist, communist country. On the flip side, only 15.6 percent of the Chinese in 2012 and 14.4 percent in 2014 view Japan as a democratic country, while 46.2 percent and 35.9 percent assess it as militaristic.

Building on this relevant statistical information, I examine how the Japanese view the actual events and trends between China and the United States based on analysis of Japanese television programs, newspapers, and magazines as well as talks with scholars and officials. There have been some major events in East Asian international relations such as the American "pivot" in the Pacific, high-profile American official visits to the region, and military exercises. A Sino-U.S. rivalry in the Pacific is intensifying, while the two countries continue to search for strategic cooperation over a broad range of issues.

The Japanese media analyses reflect Japan's specific interests, mostly from either a geopolitical or geo-economic angle. Similar to American coverage, *Asahi shimbun* (September 25, 2010, 13) focused on the Chinese *yuan* exchange issue when covering the meeting between Obama and Wen Jiabao in New York on September 23, 2010. Unlike past coverage, there was less concern about Japan passing based on the assessment that the United States needs Japan more as it has declined relative to China and faces China's growing challenge.

Japanese no longer worry much about Sino-U.S. tension being negative for Japan. Rather, they seem to prefer greater tension, consciously or unconsciously aiming to shape Sino-U.S. interaction, as in letting their own disputes with China drive the Sino-U.S. bilateral relationship, forcing the United States to take Japan's side. The Japan Institute of International Affairs (JIIA) (2012), for example, urged the United States not to "assume a neutral stance regarding territorial rights" to the Senkakus. The Japanese had a high regard for former Secretary of State Hillary Clinton, particularly for her pro-active policy toward Asia. The Japanese media closely covered her attendance at the ASEAN Regional Forum (ARF) on July 12, 2012. The Japanese shared concerns with some ASEAN countries and appeared to be disappointed that, on this occasion, Clinton was restrained. *Asahi shimbun* was disappointed, as were many in the United States, that there was no direct confrontation and ASEAN could not agree on a declaration on China due to internal division and China's influence (*Asahi shimbun* July 13, 2012, 12).

As Sino-Japanese disputes have gone multilateral, public exchanges to win support for one's supposedly reasonable positions have intensified, while making the other side look bad. The Chinese government ran ads in mainstream Western media first. The Japanese also beefed up their campaigns after privately sounding the alarm to American officials and analysts about a rising China well-before the fishing boat incident. It was in Japan's interest to make sure that the United States regarded China with ample suspicion, and well-placed Japanese strove to reshape the American view of China.

With bilateral tension so much more intense and so much more open, there is a greater push to make the Americans aware of their differences from the Chinese. As an extreme example of some Japanese appealing directly to the Americans and seeking to frame U.S.–China relations in good versus evil terms, Okawa Ryuho, the founder of the Happy Science Group, purchased a one-page ad in *The Washington Post* (December 14, 2012, A21) to urge Obama and the United States to stand together with the Japanese and fight against "China's desire for expansion and world domination." He reasoned that god-loving America and Japan are natural allies against atheist China and North Korea. However, distorted this assessment, given the much larger number of Christians in China than in Japan and the shared Buddhist tradition in these two states (Pew Research Center 2012), national identity involves imagination that may have a weak factual basis. The imagination of the Japanese nation as continuously militaristic by many Chinese, as revealed in the above Genron/*China Daily* polls, is a prime example.

If we look deeper, we find a complex Japanese identity of seeing the United States as maintaining the international rules while China is challenging them. However true this is, it is also a matter of national identity when a typical Japanese analyst talks about China not respecting the existing international rules but finds it difficult to define these rules or give concrete examples of violations, taking for granted that China is doing so.

The Japanese now focus more on differences in political regimes. A functioning democracy, Japan spawns a genuine value gap with China.[3] In particular, the Chinese government's anger over Liu Xiaobo's winning of the Nobel Peace Prize in 2010 also received much Japanese media attention. Similarly, blind Chinese activist Chen Guangcheng's dramatic escape from house arrest to the U.S. embassy in Beijing in April 2012 was covered in great detail in the Japanese media.

---

[3] See an *Asahi* editor's view (*Asahi shimbun*, October 16, 2010, 17).

Since Japanese do not think they bear any responsibility for worsening relations, one way to explain them is to argue that an authoritarian regime in China is the problem. There is no question that lack of democracy has created huge problems for Chinese domestic politics and foreign policy, including its relations with Japan, but national identity distorts the discourse. For example, Vietnam, similar to China in political regime, is portrayed positively in the Japanese media because it is viewed as a natural ally against China. It is striking that Japanese media largely portrayed Abe's visit in January 2013 to Vietnam, Thailand, and Indonesia as showcasing his value diplomacy with countries that share the values of freedom and democracy to check communist China (*Sankei shimbun* online January 15, 2013).

Some Japanese also imagine a Japanese system more democratic and open than it actually is. Similar events are narrated differently. As an example, *Asahi shimbun* noted on July 30, 2012 that Japan's ongoing anti-nuclear demonstrations were orderly in contrast to the Taisho period in Japan's past and to the Chinese demonstrations against the Japanese firm Oji's waste processing plan, highlighting the difference between a mature democracy and a non-democratic China. However, while *Asahi shimbun* (July 17, 2012) put the latest anti-nuclear demonstration on the front page, it had earlier put a major anti-nuclear demonstration on the back page while making rising eel prices a feature story. There was an even more violent anti-Japanese firm demonstration in India, with two Japanese nationals injured and one Indian employee killed, but the Japanese media chose not to highlight that story, unlike its extensive coverage of a Chinese demonstration against a Japanese firm in China. China is the other and India is not. Rivalry rather than democracy is driving Japanese thinking.

Twists in Japanese National Identity

While Japan's opinion of China has sunk ever lower and its affinity with the United States remains high, one should also note that Japanese identities are complex and evolve in a way not necessarily consistent with expressed views. This is evident in two twists in identity related to the United States and China. First, Japan has turned away from Americanization since around the mid-2000s due to a growing inward-looking tendency. Second, some reforming Japanese politicians seek, unconsciously, to adapt elements of the Chinese system as if they are more in keeping with Japan's aims.

Growing tension with China and closer security cooperation with the United States do not necessarily mean a narrower national identity gap with the United States. Politicians with such strong right-wing views as Ishihara Shintarō are politically active and influential when they would remain on the fringe in other advanced democracies. Ishihara was a highly popular mayor of Japan's capital city starting in 1999. He stepped down at the end of October 2012 to form a new national political party, which then merged with the Japan Restoration Party founded by a conservative populist politician Hashimoto Toru, the mayor of the City of Osaka. Ishihara finally bowed out after losing the general election in December 2014. Provocateurs, who stir up disputes and force issues on the national government that exacerbate disputes with other countries, have had a notorious history in recent decades.

The Japanese ultranationalists continue to fight World War II by whitewashing history. They were initially more angry at the United States than any other country. It long made them feel humiliated and agitated. Ishihara, who in 1989 co-authored the famous book *Japan that Can Say No*, termed Japan a "mistress" of the United States in a news conference at the Foreign Correspondents Club (Matsubara 2012), the cause of an extreme sense of national shame. Over time, though, Japanese nationalists have turned their anger against North Korea and China while quietly complaining about the United States with much less frequency. In the interview cited above, Ishihara mainly attacked China while observing that "our master is now on the decline — he is old and losing his physical strength."

The Japanese ultranationalists have now warmed up to the United States mainly due to their strong dislike of China. They have an exaggerated sense of national survival, now largely framed as coming from the China threat. Ishihara announced his plan to purchase the Senkakus while visiting the United States in April 2012. To make that connection even more explicit, the Tokyo Metropolitan Government purchased an ad in the *Wall Street Journal* on July 27, 2012 to appeal directly for American support for its plan to purchase the Senkakus. The ad warned darkly that "failure to support the Asian nations confronting China would result in the United States losing the entire Pacific Ocean" (*Japan Times* 2012a). Ishihara and those who share his worldview want the United States to back up Japan hundred percent over narrowly defined issues such as territorial disputes.

By picking history fights, Japanese conservatives enlarge the national identity gap with the United States. Due to the controversy over a comfort woman memorial in New Jersey in which Japanese diplomats reportedly protested to local officials, the movement is now spreading to the rest of the country. Glendale, California marked Korean Comfort Women Day in early August 2012 (*Japan Times* 2012b). American public opinion as reflected in mainstream media outlets generally views Japan as turning conservative and has reservations about its new prime minister. For example, the Abe cabinet launched on December 26, 2012 was assessed by *Economist* as one of "radical nationalists."[4] Its editors opined that while the United States should support Japan when China is aggressive, that support "should not extend to rewriting history or provoking China (let alone South Korea)" (*Economist* 2013b).

As a more tolerant democracy, the United States has been more successful in handling national identity gaps. Thus, the developments discussed above will do little to dampen security cooperation, but they do show the limits of nationalist manipulation of messages in the United States. Moreover, if Japan worsens relations with neighboring countries due to its leaders' revisionist views of history,

---

[4]Fourteen in the 19-member cabinet belong to the "League for Going to Worship Together at Yasukuni." Thirteen are members of a nationalist think that rejects "apology diplomacy" and wants to return to "traditional values." Nine cabinet members participate in an association that wants to emphasize patriotism in textbooks and denies most war atrocities. Abe and some other cabinet members also want to revise the constitution imposed by the United States (*Economist* 2013a).

that would complicate American national interests in the region. As Glen Fukushima (2012) noted, while Abe is a strong pro-American leader and intends to strengthen the alliance, "his revisionist views of history and controversial views of Asia could lead him to speak and act in ways that exacerbate tensions with neighboring countries, especially China and South Korea." More recently, critical of the revisionist movement in Japan, Richard Cohen (2014) has noted the "sudden reversals" as a feature of Japanese culture and thinks that "a more ominous reversal may be underway" now, which "would only aggravates the insult to Japan's victims and further unsettles its neighbors, China and South Korea in particular." More recently, a U.S. Congressional Service report released on January 15, 2015 warned that Abe holds a revisionist view of history and the U.S. national interests would be hurt if Japan's relations with its Asian neighbors worsen over the history issue. The report noted that Abe's electoral victory in December 2014 continues to have both positive and negative impact on U.S.–Japan relations (*Asahi shimbun* online January 17, 2015).

Indeed, some polls appear to reveal the trend discussed above. According to a joint poll conducted by *Yomiuri shimbun* and Gallop on November 17–23, 2014, only 61 percent of the polled Americans trust Japan, the lowest level for the past seven years. *Yomiuri shimbun* (online December 23, 2014) interpreted that result as reflecting America's concern about Japan's worsening relations with its neighbors and the lowering state of Japan in the United States. Conversely, only 45 percent of the Japanese polled trust the United States, decreasing from 50 percent a year earlier, reflecting distrust in the Obama administration.

More broadly, the Japanese, particularly the young, are becoming more inward-looking, which reflects a greater degree of psychological distancing with the outside world. It is noted both inside and outside Japan that Japanese young people are becoming less inclined to go abroad to study, compared to other Asian countries, particularly South Korea and China, as shown vividly in Figure 4.3. There are no incentives for them to go abroad when competition for jobs at home is becoming so time-consuming and

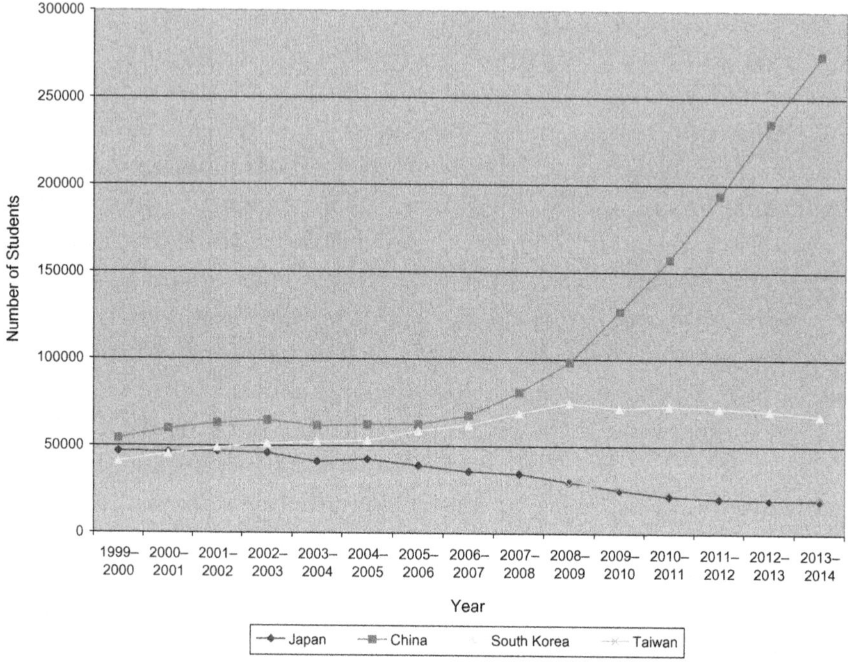

Figure 4.3　East Asian Students in the United States, 1999–2014.
Source: Institute of International Education 2014.

network-dependent. But there is also an underlying identity shift. Many find it more comfortable staying at home than dealing with difficult foreign customs. This shift has an impact on the Japanese sense of identity and will become even more pronounced when the currently young take center stage.

On the elite level, there is much confusion about Japanese national identities. As Rozman (2012, 24) noted, for Japanese, "the post-Cold War era offered tantalizing glimpses of breakthroughs in national identity, but these were increasingly submerged in bitter disappointments ... The search for new clarity about identity has led to dead ends, as those who favor revisionism centered on the war (*sensoron*) have won a following but no prospect of political consensus and those who favor the idealism of the East Asian community have found a region in turmoil under China's unwelcome quest for leadership." Some Japanese still search for a unique Japanese identity that does not derive from anti-American or anti-Chinese feelings (Togo 2012, 165–166), but growing nationalism is more based on fear than hope, particularly about a rising China.

Japan is not unique in facing identity confusion, particularly with globalization and modern communication technologies. But the Japanese sense of anxiety is arguably among the strongest in the world for the simple fact that it is the second or third largest economy in the world but feels culturally separate (e.g. Uchida 2009). Japan is still torn between the East and the West. By contrast, the Chinese often simply assume that they are the East and have fewer qualms in competing or integrating with the West at the same time. South Koreans arguably are more emphatic of the unique Korean identity than the Japanese at present, but they are also charging outward to the West and East, carving out a large economic and cultural space in Asia and the world.

Mainstream Japanese politics have become increasingly conservative, as defined in the Japanese context. Some bravely seek a synthesis. As an example, the then-ruling DPJ came up with a draft of its party program, revealed to the leadership on August 7, 2012. It emphasized that "with the imperial system as foundation," Japan should further polish its unique features that have resulted from integration and development of cultures of "ancient and modern, the East and the West" [kokon tōzai] (*Asahi shimbun* August 8, 2012, 4). But as the DPJ is formed of different ideological stocks, there was immediate dissent expressed against such a conservative view of history (*Asahi shimbun* August 9, 2012, 4). The December 2012 Lower House elections revealed a clear trend of parties moving to the right. Abe Shinzō, the party chief of the LDP, pushed a strong conservative agenda during the election campaign, mindful of an even more conservative Japan Restoration Party.

However difficult it is to draw a straight line between an expressed view and a policy outcome, we observe a continuous emphasis on Japan having unique features that are different from both the East and the West and on the centrality of those features to the way Japan must act. That partly explains a degree of uncompromising, fundamentalist thinking, particularly when it comes to Japan's disputes with other countries.

Japan is not looking at the United States or the West for inspiration right now except in the security arena.[5] Indeed, some of the earlier "Americanizing efforts" by reformers such as Koizumi Junichirō have been blamed for enlarging the wealth gap and threatening social stability in the country. The electoral reform and creation of a two-party system modeled after the United States and Great Britain is also viewed as only creating political paralysis. Japanese thinking in this regard partly reflects blaming others for reforms that were not carried out, but national identity plays a crucial role in these reflections that perceive Americanization as threatening Japan's unique qualities. Some remain critical of the United States as greedy capitalist in contrast to a harmonious Japan.

The Japanese who advocate reform to deal with Japan's supposed national crisis look up to the Meiji heroes. The American Occupation that has left a strong institutional legacy is something they would rather forget. It is striking how difficult it is to find any museums dedicated to the American Occupation in a country where everything seems to be memorialized. Moreover, as some Japanese thinkers note, the Meiji Restoration also represented partially a move towards the Chinese system (Yonaba 2011; Mitani 2006). Following the China study school founded by Naito Konan (1866–1934), they argued that Song China was the first true modernizing country with a secular state, a merit-based selection system for officials, and a competitive market economy. In their view, Tokugawa Japan took a different path than China, but Japan came to represent the Chinese system more through the Meiji Restoration, which is better translated as "rejuvenation" in English. They point out that rising political stars such as Hashimoto Toru represent an unconscious attempt to complete the transformation of the Japanese state begun in the Meiji era. While the "sinicization" argument is still a marginal academic view in a country that strongly

---

[5] Abe, for example, created a National Security Council modeled after the U.S. institution in January 2014.

dislikes China at present, it illustrates the possibilities in imagining national identity made possible because of the long Sino-Japanese interaction.

Watching Hashimoto almost daily on Japanese television for two years suggested to me that while he was one of a few Japanese leaders capable of arousing the public, he also had the potential to be a Chinese style strong leader, which may be reason to be on guard. The seemingly invincible Hashimoto began to stumble in late 2012. The December 2012 Lower House election restored power to the LDP that had not really changed. Opinion polls now showed the LDP as the most popular party, far ahead of Hashimoto's Japan Restoration Party. Abe's vision of "beautiful Japan" is winning the day. At the same time, one should watch an undercurrent of Japanese adapting to the Chinese system, which does not mean integration into the Chinese sphere of influence. In fact, those who are subconsciously adapting to the Chinese system are more likely to clash with the Chinese state.

Conclusion

With growing concerns about a rising China's attitude toward Japan, the Japanese have an increasingly lower sense of affinity with China and a higher level of affinity with the United States. The United States has an almost insurmountable advantage over China at this point. Among other reasons, as a far more tolerant democracy, it has given the Japanese a significant space for national identity discussions. Even in historical memory, the United States respects the Japanese, with the American ambassador's attendance at the atomic bombing memorials in Hiroshima and Nagasaki as a case in point. The United States does not confront the Japanese historical narrative even though the United States has its own convictions about the "Good War." The American government also does not take on Japanese nationalists or fight history diplomatically. By contrast, China's national identity-based legitimation and how it handles the history issue on the diplomatic level clash head on with the Japanese national identity process.

The Japanese are viewing Sino-U.S. relations from a multi-level complex of national interests and identities. There is now a greater mismatch between the distribution of interests, superficial affinity, and deeper national identity anxieties. Japan has a strong symmetry of strategic interests with the United States and wants the United States to side more strongly with it to manage a rising China. It welcomes and thinks it sees an enlarging national identity gap between China and the United States. At the same time, Japan continues to have a strong economic interest to leverage a rising China's rapidly expanding market, and it is unconsciously adapting to the Chinese system rather than copying the American system at present. Rather than choosing sides in this perceived clash of national identities between China and the United States, it is widening the gap with the United States on matters at the core of its identity even if that seems inconsistent with closer security ties and may be overlooked as the gap with China widens further.

Chapter 5

Sino-Japanese Coevolution

The Sino-Japanese interaction these days is akin to a not-so-shadow boxing match. In this chapter, I do not intend to act like a ringside commentator who breaks down each move for praise or ridicule. People who care about this relationship are all watching instant television and social media coverage. However, this is not a game for entertainment. If the Sino-Japanese confrontation spins out of control, we will all be paying a high price for it. My purpose here is to seek a better theoretical understanding of how the two countries ended up in this unfortunate situation in the first place.

For many Chinese and Japanese, the reason for the rising tension between the two nations is self-evident. Depending on where one sits, it is either all Japan's fault or all China's fault. It is understandable that officials insist publicly on their innocence and put blame on the other side in a confrontational situation. Why would anyone start negotiations lending support to the other side? But it would be a huge problem if these people actually believe their own rhetoric. It is wrong to take up a let-us-blame-the-other-side argument. Doing so defies explanation for why the "guilty" party has good relations with other countries. You then have to reason that the other country hates only you, which makes you dislike them even more.

Of course, it makes more sense to realize that there is something specific about the relationship between the two of you that brings out the worst in the other country. Similarly, one has to reconcile the fact of one's own bad relations with some other countries, an inconvenient detail that weakens the assumption of one's own innocence. Both the Chinese and Japanese governments have taken actions contributing to the tension in their relationship. It is then not particularly meaningful to determine whose action is more to blame. Is a blow worse than a hook? One may indeed be able to determine the salience of a particular action in a particular time frame, such as the nationalization of the islands in question or the announcement of an air defense identification zone. However, my own assessment is that both sides are to blame in the scheme of things, albeit for different actions. Government mismanagement has been a crucial reason for the worsening bilateral relationship and neither party should shift all the blame to the other side or to structural forces beyond one's control.

Some strategic thinkers have offered a variety of structural explanations for the current tensions. It is widely noted that the power balance in East Asia has shifted between a rising China and a relatively declining Japan. More broadly, one can go back to the end of the Cold War, which changed the security interests and priorities of the United States and other great powers. A perceived "power transition" situation has emerged. This theory posits that the international system is particularly volatile when a rising power challenges the privileged position of the *status quo* hegemon.

There is some truth in all these structural arguments, which are valuable if one is interested in the main tendencies of international politics over time and across space. But they are too broad for understanding a concrete case. This chapter offers a theoretical insight about the coevolution between China and Japan. I am not claiming that coevolution fully explains the Sino-Japanese relationship. Rather, I hope to expand our theoretical understanding of this important relationship and believe that this theoretical insight may also be applied to other bilateral relationships.

Why China and Japan are experiencing high tensions in their relations is not as meaningful a question as it appears. If one replaces the proper nouns of China and Japan with abstract terms of Country A and Country B, the question becomes why Country A and Country B are experiencing high tensions, which is non-specific. We know countries sometimes have tensions. A better question is why the two Asian great powers that had a better relationship in the past are now experiencing greater tensions when their much closer economic and people-to-people ties should facilitate greater cooperation.

One may address the broad question of why economic interdependence does not necessarily prevent heightened security tension from different angles. I myself argued previously that it is unrealistic to expect economic interdependence or any other arrangement including alliances to prevent military conflict, or that closer economic ties nevertheless mitigate conflict and that things would be worse without economic interdependence (Wan 2003). Quantitative researchers have run multiple regressions to examine the causal relationship between economic interdependence and military conflict, often with contradictory results. However, statistical analysis aims at probability and is therefore suggestive mainly for those interested in a more targeted analysis of a particular case.

In this chapter, I will advance a biological and evolutionary line of argument. The current tensions between China and Japan result mainly from competition going awry from an ecosystem perspective. The two Asian neighbors have coevolved over millennia with increasing intensity over time. They avoided serious tensions in the 1970s–1990s partly thanks to each being situated in a different niche. However, that separation has diminished in a globalizing world and the two countries are becoming more similar (Sinification and Japanization), which has triggered a backlash. From a generational perspective, the earlier generation of proponents of Sino-Japanese friendship sought to forge a strong bilateral relationship through economic and person-to-person ties and have succeeded on both scores, but the current generation finds it difficult politically and psychologically to manage the new reality in their relations.

Theory of Coevolution

John N. Thompson (2005, vii), an evolutionary biologist, has defined coevolution as "reciprocal evolutionary change between interacting species driven by natural selection." Coevolution covers both the internal change of the interacting species and the interaction between them. Thompson's 1982 book *Interaction and Coevolution* studies, how different kinds of interactions create different selection pressures for the interacting species. This book is particularly helpful for my discussion here because it focuses "on patterns that derive more from the mode of interaction than from the biology of a particular taxonomic group" (Thompson 1982, v). It is far easier to examine the mode of interactions in international relations than it is to create an equivalent of genetics for International relations.

One may argue that multiple interactions among political institutions are too complex to make simple causal arguments. However, as Thompson (2013, 343–368) noted, biologists faced a similar challenge but have developed various approaches since the 1980s to handle that challenge. Thompson (2005) himself has proposed a "geographical mosaic" approach, arguing that populations may exist in discreet habitat spots in a heterogeneous environment. This theory could help explain Sino-Japanese tensions as resulting from the fact that China and Japan have now moved into the same habitat patches.

While humans are part of the biophysical world, we are different in that the social and political world does not exist independent of humans as thinking agents. Our languages, thoughts, and actions constitute the world in which we live. And generations pass down knowledge through memory and learning rather than in genetic codes. But we can use biology as an analogy. And the theory of coevolution focuses on the mode of interactions.

Sino-Japanese Coevolution

We may divide the Sino-Japanese relationship roughly into four periods. The first period is the longest, lasing for about two millennia of recorded history prior to the mid-nineteenth century. Early China and Japan were different political entities from what China and Japan are today, and history could have unfolded differently, resulting in a different political landscape in Asia and the world. But both countries can trace their lineages to recognizable political entities in the distant past. For the duration of the ancient Sino-Japanese interaction and two millennia before, the political entities in what is now China largely dominated in East Asian international relations. Both China and Japan were part of a much larger Eurasian system that shared cultures, technologies, and germs (Diamond 1999). But China was geographically isolated from the rest of the Eurasian continent separated by the Himalayas to its southwest and deserts and steppes to its northwest, and Japan was more isolated still, separated by seas from the Asian continent at a distance far greater than that between the British Isles and the European continent.

An asymmetry existed in Sino-Japanese evolution, with Japan more impacted by China than the other way around. Japan interacted with a smaller number of countries directly and psychologically. Japan's world initially included only Korea and China and gradually expanded to India indirectly and to Ryukyu (now Okinawa) and Southeast Asia. Thus, Japan was engaged in what Thompson (2013, 347–348) has termed "a small web of interactions." More interacting partners would create more evolutionary solutions. Indeed, China had a much more extensive web of interactions and coevolved particularly with the nomadic peoples to its north and northwest.

One striking feature of the Sino-Japanese interaction in the past two millennia was that the two countries were quite similar in many ways, and certainly more similar than what China shared in common with the nomads, but China and Japan did not interact as intensely as did the Chinese and the nomads. On this point, it could be said that it was not obvious who was a "Chinese" and who was a "barbarian" throughout Chinese history. Between the Chinese and the Japanese the limited direct interaction took the form of extensive trade but rarely was there conflict. In fact, the East Asian countries of China, Korea, Japan, and Vietnam rarely fought wars with each other (in fact, there was almost no fighting after the

Japanese invasion of Korea in 1592 until the end of the nineteenth century) in contrast to Europe and elsewhere, which for some reflected "a Confucian long peace" (Kelly 2012; Kang 2010). While shared cultural and political norms were important, another notable factor for the extended period of peace was that Northeast Asian nations also had in common a foundation of similar ecological conditions characterized by relatively self-sufficient villages engaged in agriculture and handicraft. As I have argued elsewhere, East Asia also had a more "natural" international system measured by the regional states' shares of the total regional population divided by their shares of the total regional gross domestic income, which was in my view conducive to stability. By contrast, an international system is inherently unstable if some members take a much larger share than others (Wan 2013b).

The structure of Sino-Japanese relations was impressively stable. The mode of interaction between the Chinese and Japanese was distant, ritualistic, predictable, and basically non-violent. There has been much discussion of Chinese arrogance and Japanese defiance as reflected in a dozen or so historical incidents, but this relationship was largely peaceful for two thousand years, rare between large nations. East Asian international relations were generally characterized by continental polities largely dominating in the Asian landscape, but, while it often had to adapt, Japan could evolve without direct foreign interference thanks to a geographical and psychological separation from the Asian continent.

The second period of Sino-Japanese relations started in the mid-nineteenth century and lasted for a century. Both China and Japan now operated on a global level and simultaneously had far more intimate interaction with each other. The main story of this period was relentless evolution of both the structures and modes of interactions. While there was relative stability and peace in Europe from 1871 to 1914, much conflict and turmoil prevailed in East Asia. Then the whole world turned upside down with two world wars, sparing only Latin America. The European imperialist powers, then Russia, the United States, and finally Japan competed for hegemony in East Asia. The imperialist disorder and dramatic social changes, the turmoil generated led to reforms and revolutions throughout the region. With direct imperialist administration or indirect sphere of influence, there was little separation between the Asian countries and the global powers. The mode of interactions also changed fundamentally, from ritualistic and moralistic ways of dealing with each other as represented in the Chinese world order, to legalistic, nominally sovereign and predator–prey interactions in the imperialist Westphalian system.[1] With a greater coherence and impressive speed, Japan adapted more quickly to the new international order than China and other East Asian countries and then utilized legalistic but imperialist methods, backed by use of military power, to restructure its interaction with other Asian countries to its own advantage.

The Sino-Japanese relationship was not always hostile, but for much of that period the two nations were in conflict, with Japan taking initiative and inflicting damages on China. Thus, a predation mode of interaction existed between the two countries, which triggered a strong nationalist reaction from the Chinese, explained the instability and unsustainability of the Sino-Japanese relations structure, and were part of the reasons for their different historical paths.

The Sino-Japanese interactions were far more extensive than they had been previously. The scale of interactions changed dramatically after the mid-nineteenth century. The number of Japanese who came to China before that turning point was a rounding error, compared to other nationalities including those from European countries. By contrast, millions of Japanese, including many soldiers, had set foot in China for about half a century, more numerous than any other single foreign country. Tens of thousands of Chinese also visited or studied in Japan.

The history of Sino-Japanese relations exhibited a clear pattern of coevolution in this period. Japan was an important driver triggering domestic transformation in China, with Japan initially held up as a model and then as a threat to justify changes. Japanese aggression

---

[1] Of course, we know that China as well as some other East Asian countries also expanded, often resorting to force to achieve their objectives.

also interrupted the Chinese modernization process and affected the Chinese political equilibrium, which partly made it possible for the Chinese Communist Party to win power. Conversely, the "China problem" posed the biggest challenge for Japan, triggering events that furthered the country down a militaristic path to its eventual defeat. Following the end of World War II, the United States helped establish democracy in Japan, a country that had experienced parliamentary politics in the 1920s.

The third period of Sino-Japanese relations lasted through the second half of the twentieth century. During the Cold War, there was considerable domestic support in Japan for reaching out to other Asian countries, considered the right thing to do by the progressive forces and a smart thing to do by the conservatives. Economic and cultural interaction expanded slowly between Beijing and Tokyo but diplomatic relations were not achievable due to U.S. pressure for Japan to recognize the Republic of China in Taiwan rather than the People's Republic of China. That restriction was removed when the United States and China reached a rapprochement in 1972.

Scholars have discussed the so-called "1972 system," which was a social structure specific to China and Japan. It was reasonably stable, with an equilibrium based on different national priorities and locations in the regional and global system. Japan was apologetic for its past aggression and offered to help China modernize, an identity of an advanced country that was humble and sincere, which was acceptable for many of the older generation Japanese. The Chinese government prioritized a common front vis-à-vis the Soviet Union in the 1970s and economic modernization starting in 1979. The history issue and the territorial issue were present at the start of Sino-Japanese diplomatic relations but they were managed in both countries by influential leaders that exercised leadership and often smoothed things over behind the scenes.

To add to the familiar story told above, from an evolutionary perspective, China and Japan occupied different niches in the regional and global ecosystems. Japan competed with other advanced countries in the higher-end sectors while China began climbing up the industrial ladder from labor-intensive manufacture. The two countries complemented each other, which reduced direct competition. China had a higher political profile in the world while a rising Japan took a more cautious approach in global diplomacy. The mode of interaction was that of mutual gains or "mutualism," to borrow an evolutionary biological term.

The leaders of Sino-Japanese friendship consciously sought to increase economic and person-to-person exchange to forge a solid foundation for a strong relationship for generations to come. They were fully aware of the different national interests when it came to history and territories but they hoped to bypass those issues until the two nations were in a better position to deal with the disputes more directly. They recognized the great potential for such exchanges. People now may criticize earlier leaders for not facing up to the real problems, but I do not think that is fair. Earlier leaders did the best they could, given a very difficult situation and they left a positive legacy of economic and cultural ties. The problem we have now does not result from the fact that the previous generation failed to resolve all the problems for posterity but that the current generation has proven incapable so far of handling the challenge utilizing the positive legacy.

During this period, there were disputes that wore on the overall relationship over time. My previous research shows that there has been a cyclical pattern trending downward in Sino-Japanese relations since the decade-long "honeymoon" in the 1970s. This was an erratic, back-and-forth downward pattern. There was a rebound after each low point in the bilateral relationship, but each time it was shallower and shorter. Another feature is that the disputes were offset by incidents of cooperation (Wan 2006, 18–31). The two governments managed to make necessary compromises. In the scheme of things, while both governments continued to talk about friendship and subsequently about a strategic partnership as the overarching structure of the bilateral relationship, the actual mode of interaction would over time undermine the 1972 structure.

Current Sino-Japanese Tensions

The fourth period of Sino-Japanese relations started with the new millennium and is now into its second decade. Starting with the

Koizumi era in 2001–2006, both governments became far less willing to compromise. The bilateral relationship took a sharp turn toward confrontation with the September 2010 Chinese fishing boat collision incident, an accident waiting to happen because of the apparent growing salience of territorial issues. But poor management in both countries turned an unfortunate incident into a crisis.

Much has been said about the current tensions and much I agree with. Here I emphasize the co-evolutionary angle to this story. However one looks at it, absolutely or relatively, China and Japan are essentially going through a bilateral integration process. Some facts are well-known and much discussed, including bilateral trade, significant investment, production networks, student exchange, mutual visits, marriages, flights, and phone and internet connections. And one should keep in mind that no armed soldiers have stepped into each other's territories except for occasional mutual naval visits. That is why people discussed the "Sinification" or "Japanization" in the two countries not so long ago. These descriptions are not hyperbole, in my view, so one must ask why there is so much tension. What is the point of all these connections if they don't serve to reduce strain? This question is often framed as puzzling because it defies the expectation that closer ties should improve relations.

It is not particularly helpful to ask whether economic interdependence universally facilitates security cooperation. Economic interdependence is creating greater security among advanced democracies in North America and Western Europe, but not in East Asia. The interaction between economics and security is contingent upon time, space, and scale.

Familiarity may create contempt. But if one follows the Sino-Japanese relationship closely, one should be able to see that these connections are largely positive as intended. People who have better knowledge of the other country tend not be as negative as the general public or the media. In fact, one could sense an emergent property of near-kinship on a personal basis. Ecologists use the principle of integrative levels to organize studies of complex systems. The principle means that when components combine to form a larger whole in a hierarchical structure, new properties emerge that cannot be predicted from studies of components alone (Odum 1997, 33–34).

However, we now observe a strong backlash. Critics in both China and Japan take a moral high ground and those who are benefiting from the Sino-Japanese interaction keep quiet to avoid being criticized. The critics on both sides tap into more deeply-rooted notions shaped after the mid-nineteenth century. If China and Japan had interacted on a more intimate basis before the mid-nineteenth century, they might now be moving toward a combined new nation. But we live in a different time now. Both nations possess a strong patriotic sentiment. And both countries engage in a global web of interactions, which offer more evolutionary solutions. Both the Chinese and Japanese feel (wrongly, in my view) that they do not have to depend on the other country. In fact, many political leaders find working with third parties more attractive than with each other. This preference is liable to complicate bilateral relations.

From an ecological perspective, China and Japan now compete directly. China has moved up the technological ladder faster than most people anticipated. Even though China is still a fragile great power with uneven economic development, the country is so large that parts of it already compete with developed countries, which explains why China's advance in places like Africa is viewed as threatening to Japan's economic prosperity and national security. The two countries are grazing in the same grassland now. Politically, Japan is seeking to assert itself in the world partly in response to a rising China, which results in even more direct competition for political influence and leadership with Beijing.

An explicit biological story is the passing of the generation in both countries that personally experienced war. Watching the Sino-Japanese relationship and other cases in the world, one has to wonder how much people really learn from the past. With selective historical memory in both countries and a lack of critical thinking evident in much of both populations, no wonder government elites are finding it so difficult to manage the relationship, even though they are dealt good cards such as close economic and cultural exchange.

Looking into the Future

It is difficult to forecast what may happen in Sino-Japanese relations. Although no fortune teller, I will try to provide some perspective consistent with the arguments advanced in this article. Patterns of interactions can be explained by the processes that lead to them. Thus, to predict whether patterns will change, we need to examine whether there will be significant changes in the processes. What we can observe now is that the processes in practice for China and Japan dealing with each other are becoming entrenched as we speak, with broad support from society and the policy elites. The current leadership teams in both countries are expected to last for several more years, longer still in the Chinese case. Thus, the patterns of high tensions between the two countries are unlikely to change anytime soon. In addition, an explicit multilateralization of the disputes is a new development in the Sino-Japanese relationship. Therefore, it is harder still to shift foreign policy directions with obligations to third countries. Since President Xi Jinping and Prime Minister Abe Shinzō met briefly on the occasion of the Asia Pacific Economic Forum summit in Beijing in November 2014, bilateral official dialogues have been restored to some extent. But the fundamental tensions remain.

I offer a pessimistic forecast for Sino-Japanese relations here not because I wish to see such future development. In the end humans shape their own destiny. To prevent a gloomy future as may be inferred from observation, one has to change drastically one's expectations and mindset. In short, I wish for a self-negating prophecy in which we behave differently so as to prevent a dreaded prophecy from taking place. If the two nations are willing to do that, as they learn from the experiences of other countries, they will also leave a positive legacy that contributes to future successes in achieving reconciliation.

Part II: Issues in Sino-Japanese Relations

Chapter 6

The Forced Labor Redress Movement

A prominent feature of contemporary East Asian international relations is the history problem that Japan faces in its relations with the People's Republic of China and the Republic of Korea. One may indeed debate whether there should be a history problem at all or whether the problem is still Japan's at this point in time. But we know as a matter of fact that Beijing and Seoul have taken diplomatic actions against Tokyo over the history issue.

The history dispute has been intensely political. One can demonstrate how the Chinese and South Korean governments have used history to advance their political objectives at home and abroad judging by the inconsistency and overlapping with other disputes in their diplomatic actions. But the political motivation in the history issue is hardly surprising. After all, is there anything that cannot be used for political purposes? More important, the history dispute has its own dynamic, which cannot be reduced to other interests. One cannot use the history card continuously unless the card itself has inherent validity. In fact, most motivated activists are not seeking tangible side payments. Rather, the history issue itself is paramount for what they believe to be justice.

The history issue matters for East Asian security. For Japan, a conflict exists between normalization and historical reconciliation (e.g. Ikenberry 2006; *Washington Post* 2006). Given the current dynamic of East Asian international relations, Japan's normalization will most likely lead to greater confrontation with its neighbors, which will make the country less secure and its leadership aspiration frustrated. For those who want to see a more active Japan given its stable democracy and strong alliance with the United States, there is more than exasperation that Japan has not been able to move beyond its history problem with its neighbors. For many Chinese and Koreans, what they view as Japanese failure to address the history issue shapes their assessment of Japan's intention in redefining its defense missions and enhancing its defense capabilities. Conversely, many Japanese view what they see as endless criticism on history simply as a disguise for keeping Japan down, therefore revealing a hostile intent against their country. In response, they believe, Japan should speed up the normalization process by beefing up its defense and offering greater support for the United States in military operations outside Japan.

The importance of historical reconciliation for East Asian security was also illustrated when North Korea conducted a nuclear test in October 2006. During Prime Minister Abe Shinzō's visit to Beijing on October 8, the Chinese and Japanese governments expressed "deep concern" for the North Korean nuclear test in a joint statement. Abe did not actually promise not to visit the Yasukuni Shinto Shrine and all he did was refuse to state clearly his intention on Yasukuni visits. But that deliberate ambiguity was apparently sufficient to allow resumption of Sino-Japanese leadership exchange and thus allow the Japanese government to discuss the North Korean nuclear issue with China and South Korea on the highest level, something Abe's predecessor Koizumi Junichirō would have found difficult to accomplish. Abe's summits with the Chinese and South Korean leaders in October 8–9 paved the way for closer cooperation in light of North Korea's nuclear test. A true historical reconciliation would surely allow Japan, China, and South Korea to engage in closer security coordination.

History needs to be addressed because of the political reality in Northeast Asia, the validity of the issue, and the high security stakes but should be handled in such a way as to encourage reconciliation and to reduce long-term animosities among the three major nations of East Asia. Symbolic reconciliation — such as apologies and talks of friendship — practiced on the government level offered a modus operandi for the three nations to focus on substantive improvements in their economic and cultural exchanges. While one should not dismiss the sincerity of the advocates of Sino-Japanese friendship in both Japan and China or their major contributions to the relationship, such a friendship model no longer works given the great transformations of Chinese and Japanese societies. Moreover, despite past symbolic diplomacy, the history issue remains. One important reason is that symbolic friendship politics between the Chinese and Japanese governments does not sufficiently address societal sentiment.

We need societal pathways to reconciliation, and the redress movement is such an example. We should not be naïve and view the movement as a panacea. Reconciliation, which is broader than monetary compensation, may be achieved in different ways. Moreover, as will be shown in this chapter, the redress movement has its limits. But what is important about the movement is more what it reveals than what it has already accomplished. The movement shows that people in China and Japan can handle the history issue in an orderly and transnational fashion, which is badly needed given hardening and stifling nationalist narratives evolving in the two countries.

Compensating the Past Wrongs

The starting point for discussing the redress movement is whether such a movement has any legal basis. Different from apologies often demanded or expected by governments, redress activists turn to the court system to seek compensation as a material form of atoning for the past as well as apologies from Japanese companies and the Japanese state. This chapter focuses on the legality of seeking compensation related to the Sino-Japanese forced labor redress movement and suggests a new approach to the legal issue in light of the overall Sino-Japanese relationship.

One should note immediately that few Asian governments demand outright the legal right to state-to-state or even private monetary compensation from Japan, although they sometimes suggest that Japan has a moral obligation to do so for private citizens seeking justice and appear accepting of their citizens' demand for compensation from the Japanese government or Japanese companies. This is because the Japanese state has concluded treaties with virtually all Asian states, except North Korea, to end the war and resolve war-related issues.

The Chinese government is no exception. The Chinese Foreign Ministry treats the war reparation issue as the fifth sensitive issue in Sino-Japanese relations, along with history, Taiwan, Diaoyu (Senkaku), Japan–U.S. security cooperation, Japanese chemical weapons discarded in China, and Guanghualiao/Kōkaryō (the dispute over whether Beijing or Taipei legally owns a student dorm in Kyoto). The issue is described as follows in the ministry's website (Chinese Foreign Ministry 2002).[1]

The War of Japanese aggression against China inflicted extremely grave disasters on the Chinese people. China and its people suffered a tremendous loss. As the old saying "The past, if not forgotten, can serve as a guide for the future" goes, such a miserable history should be borne in mind. Nevertheless, it should be noted that it was a few militarists who launched the war and should take the primary responsibilities. The Japanese people were also the victims of the war. It has been always the policy of our party and government to draw a clear distinction between the few militarists and Japanese people. During the negotiation of normalization of diplomatic relation in 1972, the Japanese government stated that it keenly felt and introspected the severe responsibilities arising from the war for the Chinese people. Taking this into consideration, the Chinese government decided to waive the claim of war reparations, which was written into the Sino-Japanese Joint Statement in 1972. The Treaty

---

[1] I checked the website again on December 23, 2014. It has not been updated.

of Peace and Friendship, approved by the third meeting of the fifth Standing Committee of Chinese People's Congress in 1978, reaffirmed in the form of legal document the decision of waiving reparation. The position of the Chinese government on this issue is clear and consistent: China sticks to the position of waiving reparation stated in the Sino-Japanese Joint Statement and continues to honor her commitments of international treaty stated in the Treaty of Peace and Friendship. However, as for those realistic problems left over by the War of Japanese Aggression against China, such as the chemical weapons discarded by Japan. The Chinese government, proceeding from protecting the legitimate rights and interests of its people, requests that the Japanese side should take them into serious consideration and handle them properly.

This carefully drafted statement makes it clear that the state-to-state war reparation issue no longer exists for the Chinese government in a legal sense. A treaty commitment is binding. A country's violation of treaty commitments compromises its standing in the international community, invites retaliatory actions, and shakes the very foundation of its interaction with other countries. In fact, one does not even want to be viewed as wavering. That is why the Chinese Foreign Ministry statement emphasizes that the Chinese position is "clear and consistent," in case one wonders if the Chinese government wants to revisit the issue in the face of domestic criticism that the 1972 deal compromised Chinese interests. In Beijing's comment on war reparations issue in response to the Japanese Supreme Court's scheduled hearing in March 2007 on whether Chinese citizens have the right to pursue private compensation from the Japanese state and Japanese companies, the Chinese Foreign Ministry spokesman reiterated that Beijing's position in the 1972 Joint Statement remains unchanged and the Japanese government should treat Japan's atrocities committed during the war appropriately as a "humanitarian issue" (China News Agency online March 13, 2007). Even after the Japanese Supreme Court ruled on April 27, 2007 that the Chinese government had renounced the right to war compensation from Japan, including private claims, in the 1972 joint statement, the Chinese Foreign Ministry spokesman protested over Japan's unilateral legal interpretation of the Chinese position but did not offer an opposing interpretation that Chinese citizens do have a legal basis for lawsuits against Japan.

Since the Chinese government has not raised the lawsuit issue diplomatically, the Japanese government does not have to respond. The forced labor issue is simply not on the Sino-Japanese diplomatic agenda. From this perspective, the redress movement appears to face an uphill battle, with little chance of actually winning.

If so, why do we see the redress movement? Fundamentally, this movement is part of a global trend for non-state actors to assert themselves, to create political and legal space for their concerns, and to challenge the state-centric order.[2] Redress activists recognize the difficulty of winning in courts. But they are not practicing martyrdom. After all, one important mission for the redress activists and the victims has been to create a legal record of the Japanese atrocities, which has been a partial success since most Japanese judges have acknowledged the crimes committed by the state and companies. Moreover, it is not unreasonable for them to believe that there is a chance, slight as it might be.

Moreover, a legal route may pave the way for an extra-legal, political solution in the end. The Chinese lawsuits in the Japanese courts are political as well as legal. The judicial system enjoys a high degree of autonomy in a democracy like Japan, which explains why foreigners can sue the Japanese government in the Japanese courts in the first place. As such, a sound legal system should operate based on legality and would erode its credibility if it bends to every policy whim or diplomatic expediency. At the same time, even in a country of rule of law, policy and law are not independent of each other. The legal defense of the Japanese government reflects its policy choice not to compensate the victims for fear of opening a Pandora box. If the government finds it important to shift policy, it may resort to

---

[2] The Chinese redress activists are particularly inspired by the Jewish redress activities. For the Jewish redress movement, see Ferencz 2002. For a broader discussion of how human rights have been globalized, see De Greiff 2006; Keck and Sikkink 1998; Brysk 2002; Coicaud, Doyle, and Gardner 2003; Daly and Sarkin 2006.

extra-legal means. As a case in point, after the Tokyo District Court on January 30, 2007 rejected a lawsuit by Japanese orphans left in China after World War II on the grounds that the state did not violate the rights of the plaintiffs since their damage was caused by war, Prime Minister Abe Shinzō decided to study policy measures to provide additional assistance for the Japanese orphans who have returned to Japan (*Yomiuri Shimbun* online January 30, 2007). Thus, some Japanese redress activists have urged the creation of two funds for forced laborers and comfort women to settle their private claims. After all, in most cases Japanese judges have acknowledged crimes committed and have ruled against the Chinese plaintiffs based on legal arguments that statute of limitation has passed and that the state has no legal obligations to compensate private citizens under the Meiji Constitution in effect at the time of the crimes. Moreover, the funding could come from the unpaid wages for Chinese forced laborers the Japanese companies had deposited in the government banks and agencies after the war ended.

The German experience has been an inspiration and offers hope. The German parliament passed a law to establish the Remembrance, Responsibility and the Future Foundation in August 2000, with a commitment of DM10 billion (about $5 billion at the time) for forced and slave laborers and Holocaust victims. Half of the funds came from the government and half from German companies. The German government anticipated more than 2 million people who would qualify for compensation from the foundation (Authers 2006). In the end, the foundation paid EUR 4.37 billion to more than 1.66 million people in almost 100 countries and ended payments officially on June 12, 2007 (Remembrance and Future Fund 2007).

The Chinese redress activists can also hope to eventually persuade the Chinese state to fight on their behalf. The Chinese Foreign Ministry statement cited above has two catches. One is that "realistic" issues, which presumably include forced labor, should be handled properly. The Chinese redress activists take that kind of statement as indicating that the government does not forbid their activities. The other catch in the Chinese statement is that China gave up reparations on the understanding that Japan would face up to its past. It does not say that if Japan does not face up to the past, the Chinese government would negate its legal obligations. But what it says is that the whole relationship would be problematic. A relationship is more than legality.

If we look at the broader bilateral relationship between Japan and China, one way to atone for the past is to demonstrate the nation has completely renounced its militarist past and is firmly committed to peace and cooperation. Japan has accomplished much in democracy, pacifism, and economic development in the past six decades. Since Japan normalized its diplomatic relations with the People's Republic of China in 1972, the Japanese government and society have offered assistance to China, particularly China's modernization effort since the late 1970s, partly to reconcile with its important neighbor.

Much of Japanese reconciliation effort has come from the private sector, including Japanese enterprises. But the more discussed way of compensating indirectly for its past aggression is Japan's Official Development Assistance (ODA). Japan's ODA is no charity, and certainly is not perceived as such by the Japanese government and the recipient governments. ODA serves Japan's broad foreign policy objectives. It helps Japanese companies and consultants in competition with other advanced countries. And most Japanese ODA money comes in the form of loans that have to be repaid with interest. Japan's ODA has few political strings attached. Recipients can save money because the terms of ODA loans are more generous than the money they can raise from the private capital market if they can at all. ODA as seed money for infrastructure projects also paves the way for other things East Asians want, namely investment and technologies. For China, Japanese ODA was offered in particularly favorable five-year packages, which coincided with Beijing's five-year plans and diverged from Tokyo's typical practice of offering ODA on a yearly basis. Moreover, Japan's ODA amounted to about half of total foreign bilateral aid to Beijing, which facilitated China's modernization at a crucial stage (Wan 2006, 263–264).

Official Chinese and Japanese documents have not mentioned a substitution of ODA for wartime compensation. But such a rationale was intended and understood thanks to countless Sino-Japanese exchanges of views. If so, why has Japanese ODA not affected Chinese attitudes toward Japan over the history issue, as many in Japan see it? To answer this question, we should first step back and think about the overarching objective of Japanese ODA for China to which an implicit compensation for the past contributes. Japan's ODA was ultimately intended to advance its overall relationship with China. From that larger historical perspective, Japan's ODA served as an important and positive anchor for its relations with China. Sino-Japanese economic and socio-cultural exchange has expanded tremendously since 1972. One can also ask a counterfactual question of whether an absence of ODA would have made things worse. A good case can be made that the answer is yes.

To zoom in on the history question, Japanese ODA has contributed to reconciliation. One can demonstrate based on anecdotal evidence and surveys that the Chinese who have engaged in interactions with the Japanese tend to have more positive and more nuanced views of Japan than those who have not done so (Wan 2006, 74–78). Moreover, while it is difficult to prove empirically it is reasonable to argue that a substitution effect was felt on the Chinese state level. For Chinese economic planners, Japanese war reparation and ODA would indeed serve a similar function of financing state projects deemed important for the nation. Therefore, when Chinese officials frequently expressed gratitude to the Japanese for the aid projects, the chance is that they were truly being grateful for the financing of "their" projects rather than being disingenuous.

Still, it is a fact that Japanese aid has not changed Chinese views as much as some Japanese hoped. One explanation that has been offered is the propaganda of a Communist Party government or lack of it to publicize the Japanese ODA projects. This is partly true. The Chinese government did not publicize the Japanese ODA projects that much. But it is not clear how much an average recipient government has publicized the aid projects. A recipient government has a strong incentive to thank the Japanese government to keep aid money flowing while having little incentive to tell its own citizens why foreign money is so important since that presumably reveals its own inadequacy. Understandably, the Japanese government did not particularly push on this issue either since that would appear overly self-serving.

The main reason for the failure of the substitution approach is that the in-lieu "compensation" does not go to those who suffered. If you were forced to do hard labor in Japan during the war, the fact that Japanese aid money has contributed to the construction of a new terminal in the Beijing Capital International Airport does not soothe your pain. With the benefit of hindsight, it would have been more conducive to Chinese belief in Japanese atonement if some money had been paid as direct reparations for individual victims.

Compensating the surviving victims could still work. For the sake of justice and a good relationship with neighbors, survivors should be compensated before they die. Direct compensation for Chinese forced labor and comfort women victims would generate a far greater and positive impact on average Chinese citizens' view of Japan than billions of dollars of ODA have. The German and Austrian cases mentioned earlier have shown the power of reconciliation efforts that combine monetary compensation and moral responsibility. The power of direct interaction with ordinary Chinese citizens was also vividly demonstrated when the Chinese government permitted a Japanese rescue team to the disaster area in the aftermath of the Sichuan Earthquake in May 2008. The Chinese Internet forums which have been overwhelmingly critical of Japan in recent years were mostly appreciative of Japanese assistance in time of need.

Chinese Private Lawsuits in the Japanese Courts

The Japanese army forced Chinese prisoners of war and civilians to do hard labor in Japan during World War II. In 1946, the Japanese Foreign Ministry compiled a list of 38,935 Chinese forced laborers brought to Japan, with a death ratio of 17.5 percent in the labor camps, which was particularly high considering the fact that most

Chinese were brought to Japan after March 1944, the last year of the war (Tanaka and Matsuzawa 1995). Some Chinese researchers consider the official Japanese account too small. China was not alone in that misery category. The Japanese state used forced labor from a large number of Asian countries, particularly Korea (Kratoska 2005). To illustrate that forced labor is not a Chinese concern alone, much has been written in the West about the abuse of American and European prisoners of war in the Japanese labor camps (e.g. MacArthur 2005; Holmes 2001; Wodnik 2003; Jacobsen 2004).

PRC citizens have so far filed 16 forced labor lawsuits against the Japanese companies and the Japanese state in the Japanese courts since June 1995.[3] These cases account for most of the lawsuits by PRC citizens in Japan. Besides the forced labor cases, there are four cases by comfort women and nine over war atrocities. Unlike the war-atrocities and comfort-women cases that are all filed in Tokyo, the forced labor cases are spread throughout Japan, including Tokyo, Sapporo, Niigata, Gunma, Nagano, Fukuoka, Hiroshima, Kanazawa, Kyoto, Nagasaki, Miyazaki, and Yamagata.

The 16 Chinese forced labor cases are evenly distributed over time: 1995 (1 case), 1996 (1), 1997 (2), 1998 (2), 1999 (2), 2000 (1), 2002 (2), 2003 (2), 2004 (2), and 2005 (1). There has not been an avalanche of Chinese forced labor lawsuits in the Japanese courts. Whereas earlier cases might encourage future ones, a lack of success also discourages would-be plaintiffs. More important, it is costly to file a lawsuit due to the need to collect evidence in China and to bring Chinese plaintiffs to testify in Japan.

It is difficult to have a precise tally of the number of Chinese involved in the lawsuits and the amount of money demanded. My best estimate is that the Chinese forced labor lawsuits involve 236

---

[3] Much of my discussion in this section comes from Wan 2006, 304–327. The information has been updated based on information from media reports and from the Web site of Chūgokujin sensō higaisha no yōkyū o sasaerukai [Society to Support the Demands of Chinese War Victims], available online at http://www.suopei.org/index-j.html, and the Web site of the Chinese nongovernmental network Zhongguo jiuyiba aiguowang [China 9.18 patriotic dotcom], available online at http://www.china918.net.

plaintiffs who demand about ¥4.9 billion, which is slightly over $40 million. Chinese plaintiffs typically ask for ¥20 million each.

By early 2007, of the 16 cases, two cases were pending at the district court. Of the other 14 cases, the very first forced labor case lost in the Tokyo District Court but was settled out of court in 2000. Three cases won and ten cases were lost in the district court. The high court had ruled on seven district court decisions, six negative, and one positive ruling for the Chinese plaintiffs. Three favorable district court rulings and one negative district court ruling for the Chinese plaintiffs were reversed by the high court. But in a decisive turn of events, the Supreme Court ruled against Chinese plaintiffs in the Nishimatsu case and two other forced labor cases on April 27, 2007, which essentially ended the hope that Chinese wartime victims will ever be compensated through the Japanese court system. As a case in point, the Maebashi District Court ruled against the Chinese plaintiffs on August 29, 2007, citing the Supreme Court ruling. The Supreme Court rejected more cases on June 12, 2007, June 4 and July 8, 2008.

Most court rulings have recognized wrongdoing by the Japanese state and the companies but have largely ruled against the Chinese plaintiffs based on two legal arguments. One is that the state has no obligation to compensate private citizens based on the Meiji Constitution in effect at the time and the other is that the 20-year statute of limitation has passed, which is a preferred defense for the Japanese companies. But the few favorable court rulings maintain that the Japanese state and the companies do have responsibilities to compensate victims. The rulings typically lump the state and the companies together. As an exception, Fukuoka District Court ruled on April 26, 2002 that Mitsui Mine Co. pay ¥165 million to 15 Chinese plaintiffs but did not rule against the state. In response, Mitsui appealed to Fukuoka High Court. The Chinese plaintiffs also appealed for state compensation. Fukuoka High Court rejected the lower court ruling on company compensation on May 24, 2004. The April 27, 2007 Japanese Supreme Court ruling also recognized wrongdoing but took a legal position that the Chinese government had abandoned the right to war compensation in the 1972 Joint

Statement that normalized diplomatic relations between Tokyo and Beijing.

I will discuss three cases in greater detail here. The first Chinese lawsuit was filed by 11 Chinese plaintiffs led by Geng Chun. Geng, a Kuomintang military officer, was captured by the Japanese army in May 1944 and was taken along with almost one thousand Chinese to Japan to do hard labor at the Kajima Corporation-run Hanaoka Mine in Odate City, Akita Prefecture. Due to particularly harsh conditions and cruel treatment, almost half of the Chinese forced laborers died before the war ended. On June 30, 1945, Geng led about 700 Chinese in an uprising, which was repressed the next day. Geng and some other Hanaoka survivors sent a letter to the Kajima Company for compensation and apologies in December 1989 and formally filed a lawsuit against Kajima in the Tokyo District Court on June 28, 1995. They sought monetary compensation, commemorative museums, and public apology. Unlike the following cases, Geng and his co-plaintiffs did not sue the Japanese government. On December 10, 1997, the Tokyo District Court ruled against the Chinese plaintiffs. Geng appealed to the Tokyo High Court. Urged by the Tokyo High Court, Kajima accepted a settlement on November 29, 2000, paying ¥500 million for all the Hanaoka Chinese survivors and descendants but admitting no guilt. Whereas, the settlement was hailed as a partial victory by some and many survivors collected their share of the money, some Hanaoka survivors including Geng and some activists have criticized the settlement for not acknowledging the crimes committed.

The second case is Liu Lianren verus the Japanese state filed on March 25, 1996 in the Tokyo District Court. Like Geng Chun, Liu Lianren received much media attention because of his extraordinary suffering as a forced laborer. A peasant in Shandong Province, Liu was forcibly taken to Hokkaido for forced labor in a mine in November 1944. Due to harsh living and working conditions, Liu fled into the mountains on July 31, 1945. Without knowing the end of the war, Liu hid in the mountains for 13 years. Found in February 1958, Liu returned to China in April that year. Liu sued the Japanese state for failure to protect him after the war ended. He sought ¥20 million of compensation and apologies. He last testified in the Tokyo District Court in 1998. Liu died in September 2000. On July 12, 2001, the Tokyo District Court ordered the government to pay ¥20 million in compensation to Liu's descendants. But on June 23, 2005, the Tokyo High Court acknowledged wrongdoing but rejected the lower court ruling on the ground that the Japanese and Chinese governments had no legal arrangements at the time that would allow citizens of one nation to receive compensation from the other. On April 27, 2007, the Supreme Court ruled against Liu's descendants.

In the third case, five Chinese filed a case against Nishimatsu Construction Co. and the state at Hiroshima District Court on January 16, 1998, seeking apology and ¥27.5 million in compensation. The Chinese plaintiffs were among the 360 Chinese laborers were brought by the company to Hiroshima Prefecture to work for hydroelectric construction in 1944. On July 9, 2002, the Hiroshima District Court ruled against plaintiffs, citing statute of limitations while recognizing wrongdoing. On July 9, 2004, Hiroshima High Court ruled in favor of plaintiffs.

This case became significant because the Japanese Supreme Court decided to review it, the first time the court had done so for a Chinese forced labor case. Court debates were held on March 16, 2007. The Supreme Court decision would have a profound impact on all pending Chinese lawsuits because the Supreme Court wanted to determine whether the 1972 Joint Statement includes right to private compensation. From a legal perspective, this was a moment of truth, and it was recognized as such by Chinese and Japanese activists. It was speculated that the Supreme Court might reverse the verdict of the high court. If it intended to maintain the verdict, there would be no reason for court debates again. Moreover, of the five forced labor cases that had been decided by the high court prior to the Supreme Court's decision to hold a hearing, only the Nishimatsu case was decided in favor of the Chinese plaintiffs. The Supreme Court chose only the Nishimatsu case for review (Underwood and Kang 2007). In the end, as mentioned earlier, the Supreme Court ruled against the Chinese plaintiffs.

However, even with the Supreme Court ruling against Chinese forced labor cases, the redress movement is expected to continue outside the Japanese court system in Japan and is actually gathering momentum in China. In a way, the fact that the legal path has been blocked led to more intensive efforts to seek a political solution to the forced labor issue, showing signs of promise by the end of 2008. Indeed, Nishimatsu Construction Co. initiated negotiations for a settlement with the five Chinese plaintiffs and reached an agreement on October 23, 2009 to create a ¥250 million yen trust fund from which the over 300 Chinese forced laborers could receive compensation. To be sure, this out-of-court settlement was not exactly a political solution involving the Chinese and Japanese governments, but it took place in a political context that such settlements were deemed desirable. By late 2014, 248 former forced laborers (out of 360) and descendents received ¥600,000 each (China News Agency online October 19, 2014).

A Transnational Redress Movement

The Chinese redress movement should be properly termed the Sino-Japanese redress movement because of the dominant influence of the Japanese supporters. To start with, only Japanese lawyers can represent foreign plaintiffs in the Japanese courts. Most of the Chinese lawsuits are handled by the Lawyers Team for Chinese War Victims Demanding Compensation (*Chūgokujin senso higaisha songai baishō soshō bengodan*), started by Onodera Toshitaka after a visit to the Nanjing Massacre Museum in May 1994. Upon return to Japan, he organized more than 300 lawyers to support Chinese lawsuits in Japan. The Japanese lawyers involved in the Chinese lawsuit cases are working *pro-bono*. They do not just wait for the cases to come to them. They often initiate cases themselves. The Chinese lawsuits are particularly demanding given the need to collect evidence in China and to bring Chinese witnesses to Japan. Su Xiangxiang, a Chinese veteran activist who has been involved in the movement from the beginning, says it has been largely Japanese lawyers who use their own money to help the Chinese plaintiffs sue the Japanese government and the Japanese companies, and he estimates that the Japanese lawyers have used 10 million yuan ($1.25 million) of their own money to support the suits (*Jinghua Shibao* online 2006).

The Chinese lawsuits are supported also by some Japanese academics like Tanaka Hiroshi who have uncovered relevant historical documents, conducted field research in China, and offered valuable advice. Japanese citizens have also formed local support groups for the Chinese plaintiffs under the umbrella of the Society to Support the Demands of Chinese War Victims (*Chūgokujin sensō higaisha no yōkyū o ssaerukai*). These citizen groups rally support for the Chinese cases, raise funds, attend the hearings, and help arrange visits by Chinese witnesses. Much of the support in Japan also comes from the Chinese Diaspora in Japan.

The Japanese lawyers and supporters want to achieve a genuine reconciliation with the Chinese by righting the past wrongs, and they want to put on record the Japanese atrocities committed in Asia as a way to counter a revisionist trend in Japan. The Chinese plaintiffs, lawyers, and supporters share the same objectives. That is why redress activists pay particular attention to the wording of the court rulings, namely whether the judges acknowledge crimes committed and how much.

The Chinese private lawsuits in Japan are highly popular news stories in China. Chinese readers follow the stories closely and Chinese journalists chase after the stories accordingly. In that context, the support by the Japanese lawyers and citizen groups has received extensive Chinese media coverage. For an example, Onodera's launch of the Japanese lawyer group to support Chinese victims after visiting Nanjing in 1994 is a story told in detail time and again. Oyama Hiroshi, the president of the Lawyers Team for Chinese War Victims Demanding Compensation, was selected as one of the ten people who "emotionally moved" the Chinese people the most in 2003, along with China's first astronaut Yang Liwei. To illustrate the high profile nature of the Sino-Japanese redress movement, Wang Xuan, a Chinese redress activist who received graduate education at Tsukuba University, was selected for that celebrity status the previous year.

The Chinese media coverage of the activities of the Japanese lawyers and supporters has been highly positive. One often reads about the supposedly Japanese characteristics of meticulous attention to details and perseverance to the end. Needless to say, any stereotyping of "national characteristics" is highly problematic, but such openly expressed admiration for some Japanese serves as a badly needed corrective in the Chinese context in which negative stereotyping of the Japanese prevails.

The Chinese public reaction to the Sino-Japanese redress movement reveals the power of seeking justice directly through societal players, which an indirect or implied compensation such as ODA cannot hope to match in terms of influencing public opinion. There are simply no spontaneous social groups in China to publicize Japanese ODA projects, let alone a Sino-Japanese movement for that purpose. One cannot point to Chinese government propaganda or media control to explain this. The Chinese redress activists and groups began to operate on their own initiative against the apparent wishes of the government. While the Chinese government does not have strong incentives to publicize Japanese ODA projects, it also has no reason to restrict societal discussion in this area. In fact, the Chinese government should be logically more concerned about anti-Japanese activities that often lead to street demonstrations, which threaten social stability the government considers to be paramount. If some Chinese ODA activists want to highlight the contribution of Japanese ODA to Chinese modernization, it would not be politically risky or technically challenging to do so. The simple reality is that there is no market for such information when the Chinese public is focused on the history issue. Chinese media reaction to Japanese supporters of the redress movement compared to the reaction to Japanese ODA shows that when it comes to historical reconciliation, the best strategy is to face the history issue head on.

At the same time, we should not consider the Sino-Japanese redress movement to be the solution. There are limits to the movement. Whereas the Chinese media coverage has been positive, that may or may not change Chinese public's view of Japan as a whole. The Chinese stories on the redress movement often have a "reality check" in their discussions, that is, we trust Japanese people like Onodera, but how representative are they in Japan? Isn't the Japanese government opposed to the compensation to the victims?

Society and State

The redress movement is a grass-roots transnational social movement, unlike the past friendship networks orchestrated by the state, particularly on the Chinese side. As a social movement, the redress movement interacts with the state-to-state relationship. In a democracy like Japan, the government does not take actions against the Japanese redress activists, and local governments may be supportive. The activities of these redress activists and citizen support groups against their own government are a strong testament to Japan's dramatic and successful post-war democratization. Political values aside, Japan's strong democracy gives it a significant edge over China in contemporary international relations where first-class powers are virtually all democracies. Ironically, any effort to stifle such dissent against the state in the name of national unity would necessarily neutralize that advantage because Japan would then be viewed as not so democratic.

The Japanese government has been resistant to private redress claims. It sees the lawsuits as a Pandora's Box that would allow a flood of new claims over forced labor and other wartime atrocities in Japan and elsewhere against the Japanese state and companies. There is also a Japanese perception that the Chinese pursuing the claims may not represent the true victims and are in this effort for monetary gains.

Unlike in Germany, a "civil war" regarding history exists in Japan and the tide appears to be tilting toward the revisionist view of history. The high point for the redress movement in Japan arguably took place in the mid-1990s, with Prime Minister Murayama Tomiichi offering a more explicit apology than previous prime ministers and the Asian Women's Fund established. But with rising nationalist sentiment in Japan and a relationship with China that remains deeply strained despite recent improvements, Chinese forced labor plaintiffs have made little progress. As a case in point, in the second Chinese forced labor lawsuit filed at the Fukuoka District Court in 2003, Mitsubishi Materials defense lawyers adopted an aggressive tactic based on an explicit revisionist line of arguments that deny Japan's wartime crimes. By contrast, the Japanese companies being sued had typically used legal technicalities such as the statute of limitations or the contention that they are different companies now (Underwood 2006).

In a non-democratic country like China, the relationship between any social movement and the state is complicated, to say the least. The redress movement in China was a product of China's own transformation. Reform opened up some space for activism in Chinese society. Chinese citizens wanted to air their grievances, and they wanted the government to address the past wrongs done to them. In that context, it was natural that some people would want to deal with Japanese atrocities. But the Chinese government initially viewed redress activists with strong suspicion and treated them almost like dissidents that threaten the country's order and stability (Wan 2006, 321–322).

Official support for private lawsuits is slowly emerging in China. One major complaint of Chinese redress activists was the difficulty in setting up foundations in order to raise funds to support lawsuits against Japanese companies and the Japanese state. The situation improved for them in August 2005 when the China Legal Aid Foundation and the All China Lawyer Association jointly launched an initiative to provide legal aid to Chinese private lawsuits against Japan and to create a special fund for the purpose. The group held a highly publicized ceremony to accept donations in the Great Hall of the People in February 2006. The ceremony was attended by retired senior Chinese officials. All together, the foundation received 2.56 million yuan or slightly more than $300,000 (*Jinghua Shibao* online 2006).

As another sign of relaxation, the Chinese Association for Private Lawsuits against Japan (*Zhongguo minjian duiri suopei lianhehui*) was formally allowed to operate in April 2006. The group was formed in 1992 but could not register for the following decade.

The association was headed by Tong Zeng, one of the pioneers for lawsuits against Japan in China. Earlier, Tong was "asked" to leave Beijing during the Japanese imperial visit to China in 1992. Beginning around 2005, some of the activities by redress activists have been highly publicized and attended by senior officials (some retired) and celebrities. Local governments have built monuments or museums and held memorial meetings for Chinese forced labor victims. Some company executives have donated large sums of money to the redress cause. All of these highly publicized activities reveal calculations that such activities will not cause political trouble for the people involved.

The Chinese government's subtle shift in attitudes toward the Chinese redress activists should be understood in the larger context of China's growing tensions with Japan during the Koizumi administration. While still suspicious of any social groups independent of the state, the Chinese government could utilize to some extent the societal sentiment in exerting pressure on Japan. At the same time, the government felt hindered by overly strong anti-Japanese discourse on the Internet and particularly by anti-Japanese demonstrations. Thus, the government continued to crack down on some more extreme internet groups.

The Battle Field Shifting to China

One significant development in the redress issue is that Chinese forced labor victims and their descendents are beginning to sue the Japanese companies and the Japanese state in the Chinese courts. There has always been discussion about moving lawsuits elsewhere since the chance of winning in the Japanese courts has been slim. There was at one point hope that the Chinese could sue the Japanese state and companies in the Californian court system but that route is no longer viable given the U.S. Supreme Court ruling in Japan's favor and the continuous opposition to such lawsuits by the American executive branch.

It makes sense on one level for the forced labor Chinese plaintiffs to sue in the Chinese courts because they would have the advantage in terms of public sympathy and because the Chinese courts may conceivably collect compensation from the Japanese companies operating in China. However, such an approach also presents potential problems for the Chinese government. For one thing, Chinese civil lawsuits for labor abuses would also open the door to lawsuits being filed in the foreign courts against the Chinese state and Chinese companies and make it possible to collect from a growing presence of Chinese companies operating in foreign countries. Even without reciprocal lawsuits that potentially exact high compensation from China, punitive actions against major Japanese companies for the past wrongdoing would also discourage Japanese direct investment in China, which would be potentially far more costly economically for the Chinese state. The first incidence of lawsuit against Japanese firms occurred in December 2000 in Hebei Province, but the court refused to take the case on the ground that China does not have corresponding laws or relevant legal interpretations.

With growing tensions between the two countries since the September 2010 fishing boat incident, the Chinese government is shifting its position somewhat by recognizing the private citizens' right to seek redress and by not preventing lawsuits. Thus, Tong Zeng and some other Chinese redress activists believe the time has arrived to file lawsuits against Japan in Chinese courts. Some Chinese legal experts also support such a move (e.g. Chen 2014). In a highly publicized case, a class-action case representing 9,415 plaintiffs against Japan's Mitsui and Mitsubishi was filed in the Beijing Number 1 Intermediate court on February 26, 2014. It would be difficult to tell how well the case would move forward even if the court accepts the case because of lack of laws for such a case. The Republic of China laws that might be relevant for the cases are no longer in effect. Thus, some activist Chinese lawyers think that the court would have to refer to international law (*Huanqiu shibao* online February 27, 2014). The Chinese activists have been encouraged by similar legal actions taken in South Korea. On April 15, 2014, the seventh Chinese forced labor suit against Japanese companies was filed in a Shandong court. It is not just forced labor redress either. We should expect to see more legal dealings between the two countries in the future. The Chinese lawsuits in the Chinese courts are already having an impact on the Japanese companies. After being sued in the Beijing court in February 2014, the two Japanese companies sought settlement with the Chinese plaintiffs proposing the establishment of a fund to pay about 1.9 million yen for each of the 3,765 former laborers and the bereaved plus compensation for lawsuit expense. But the plaintiff side stopped the settlement discussion on February 11, 2015 arguing that the Japanese companies have not agreed to admission of direct involvement in forced labor or to acknowledge payment as compensation (*Asahi shimbun* online February 11, 2015). Thus, Chinese plaintiffs may expect settlement with the Japanese companies but admission of guilt would be difficult.

While Chinese societal actors have become more engaged over the forced labor issue, the Japanese social atmosphere has shifted drastically. A revisionist view of history has become ever louder and seems dominant at times, supported and urged by powerful revisionist politicians. They are particularly opposed to the comfort women issue, viewing any mention of this shameful institution and practice as offending Japan's honor. Japanese revisionists also seek to whitewash the forced labor issue.[4] It is regrettable that efforts by many Japanese citizens for genuine reconciliation have yielded few concrete results and are currently overwhelmed by the revisionist tide.

---

[4]As a case in point, a textbook publisher in Tokyo has recently received government permission to remove any mention of comfort women or forced labor from high school social studies textbooks (*Asahi shimbun* online January 9, 2015).

Chapter 7

Japanese Strategic Thinking toward Taiwan

Japan's strategic thinking toward Taiwan should tell us much about Tokyo's overall strategic thinking. Strategic thinking is often narrowly defined as thinking about a country's national security. More broadly, it may be seen as a calculated approach to advance a country's core national objectives. Security thinking toward Taiwan has become important to Japan since the mid-1990s. It is viewed in the context of relations with the People's Republic of China (PRC) and the world. The United States, Japan's security ally, has taken on the responsibility of defending Taiwan against unprovoked attacks from the PRC. Taiwan is strategically located on Japan's shipping lanes to Southeast Asia and the Middle East. Taiwan has become a high-stakes issue. To know a country's strategic thinking, it is crucial to see how it views high-stakes issues.

The chapter also examines Japan's general attitude toward Taiwan as well as the PRC. On the one hand, public sentiment in Japan often exerts a major impact on policy. Thus, anyone who studies Japanese foreign policy has to pay close attention to Japanese public opinion. On the other hand, one should not confuse sentiment with strategic calculations. Similar to other countries, much of Japanese writing about the Taiwan issue is a reflection of public sentiment rather than strategic thinking, as the term strategy normally means. Thus, to identify what is public sentiment is to sharpen our understanding of what is strategic in Japanese thinking.

Japanese views on Taiwan have been diverse and evolving. Broadly speaking, Japanese have become more sympathetic to Taiwan since the outcry over the PRC's handling of the 1989 Tiananmen demonstrators, and they have become worried about the security implications of the Taiwan issue since the Chinese military exercises in the Taiwan Strait in the mid-1990s. Some Japanese have become verbally supportive of Taiwan's separation from China in the past decade, viewing Taiwan as more strategically important for Japan than for the United States.

Japanese sympathy for Taiwan and concern over the PRC's rise have translated into upgraded official exchange with the government in Taiwan and stronger public support for Taiwan's security. In a highly publicized joint statement issued on February 19, 2005, the Japanese foreign minister and defense agency director general along with the U.S. secretary of state and defense minister declared that Japan and the United States have a common security objective to "encourage the peaceful resolution of issues concerning the Taiwan Strait through dialogue." At the same time, the Japanese government remains committed rhetorically to the One China Principle in the 1972 Joint Statement.[1] Japan remains convinced that U.S.–China relations rather than Japan–China relations are central to the Taiwan question. Japanese know that Japan will side with the United States if conflict occurs in the Taiwan Strait but would rather not face that stark scenario and that Japan is in no position to fight for Taiwan at this point without the United States taking the lead.

Japan is being defensive rather than offensive at this point, but the possibility exists of Japan taking a stronger stance depending on

---

[1] In an important speech on Japan's Asian strategy delivered on December 7, 2005, Foreign Minister Asō Tarō stated, "Japan will keep the position that was stipulated in the Japan–China Joint Communiqué, in the understanding that there is but one China." In a more recent document on Japan–Taiwan relations, Japan Ministry of Foreign Affairs (2013) reiterated the basic stance on its relationship with Taiwan as set out in the 1972 joint communiqué with China.

what China does and how international politics evolve. Taiwan is not the only worst-case scenario for a possible Japan–China conflict: Territorial disputes over the Senkaku/Diaoyudao and the East China Sea and competition over energy, being other scenarios. The Taiwan issue complicates Japan's relations with China. Conversely, the state of the relationship with Beijing affects Tokyo's strategic thinking toward Taiwan; a bad relationship with China would make the "loss of Taiwan" a far more significant security concern for Japan than would be the case if relations were friendly.

The chapter includes six sections. The first section provides a brief historical overview of Japan's relations with Taiwan through the 1980s. History provides a reference point to determine where current Japanese thinking toward Taiwan comes from and it is also a present issue in Japan's relations with China. The next three sections examine Japan's public sentiment and strategic thinking toward Taiwan in three periods: From 1989 to the mid-1990s, from the mid-1990s to 2001, and from 2001 to the present. The fifth section offers a focused discussion of the current triangular dynamic among Japan, Taiwan, and the PRC. The last section concludes the chapter.

Historical Overview

Meiji Japan launched its first overseas military expedition to Taiwan in 1874. Annexation of Taiwan from China in 1895 was the beginning of a Japanese colonial empire. In the early days after Meiji, Korea was viewed as Japan's lifeline, a dagger pointed at its heart, and was thus far more important strategically than Taiwan. Japan fought a war with China in 1894–1895 over Korea, not Taiwan. Nevertheless, once Taiwan became Japan's colony, it acquired strategic importance as a Japanese territory and as a support base for Japan's rivalry with the West. Also, Taiwan would later become an important strategic launching platform for Japan's invasion of southern China and Southeast Asia in the 1930s–1940s.

Today many Taiwanese endorse the view that Japan's colonial rule in Taiwan improved human and institutional resources and facilitated economic progress, self-serving though it might have been. They see China unfavorably by contrast.[2] Japanese opinion of China has worsened continuously since 1989. Thus, we see a triangular dynamic in terms of public sentiment between Japan, Taiwan, and the PRC. A favorable view of Japan among Taiwanese and an unfavorable view of Japan among Chinese contribute to reciprocal positive sentiment toward Taiwan among Japanese, which only serves to increase China's suspicion of Japanese intention toward Taiwan and Chinese distrust of Taiwanese "traitors" to the motherland.

Prime Minister Yoshida Shigeru was initially interested in making diplomatic gestures to the PRC. The ideal situation for Japan would have been to have official relations with both China and Taiwan to secure resources, markets, and diplomatic status wherever available. However, under U.S. pressure Japan established a diplomatic relationship with the Nationalist Government in Taiwan in April 1952. Throughout the 1960s, Japanese public sentiment toward the PRC was generally favorable, but that alone was not enough to overcome Japan's paramount strategic interest in maintaining a security alliance with the United States.

Taiwan was not central to Japan's strategic thinking during the Cold War.[3] Taiwan should have been important for Japan's security. Americans certainly saw a clear connection between defense of Japan and defense of its other allies in Asia including Taiwan. But like other security issues, Japan could avoid acknowledging Taiwan's strategic importance because it was shielded by the Japan–U.S. security alliance. Through the 1960s, Japan made accommodating gestures to the United States over the Taiwan issue, but it had no strategic planning for Taiwan *per se*.

---

[2] One finds many titles in Japanese bookstores. For samples, see Kō 2001; Kin and Shu 2001; Kobayashi 2000. For a critique, see East Asian Network of Cultural Studies 2001.

[3] Some recent Japanese research suggests that there was indeed a strong view within the Japanese Foreign Ministry that accepting Beijing's condition that Taiwan is an inalienable part of the territory of the PRC would impede the ability of the Japan–U.S. alliance to cover Taiwan (Inoue 2012, 46). But this assessment was not apparent at that time.

Taiwan was important in Japanese domestic politics. In 1965, 160 LDP Diet members formed the "Asian Problems Study Group," which supported relations with Taiwan and opposed China's membership in the United Nations. Some of the anti-communist Japanese politicians such as Kishi Nobukuke and Satō Eisaku wanted to maintain a good relationship with Taiwan. There was also a smaller, 100-member group "Asian–African Problems Study Group" within the LDP that supported expanding ties with China. Furthermore, the Japan Socialist Party (JSP) and other progressive groups and parties supported better relations with China. The Japanese business community was interested in the China market, but they also had significant economic ties with Taiwan. That division in Japanese domestic politics explains why Japan sought to establish diplomatic ties with Beijing while maintaining a substantive relationship with Taiwan in its negotiations with China in 1972.

In September 1972, Japan and China established diplomatic relations and issued a joint communiqué. Article Two of the communiqué states that, Japan "recognizes that Government of the PRC as the sole legal Government of China." Article Three says: "The Government of the PRC reiterates that Taiwan is an inalienable part of the territory of the PRC. The Government of Japan fully understands and respects this stand of the Government of the PRC, and it firmly maintains its stand under Article 8 of the Postsdam Proclamation." Taiwan was a main negotiation issue during Prime Minister Tanaka Kakuei's visit to Beijing, which centered on Premier Zhou Enlai's "Three Principles" for diplomatic normalization, namely that the PRC is the sole legitimate Chinese government, that Taiwan is a province of China, and that Japan must abrogate its illegal peace treaty with Taiwan.

Japan made a cleaner break with Taiwan than the United States. It took six more years for the United States to establish diplomatic relations with Beijing, and even then the Congress enacted the Taiwan Relations Act to authorize arms sales to Taiwan. At the same time, Japan succeeded in maintaining unofficial ties with Taiwan and ensuring its economic interests in Taiwan, and the Japanese model would later be adopted by the United States to handle the Taiwan issue.

Negotiations for the Sino-Japanese Civil Aviation Agreement, signed April 1974, were complicated by the Taiwan issue.[4] China wanted Japan to sever its state-to-state arrangement with the Nationalist Government in Taiwan. Japan met Beijing's demand by creating a "separate airline" for Taiwan flights and letting the Taiwan airline land in a different airport (Haneda) from the PRC airline (Narita). In essence, Japan maintained substantive relations with Taiwan while allowing Beijing to save face.

For the rest of the 1970s, China was content with Japan's position on Taiwan, which explains why Taiwan was a non-issue in the difficult negotiations for the Treaty of Peace and Friendship, signed in 1978. In fact, as Chinese understood it, the Japan–U.S. security treaty now no longer covered Taiwan, given the changing nature of Sino-Japanese relations and the common security interest against the Soviet Union (Liu 2000, 271).

In the 1980s Beijing voiced concerns over Japan's policy toward Taiwan. In particular, the Chinese Government turned a lawsuit on a student hostel in Kyoto into a major diplomatic dispute (Kojima 2012). The Kyoto district court ruled in February 1986 that it belonged to the Taiwan government. The Chinese government protested that the property should be transferred from the Nationalist Government to the PRC government and characterized the civil suit as a political issue involving the legal rights of the PRC and the nature of Sino-Japanese relations. So the real issue was Beijing's concern that the Japanese government was offering the Nationalist Government *de facto* recognition in the court decision. In the scheme of things however, Taiwan was largely a non-issue between Beijing and Tokyo, sharply different from Sino-U.S. relations. Chinese analysts admit now that Japan was largely faithful to the terms of the 1972 Joint Communiqué through the early 1990s. In a way, Beijing did not appreciate how good it had it before the end of the Cold War. The fact that China belatedly appreciates Japan's past efforts in this regard reflects concern that Japan may adjust its strategic thinking toward Taiwan, which is indeed the case now.

---

[4]For a recent Japanese analysis, see Fukuda 2012.

Japanese Strategic Thinking toward Taiwan in the Early 1990s

Japan had limited strategic space in policy making toward Taiwan after World War II. First, Japan's imperialist strategic thinking was discredited by its total defeat. Second, the Japan–U.S. security alliance since 1952 provided a strong constraint on Japan's ability to maneuver on the Taiwan issue independently, which suited Japan just fine. Third, the 1972 Sino-Japanese Joint Statement added yet another constraint on Japan. Logically, limitations on strategic action should limit strategic thinking in the core of a country's policy community. It would be a waste of time to think about issues beyond one's control. Factually, there was not much strategic discussion about Taiwan in Japan through the 1980s.

The world changed after 1989. The removal of the Soviet threat as a common strategic interest, combined with the 1989 Tiananmen crackdown, led to heightened tensions in U.S.–China relations in the early 1990s. At the same time, the democratization and Taiwanization process in Taiwan that had begun before the end of the Cold War accelerated.

Japan was in an improved strategic position in the early 1990s. It was a rising economic superpower vis-à-vis both the United States, perceived to be in decline, and China, isolated due to Tiananmen. The mounting U.S. pressure on Japan in trade negotiations eroded the Japan–U.S. security arrangement, leading to greater Japanese interest in the UN and in East Asia. China's isolation from industrial countries potentially also allowed Japan to play a brokerage role, which would enhance Tokyo's diplomatic prestige. Thus, there was much discussion about Japan's role in the world. One school of thought urged Japan to "re-enter" Asia. Some wanted Japanese foreign policy to be centered on the UN. A few commentators wanted to say "no" to the United States. Yet another view point emphasized the importance of maintaining a strong U.S. alliance. But a common denominator in the debate was a strong yearning for greater Japanese influence in Asia and in the world, which would have significant implications for Japan's view of China and Taiwan.

In the context of becoming a great power again, Japan reached out to China out of self-interest. The Japanese government now sought to situate the Japan–China relationship in the global context, which essentially meant the end of a special relationship perceived by many Japanese to be disadvantageous to Japan; further, some Japanese wanted to utilize its closer relations with China to advance Japan's influence in the world (Nakai 2000; Kokubun 2001). Moreover, since Japan was helping China after Tiananmen, its bargaining position vis-à-vis China improved. Both developments meant that Japan had the desire and confidence to end the special relationship with China. It follows then that taboo issues such as history and Taiwan became less salient for Japanese.

There was always a reservoir of goodwill for Taiwan in Japan, but Japanese public affinity for Taiwan has grown across the political spectrum since 1989. There are no annual tracking surveys on Japanese public opinion toward Taiwan; but there are polls that show a warming trend. In particularly, the Taipei Economic & Cultural Representative Office in Japan has conducted some polls. According to its commissioned poll conducted in May 2011, 66.9 percent of the Japanese surveyed felt much affinity or affinity for Taiwan, an increase of 10.8 percent from a similar poll conducted in 2009 (*Taipei Times* 2011). As a result, we do not have a precise picture of trends in public opinion. A broad consensus among Taiwan and China watchers in Japan and Japan watchers in China also exists regarding such a trend.

There are different explanations for this. First, Taiwan's democratization that had begun in the late 1980s accelerated in the early 1990s and inevitably led to Taiwanization of the ruling elite given the fact that Taiwanese are the absolute majority in the island (Wakabayashi 1992). Critics of China often start by contrasting the repressive communist regime in China and the vibrant democracy in Taiwan. Many Japanese hold it as an article of faith that the difference in political regimes explains why the view of Japan is worsening in China while Taiwanese are friendly toward Japanese; the anti-Japanese propaganda by a communist government in order to divert public attention from domestic problems is the root cause of recent Japan–China tensions. In fact, Taiwan's democracy explains why

Japanese appeared calm in a dispute with Taiwan over fishing rights near Senkaku/Diaoyudao in June 2005, unlike their more emotional reaction to Chinese demonstrations a few weeks earlier. The Japanese coast guard chased out some Taiwanese fishing boats from the disputed area in early June 2005. Dozens of Taiwanese fishing boats subsequently massed in the area in protest, creating a standoff with Japanese ships. On June 21, two Taiwanese warships were dispatched, having senior officials and legislators aboard. The ships did not enter what Japan claims to be its exclusive economic zone. As a senior Japan Defense Agency official put it five days later, Taiwan's action "was a political show" common in a democracy and there was simply no reason to be concerned about it.[5] Japan and Taiwan held negotiations over fishing on July 29, but did not reach any consensus. Arguably sending a signal that Taiwan worries about China rather than Japan, President Chen visited the Dongsha islands, in dispute with the PRC in the South China Sea on the same day.

Second, an improved image of Taiwan virtually mirrors the worsening image of China in Japan. The events of June1989 on Tiananmen Square changed the public perception of the PRC and Taiwan. Observing Chinese government repression of dissent with regular army units in the nation's capital, Japan's public sentiment toward China began a steady decline while becoming more accepting of some Taiwanese's desire for independence. There is a triangular dynamic among Japanese, Taiwanese, and Chinese public opinion; worsening Chinese perception of Japan and warming Taiwanese views of Japan help to improve Japan's opinion of Taiwan and worsen its view of China.

Third, the favorable view of Taiwan held by Japanese stems in a major way from the warm reception given to Japanese officials, scholars, and opinion leaders by the Taiwanese government.[6]

---

[5] Conversation with the official, June 27, 2005. Still, a senior Japanese diplomat expressed surprise by the Taiwanese action and criticized it as dangerous. The Japanese government privately complained to the Taiwanese government. Conversation, July 15, 2005.

[6] In interviews in Tokyo in October 2004, Japanese officials and scholars familiar with China and Taiwan all emphasized this factor.

President Lee Teng-hui, in particular, was willing to talk to Japanese visitors on all levels and was sensitive to Japanese concerns. Japanese visitors would leave meetings content and appreciative of Taiwanese concerns. Lee continues to engage Japanese visitors. He is often compared to Zhou Enlai in his ability to relate to Japanese. Like Zhou, Lee spends much time cultivating relations with Japanese and knows what buttons to push. This reversal of roles partly reflects the fact that China was isolated diplomatically before and Taiwan is now. Chinese officials now simply have more foreign visitors to meet. Nonetheless, it is no secret that Taiwanese politicians tend to have a favorable view of Japan while Chinese leaders generally distrust Japan.

Fourth, Japan's colonial rule in Taiwan serves as a basis for sympathy. This is not a case in which Japanese are interested in reclaiming the island; rather, it is part of general Japanese nostalgia about their past experience. One sees a good number of books and articles published in Japan in this regard. More significant, Japan's 50-year colonial rule in Taiwan contributes to a general sense that Taiwan is different from China, thus making a good case that it should shape its own destiny. According to Japanese perceptions, prior to Japan's colonization Taiwan was an uncivilized place the Dutch helped to cultivate, frequented by Chinese and non-Chinese pirates, connected in an East Asian regional trade network, ruled passively and briefly by Qing emperors all of which makes Beijing's claim over Taiwan problematic (Izumi 1998; Nakamura, Yō, and Akino 2003). This Japanese view coincides with Taiwan's Democratic Progressive Party's own view of Taiwanese history as distinct from that of China.[7]

Japanese analysts understood that Taiwan's democratization meant the end of the Chinese civil war, which had been the foundation of the One-China principle underlying the 1972 system that favored Beijing. Put simply, once a large segment of Taiwanese society no longer wanted to be part of China, the logic for recognizing one China began to disintegrate (Wakabayashi 2000).

---

[7] In fact, some Western historians agree as well. See for example Andrade (2005).

Taiwan's new political reality posed a challenge to Japan's policy. Japan had to balance between Taiwan and the PRC. Japan wanted to upgrade ties with Taiwan while remaining sensitive about Beijing's reaction. But it was not unreasonable to believe that Japan now had some policy space because China now needed Japan more and Beijing itself had shown flexibility toward Taiwan for peaceful unification.

Japan's search for greater maneuver room on Taiwan fit nicely with Taiwan's effort to expand its international space. Taiwan eagerly reached out to Japan (Kojima 1997, 138–144). Tokyo accommodated Taiwan by allowing Vice Premier Hsu Li-The, to attend the Asian Games opening ceremony in Hiroshima in September 1994 even though China had protested strongly. At the same time, Japan remained cautious and tended to retreat somewhat when Beijing protested. After all, Japan was also trying to maintain a good relationship with China, knowing well that Taiwan mattered to China.

Japan's security concerns about China emerged with the end of the Cold War. In the early 1990s China began to increase military spending and asserted its territorial claims. Some Japanese, particularly defense specialists, voiced concerns about China's potential military threat to Japan. Tomohide Murai, a professor at Japan's National Defense Academy, wrote an article about China as a potential threat in the May 1990 *Shokun* magazine. His colleague Kawashima Kōzō (1990) saw China expanding into a maritime power and argued that China would view Japan as its principal enemy. Hiramatsu Shigeo (1991), formerly of the National Defense Agency, published a book on the emerging Chinese navy in 1991. Japan's worry increased after the Standing Committee of the Chinese National People's Congress adopted the Law on the Territorial Waters and their Contiguous Areas (Territorial Waters Law) on February 25, 1992. The new law said that the PRC's territorial islands include Senkaku/Diaoyudao, Taiwan, the Penghu islands and the Spratly Islands in the South China Sea. The Japan government protested.[8]

---

[8] Hiramatsu (1993) expressed concern about China's new territorial waters law and its maritime strategy in his 1993 book.

Taiwan was principally a political challenge for Japanese thinkers at this stage, however. The Japanese security thinking discussed in the previous paragraph was largely a minority view on the margin of Japanese policy thinking. Japan had a stronger interest in contributing to international peace after the experience of the first Persian Gulf War, but there was little interest in taking on bilateral security challenges. The 1992 Chinese territorial waters law did not cause immediate tension with China. After all, 1992 was a good year in Japan–China relations, with Chinese party chief Jiang Zemin's visit to Japan in April and the Japanese Emperor's visit to China in October. Some contemporaries actually considered 1992 the best period in Japan–China relations. If the Chinese territorial waters law had been enacted in a time of tensions between China and Japan as it is now, it would have surely caused far more serious tensions between the two nations.

Japan's security concerns about China would increase, as is shown in the following sections. In that context, Taiwan would shift from a diplomatic and political issue to a security one. China's growing military strength contributed to a renewed U.S. interest in strengthening the U.S.–Japan alliance. The March 1996 Taiwan Strait crisis helped to illustrate the strategic importance of the alliance.

Japanese Strategic Thinking toward Taiwan in the Late 1990s

Japanese began to be seriously concerned about the security dimension of their relations with China during the 1995–1996 Chinese military exercises aimed at Taiwan (Funabashi 1999; Ijiri 1997). Japanese now realized that their country could be dragged into a U.S.–China military conflict. Japanese had previously ceased to consider security to be an important issue in relations with China and in the cross-strait relationship because the last crisis took place in 1958 when the People's Liberation Army (PLA) shelled two islands controlled by the Nationalist Government in Taiwan and because Japanese thought China had changed with economic reform and opening. A dominant view in the Japanese policy community was that the Taiwan Strait crisis was a wakeup call for Japan.

Japanese attitudes toward Taiwan became more favorable and views of China worsened still after the mid-1990s. Beijing's military intimidation tactic made Japanese more sympathetic to Taiwan and more negative about China. Also, due to fatigue over the history issue, more Japanese began to feel, based on exchange with Taiwanese, that many Taiwanese express affinity for Japan, in turn making them feeling close to Taiwanese (Amako 2003, 212–213). The Japanese media, both reflecting and shaping Japanese public opinion, also became more critical of China.

Critics of China became more energetic after the mid-1990s. They wrote a large volume of books, journal articles, and editorials advocating a tougher policy toward China and an improved official relationship with Taiwan. The leading thinkers along this line include Hiramatsu Shigeo, Hasegawa Keitarō, Ishihara Shintarō, Kase Hideaki, Nakajima Mineo, Nakamura Katsunori, Nakanishi Terumasa, and Okazaki Hisahiko.[9] The thrust of their arguments is that China is trying to revive the Chinese world order in Asia and Japan must resist it. In that context, Taiwan shares a common destiny with Japan. Taiwan is a democracy, and the most pro-Japan country in Asia. Thus Taiwan's survival is essential for Japan's defense of sea lanes. On the other end of the political spectrum, some Japanese still advocated good relations with China and urged Japan to be sensitive to Beijing's concern over history and Taiwan, but their influence began to decline.

The mainstream view in Japanese policy making sought a compromise position. On the one hand, Japan strengthened the alliance with the United States beginning in 1995, with direct security implications for the Taiwan issue. Japan also paid greater attention to its defense doctrine and capabilities. On the other hand, Japan tried not to attract attention to its role in Taiwan in this period and tried to be vague about whether its expanded security arrangement with

---

[9]For sample works of these prolific writers, see Nakamura 1998; Izumi 1998; Hasegawa and Nakajima 2001; Nakajima and Komori 2004.

the United States would cover Taiwan. Japanese officials emphasized the legal obligation of the 1972 Joint Statement. They also recognized that Taiwan was a sensitive issue that needed to be dealt with carefulness. While Japanese might confront China over the history issue, they knew the importance of Taiwan for China. Tokyo's strategy worked to some extent as China protested over the strengthened Japan–U.S. alliance but continued to cooperate on other issues.

It made sense strategically for Japan to tread lightly in the Taiwan issue. The United States, the world's sole superpower with a security treaty with Japan, was committed to Taiwan's defense by law if China used force against the island. Beijing was asserting its claim to take Taiwan by force if necessary. China's military exercises in 1995–1996 increased the danger of a military conflict in the Taiwan Strait. Moreover, China was a rising economic and military power. In this situation, Japan had little incentive to take rash actions, particularly when the two principals themselves were yet to come to the point of an explicit military confrontation. Instead, Japan continued to use its tried and true approach of coping in foreign relations.

This coping strategy became difficult to maintain due to developments in Taiwan. Taiwan became a direct democracy and was moving further away from China politically and psychologically. Thus, Taiwan would force the issue. Moreover, Japan–China relations had also changed. Japan's relations with Beijing continued to deteriorate, which would put the Taiwan issue in a different light. The second half of the 1990s was dominated by frequent disputes and repairs. The 1998 visit to Japan by Jiang Zemin furthered this negative trend of worsening Japanese opinion of China. Jiang was viewed as unreasonably pressuring Japanese over the history issue to keep Japan down and to advance China's own great power ambitions. Taiwan was one of the underlying sources of growing tension between Beijing and Tokyo. In fact, one of Jiang's principal objectives for his 1998 trip to Japan was to have the Japanese government accept the principle of "Three Nos," namely no to Taiwan's independence; no to one China, one Taiwan or two Chinas; and no to Taiwan's membership in the United Nations or other international organizations that include only sovereign nations. Even though

President Bill Clinton had just verbally accepted the principle during his visit to China, the Japanese government soundly rejected the Chinese demand.

Japanese Strategic Thinking toward Taiwan since 2001

Japan's strategic thinking toward Taiwan since 2001 maintains a clear continuity with its previous thinking. What has changed is that security thinking regarding Taiwan has been fleshed out more and has become more salient in Japanese discourse in the context of a worsening top-level political relationship with China, that Taiwan is now a security concern for Japan, not just as a derivative of the U.S.–Japan alliance, and that Japan has become more explicit in its policy position on Taiwan and is taking precautionary measures in case of a Taiwan contingency.

Japan's policy toward Taiwan began to shift in 2001 with former Taiwanese President Lee Teng-hui's visit to Japan in April. Lee had tried to attend the Asia Open Forum in Matsumoto in October 2000 but failed due to Beijing's protest. Support for Lee's visit in Japan grew in 2001. Prime Minister Mori Yoshiro asked the Foreign Ministry to grant Lee a visa. Concerned about Japan–China relations, the Foreign Ministry decided against it initially. However, on April 20, the Japanese government allowed Lee to come to Japan for medical treatment.[10] Lee visited Japan on April 22–26, a major breakthrough for Taiwan and a major setback for China. Significant for future handling of China, Japanese felt that Japan survived this test of political will with China with little damage. In fact, some critics of China simply called China a "paper tiger" since it did not carry out retaliations as moderates in Japan had feared.[11]

---

[10] For Japanese domestic politics over the visa issue, see Okada 2003, 221–225; Hasegawa and Nakajima 2001, 14–47.

[11] Critics of China frequently make this point in their writings. A senior Japanese journalist who had been posted in China used the expression "paper tiger" in an interview I conducted in Tokyo in June 2001. The Chinese government postponed a planned visit by Li Peng, and Japanese officials and analysts with whom I talked expressed the feeling that they did not consider the cancellation a serious retaliation.

Koizumi Junichirō, who assumed office the day Lee left Japan, did not make the decision on Lee's visit. What was significant about Sino-Japanese relations since Koizumi became prime minister was political coolness on the top level. Koizumi's annual visits to Yasukuni led to a suspension of mutual visits by government leaders since 2002. Taiwan emerged as a top political issue between the two nations in that context. Japan began to talk about the security of Taiwan in an open fashion around 2004, which reflected worsening Japan–China political relations and, in turn, further strained the relationship.

Japan's public sentiment has come to exert an unusually large impact on Japanese foreign policy toward China. As an often-cited example of Japan's broad sympathy for Taiwan, even *Asahi shimbun*, the most pro-China newspaper in Japan, supported granting former president Lee Teng-hui a visa to visit Japan as a private citizen.[12] In another case, Japanese newspapers virtually all criticized China's anti-secession law enacted in March 2005 as destabilizing.

Japanese public opinion also has a major effect on politicians who have become ever more important in decision making in Japan at the expense of elite bureaucrats since the mid-1990s. In Japan's relations with China, there is a larger tendency of the public and politicians to feed off each other in a way that is unfavorable to China. The Japanese public has urged the government to be firmer over a number of issues, particularly over territorial disputes. Such sentiment has made a number of policy changes possible. For example, while the Ground SDF considered plans to strengthen the defense of Okinawa and other southwestern islands in the mid-1990s in light of China's 1992 territorial waters law, they did not carry the plans out due to concern over negative public reaction from Okinawans. But by the end of 2004 Japanese defense officials were planning to replace F-4 fighters with more powerful F-15s in Okinawa and to upgrade the GSDF troops to a brigade, anticipating little public negative reaction or protests from the ruling parties (*Asahi shimbun* 2004).

---

[12] Several Japanese journalists I interviewed in Tokyo in June 2001 all emphasized this trend, whatever their attitudes toward China.

Japanese sentiment for Taiwan continues to improve partly reflecting a sharper decline in affinity with China after the September 2010 fishing boat incident and growing territorial tensions. Japanese also felt warm toward Taiwan after the Great East Japan Earthquake on March 11, 2011. Japan was actually supported for its response to the unprecedented disaster by the international community, including China. But the Japanese were particularly appreciative of the U.S. military assistance and the public outpouring of compassion and donations in Taiwan. To this day, news stories about Taiwan often have the refrain that Taiwan is the most pro-Japan country in the world, citing the Taiwanese public's donation of around ¥20 billion for the March 11 disasters as a primary example.[13] And the Japanese performing groups go to Taiwan to express appreciation for Taiwanese support.[14] Conservative Japanese media commentators assert that the Taiwanese prefer Japanese colonial administration over the Chinese mainlander rule (e.g. *Sankei shimbun* online December 25, 2014).

For the past few years some Japanese have come to support Taiwan's separate path from China, converging with pro-independence Taiwanese activists.[15] For example, 47 junior Democratic Party of Japan parliamentarians reportedly expressed support at a meeting held in November 2004 for the right of Taiwanese to revise the constitution and to correct the name of the state based on public will. Support for Taiwan has also grown within the ruling LDP, particularly among younger politicians many of whom have built strong personal ties with Taiwanese leaders (Sina.com November 25, 2004). Beijing considers revision of the constitution and correction of state names as moves toward independence. There is even greater support in Japan for Taiwan's effort to seek greater international space.

---

[13] Observers based outside Japan have made similar observation. See for example Laskai 2014.

[14] As a recent example, Japan's highly popular girl group AKB47 held a concert in Taipei on December 8, 2014. A group member started the concert by thanking Taiwan for its support of Japan during the disasters (Wireless Wire News December 9, 2014).

[15] Interview with a leading Taiwan specialist in Japan, Tokyo, October 26, 2004.

The idea of geopolitics has come back in Japan. When reading Japanese publications and news stories or talking with Japanese officials and analysts, one reads or hears frequently the analysis that if China takes Taiwan, the Taiwan Strait would become China's internal waters and can thus control Japan's shipping lane. And if the United States and China ever fought over Taiwan, Japan would be dragged into the conflict.

Japan's defense community now more openly expresses security concerns about China. Retired SDF officers, who are presumably freer to talk about issues that active-duty officers cannot, express alarm over China's apparent maritime expansion and increasing military spending. They typically use geopolitics, Chinese history as the Middle Kingdom, and Chinese Communist Party rule to explain China's behavior (e.g. Ishizuka 2000; Yoshida 2001 and 2004). Gomi Matsuyoshi (e.g. 2004), a retired vice admiral of the Maritime SDF, sees China as positioning itself to seize natural resources in Japan's economic zones down the line and urges Japan to acquire the independent defense capacity in case of military clashes with China based on the argument that Japan needs the maritime resources in the disputed areas for survival and prosperity in the twenty-first century and that the United States might not come to Japan's assistance over disputes in the East China Sea. Furusawa Tadahiko (2001 and 2004), another retired vice admiral, sees China as shifting from a continental country to a maritime one and as seeking to recreate a Chinese world order in which neighboring countries are obedient to Chinese. In this context, he sees Taiwan as central to China's objective to establish a Chinese empire and to seek maritime resources. He argues that it is far better to see Taiwan maintaining the *status quo* than becoming part of China since the island is strategically located along Japan's sea lanes. China's seizure of Taiwan would mean that the South China Sea and the East China Sea would become Chinese waters, which would restrict traditional maritime states in the region. Besides, Taiwan is a fellow maritime democracy that would serve as a check on China's maritime expansion. He also recommends that Japan formulate its own defense strategy to deal with security threats while improving its alliance with the United

States. Okazaki Hisahiko, a noted diplomat and Defense Agency official, observed that the Japan–U.S. defense strategy was ultimately about defending of Taiwan. If China seizes the island, America would lose its credibility and Japan would lose Southeast Asia, the source of its post-war prosperity (Okazaki and Nishimura 2012, 72–73).

Japanese government officials and politicians seem to share security concerns over the Taiwan question. Not surprisingly, more serious discussion takes place under the surface, which one can only infer by examining media-reported government studies and documents. For example, *Tokyo shimbun*, a paper considered to be close to the defense policy community, reported on November 8, 2004 that in a report completed in September in preparation for the new National Defense Program Outline to be issued by the end of November Japanese Defense Agency officials had established three scenarios in which China might decide to attack Japan. The first scenario is that China might attack American bases in Japan if American troops use bases in Japan to assist Taiwan in a serious military confrontation in the Taiwan Strait. The second scenario is that China might seize Senkaku, triggering a military conflict with Japan. The third is that China might resort to force over the territorial dispute in the East China Sea. The new national defense strategy issued on December 10, named North Korea and China as Japan's potential security concerns, the first time China was named as such by the Japanese government.

A Chinese nuclear submarine trespassing in Japanese territorial waters on November 10, 2004 only enhanced Japan's security worries. The action of the Chinese navy is interpreted as seeking domination over Taiwan and testing Japan's capacity to respond to a military conflict. *Sankei shimbun* reported on November 14 that a top secret simulation-based analysis had recently been submitted to the Prime Minister's Office by the Japanese Defense Agency. The report predicts China's comprehensive military domination over Taiwan by 2009.

A series of Japanese actions, including alliance enhancement with the United States, adjustment of Japan's defense priorities, and greater defense capabilities, reveal the fear of a belligerent China as an important motivating factor in Japanese strategic thinking. The 2004 *Defense White Paper* issued on July 6, 2004 emphasized that Japan's SDF should play a role commensurate to Japan's international standing. The paper also expressed concern over China's military modernization and Chinese research ship activities in waters close to Japan. There were also reports of shared intelligence regarding Chinese submarines between the American, Japanese, and Taiwanese military forces (Xinhua News Agency online November 26, 2004). Japan's new National Defense Program Outline approved by the cabinet in December 2004 mentioned China's name, calling attention to China's military modernization and maritime activities. Japanese officials emphasized that their February 2005 joint statement with the United States to express a common security interest in the Taiwan Strait did not amount to a dramatic shift in its Taiwan policy. In fact, they argued that Japan's position on a peaceful solution to the Taiwan issue has been consistent since 1972. However, Japan was clearly much more explicit and bolder in expressing its position on Taiwan, which has been perceived by China as a major hostile move. The 2005 *East Asia Strategic Review*, issued by the National Institute for Defense Studies of the Japan Defense Agency in March 2005, expressed concern over the PLA's intense training for attacking Taiwan and preventing American intervention as well as Chinese ship activities in the disputed waters in the East China Sea (*Yomiuri shimbun* online March 28, 2005). Also in March Moriya Takemasa, the deputy director general of the Defense Agency, raised the issue of the anti-secession law during his security discussion with Xiong Guangkai, a deputy PLA chief of staff (*Guoji xianqu daobao* online April 1, 2005). On April 29 Foreign Minister Machimura Nobutaka said that the Japan–U.S. alliance covers Taiwan when answering questions at a speech in New York City (*Asahi shimbun* online April 30, 2005).

While there was shared concern about China's rise and some hedging moves, there did not seem to be a consensus on how Japan should deal with the situation through the 2000s. Japanese scholars and officials generally did not believe that Japan was that strategic about the Taiwan question. The gap between positive public opinion on Taiwan and a cautious policy not to rock the boat was often used as an indication of such a lack of strategic vision.

Japan's cautious policy toward Taiwan reflected two major strategic calculations. First, Japanese recognized U.S.–China relations as central to the Taiwan question. In a way, the U.S.–Japan alliance was now really about Taiwan (not to diminish the strategic importance of the Korean peninsula). It made strategic sense for Japan to let Americans deal with this very difficult question. There has been a basic dynamic of entrapment and abandonment in Japan's alliance with the United States. Specifically over Taiwan, there was mainly fear of entrapment since Japanese recognize that the United States was not going to hand Taiwan to China even if U.S.–China relations improve.

Second, Japanese understood that overt support for Taiwan would aggravate the situation, creating a self-fulfilling effect. Tokyo should play it cool diplomatically while taking precautionary moves in alliance formation and defense capabilities. In fact, Japanese often saw the Taiwan issue as one involving Chinese and Taiwanese nationalisms, which meant that the issue would take a long time to resolve.[16]

Japan was still largely reactive than taking things into its own hands, based on the strategic calculations behind Japan's largely faithful adherence to the one China principle in its relations with Beijing. Despite their strong interest in the outcome of the Taiwan game Japanese still believed they had limited ability to influence how the game plays out. Awareness of Japan's own limitations constrained their strategic thinking; some policy elites did not want to think about things that they had no control over. Nevertheless, there

---

[16] A senior Japanese diplomat who has been handling the Japan–U.S. alliance differentiates the Taiwan issue from the North Korean crisis. He sees the Taiwan issue as political in nature, which can turn military, because it is about nationalism. By contrast, he sees the Korean situation largely as military. Thus, the Taiwan dispute would last a long time with the U.S. as the main player. Interview, Washington, D.C., March 22, 2005.

were people in Japan who were thinking about this issue, and if the situation in the Taiwan Strait and China–Japan relations changed, Japan's thinking and action regarding Taiwan would change quickly.

At the same time, what was important overall about Japan's strategic thinking through the 2000s was a revealed strong preference to compete with China. Unlike other East Asian countries, Japan was competing and would compete for regional leadership with China. This was a reflection of an identity as a proud country that has always been largely outside the Chinese world order politically, as the first non-Western nation to modernize, as a first-rate economic power, and now as a country that should take its rightful place in the international community and step out of the shadow of other major powers. Indeed, there was mounting criticism in Japan of what was viewed as a weak Democratic Party of Japan administration policy response to an increasingly asserting China. That was the larger context for the comeback victory by the Liberal Democratic Party led by Abe Shinzō.

Taiwan, China, and Japan

Taiwan has not been a passive actor in Sino-Japanese relations, having its own identities, interests and domestic politics. Chen Shui-bian of the pro-independence Democratic Progressive Party (DPP) won a plurality in the presidential election in March 2000 and was re-elected again with a narrow margin in 2004 for another four years. Chen's eight years saw high tension with mainland China. The Chen government sought to entrap Japan, an approach that made obvious strategic sense to secure an ideal trilateral alliance including the United States. Taiwan benefited from worsening Sino-Japanese relations. China's military pressure would create more room for Japan–Taiwan cooperation (Chao and Ho 2004). The Taiwan government periodically expressed support for Japan, supporting its candidacy for a permanent seat at the UN Security Council. At a forum of Taiwanese and Japanese think tanks held in Taipei in October 2004, Taiwan's Premier Yu Shyi-kun stated that "the security of the Taiwan Strait is closely linked with the security of Japan."

Taiwan's National Security Council Secretary-General Chiou I-jen supported Japan's revision of the Peace Constitution to participate in peace-keeping missions abroad (Taiwan News.com 2004). Chen Shui-bian told visiting Japanese that Taiwan had alerted Japan about China's submarine entering into Japanese waters (*Taipei Times* 2004).[17] He also urged Japan to say "no" to Beijing and to act as a normal state (China News Agency online March 3, 2005).[18] Taiwan was particularly interested in lobbying for the Japanese Diet to pass a law similar to America's "Taiwan Relations Act."

The Chen government was successful in cultivating relations with influential Japanese, but sympathy had its limitation. Japan's policy toward Taiwan was realpolitik. Neither Lee nor other leaders could change Japan's fundamental policy, which was constrained by the alliance with the United States. Japan wanted to create more room for its diplomacy, but it operated within constraints that it remains happy to respect.

The Chen government stood little chance of entrapping Japan. Since Japan was in a strengthened alliance with the United States that covers Taiwan, the basic dynamic between security and autonomy in an alliance was extended to its relations with Taiwan. Taiwan now wanted to have greater security and autonomy to walk its own path, which had enhanced the danger of insecurity for the United States, and for Japan by extension. That position logically caused some distancing from the United States. Japan was behaving similarly to the United States, another indication of clear-headed strategic calculations.

Japan would enhance official relations with Taiwan in an ideal world. A major foreign policy document produced by a task force on foreign policy for Koizumi, stated matter-of-factly that changes in Japan–Taiwan relations were "natural" given China's economic reform and opening and Taiwan's democratization and participation

---

[17] However, as a senior Japanese diplomat pointed out, Japan had not heard from the Taiwan government about the submarine beforehand. Conversation with the official, July 15, 2005. This was confirmed by others who were familiar with the case.
[18] He said so in the context of complaining about his inability to make a transfer stop in Japan.

in the APEC forum and WTO (Task Force on Foreign Relations for the Prime Minister 2002). Japan did more for Taiwan. Former Prime Minister Mori visited Taiwan in December 2003. Japan cast its vote for the failed resolution to invite Taiwan to the World Health Organization as an observer in May 2004. Tokyo Mayor Ishihara Shintarō visited Taiwan in October 2004. Lee Teng-hui came to Japan as a tourist in late December 2004. Japan was also critical of China's anti-secession law in March 2005.

At the same time, China viewed Japan's warming ties with Taiwan as anything but natural. Beijing reacted quickly and strongly over Tokyo's periodic attempts to upgrade official ties with Taiwan. Japan generally retreated in reaction to China's objection. After all, China was a rising political and economic power, and Japan had interest in avoiding unnecessary tensions. Japan also had a huge economic stake in China. Its trade with China and Hong Kong combined almost matched its trade with the United States and almost three times its trade with Taiwan in 2004 (Japan Ministry of Finance).

Thus, the cost of Taiwan's entrapping depended on how far the Taiwanese government pushed for independence and on how hard the PRC was prepared to fight to prevent such a movement. Chen Shui-bian's narrow victory for a second term in March 2004 increased the danger of cross-Strait conflict when Chen continued to take measures toward independence while giving inadequate attention to the concerns of the United States. The danger was partially eased when Chen's DPP failed to win a majority position in the December 10, 2004 parliamentary election, a surprising setback due to high expectations before the election and a sign of Taiwanese voters' wariness of causing conflict with the Mainland.[19] Beijing clearly saw a welcome setback for the Pan-Green forces in Taiwan, reflected in the statements by the spokesman of the Taiwan Affairs Office of the State Council and Chinese media analysis. The election lowered the danger of immediate military conflict. The PRC showed greater

---

[19] The DPP interpreted the setback as resulting from executing a vote reallocation plan to channel votes from popular incumbents to new candidates, but Chen had used the independence theme heavily in his election campaign.

flexibility in early 2005 as revealed by its invitation for Lien Chan, the chairman of the Chinese Nationalist Party, to visit in late April. With the Nationalist Party winning an overwhelming victory in municipal elections on December 3, 2005, a more confident Chinese government under Hu Jintao now felt vindicated by its strategy of demonstrating resolve to prevent Taiwan's independence while not reacting every time to Chen's particular moves. But Beijing would continue to watch closely Taiwan's relations with major powers such as Japan.

Chinese and Japanese became deadlocked politically over Koizumi's annual visits to Yasukuni shrine. The Yasukuni dispute was now a test of wills. Even those in Japan who did not approve of Koizumi's visits to Yasukuni did not want to send a signal that China can dictate what a Japanese leader can do in what is considered a domestic issue. On the other side, China also did not want to show weakness. Even Japan-knowledgeable moderates did not want to make concessions for fear that such a weak move would only encourage Japanese assertiveness elsewhere while triggering a major public backlash in China. This situation reflected a combination of both confidence and insecurity on both sides. It also revealed the basic nature of an emerging strategic rivalry between the two nations. The anti-Japan mass demonstrations in Beijing and several other major cities in China in April 2005 marked the lowest point in Japan–China relations since 1972. With Koizumi's Yasukuni visit on October 17, Japan's relationship with China deteriorated further. Chinese leaders now did not want to meet with Koizumi for bilateral talks even at multilateral summits as they did for the previous three years.

From a political perspective, a worsening relationship with China meant that Japan would need more allies. Since South Korea and Southeast Asian nations largely indicated neutrality in Japan–China disputes, Japan shared common interests with Taiwan. From a strategic perspective, a hostile relationship with China would enhance Taiwan's strategic value. As a senior Japanese diplomat summarized it succinctly, "Taiwan is a strategic asset between the East China Sea and the South China Sea.... Japan of course does not want to see Taiwan seized by a hostile power."[20] The explicit expression about Taiwan in the joint statement with the United States in February 2005 should be seen as a warning to Beijing that Japan has a stake in the Taiwan issue. Whether Japan will stand more firmly for Taiwan's defense depends on China's relations with Taiwan and with Japan. But in a vicious cycle, Japan's Taiwan policy shift would contribute to a worse relationship with China. Conversely, Taiwan may also act as a check on China, making it less willing to confront Japan in order to prevent driving Japan and Taiwan together.[21]

Sino-Japanese relations improved somewhat after Koizumi stepped down in September 2006. Ma Ying-jeou won the presidential election in March 2008, bringing the Nationalist Party back to power. With his re-election in January 2012, he is currently in his second and final four-year term. Ma had been a student activist asserting Chinese claim to Tiaoyutai (Diaoyudao for mainland China and Senkaku for Japan) and had expressed his wish to improve relations with Beijing. He has indeed improved relations with Beijing drastically, particularly in the economic arena. At the same time, there has been some tension with Japan. After a Taiwan fishing boat was sunk when colliding with a Japanese patrol boat near Tiaoyutai in June 2008, Ma sent in patrol boats to the disputed area. With rising tension between China and Japan after Prime Minister Noda's nationalization of Senkaku, Taiwan also asserted its claim and symbolically sent patrol boats to the area on September 13, 2012.

Nevertheless, Japan remains positive about Taiwan, trusting Taiwanese affinity with Japan and Taiwan's divergent political path from China's. Ma himself has carefully cultivated relations with Japanese, emphasizing that he is not anti-Japan. Focusing on what they view as Beijing's conspiracy to drive a wedge between Taiwan

---

[20] Interview, Washington, D.C., March 22, 2005.

[21] As a sign that the Chinese government is worried about this connection, in the aftermath of the anti-Japan demonstrations leading media outlets emphasized the importance of the Taiwan issue as well as economic cooperation in Sino-Japanese relations. On May 1, 2005, Xinhua News Agency issued a commentary urging Japan to keep its commitment to China over the Taiwan issue.

and Japan and to ultimately swallow Taiwan, the Japanese government made its own move to shore up friendship with Taiwan (*Yomiuri shimbun* online March 14, 2013). In particular, Japan reached a fisheries agreement with Taiwan in April 2013, which angered Beijing (*Sankei shimbun* online April 11, 2013). Ma had already ruled out a common front against Japan and took a more neutral, peacemaking position when he proposed a code of conduct for the East China Sea in February 2014.[22] The "Sunflower" student movement that protested Ma's Cross-Strait Service Trade Agreement in March–April 2014 caught much media attention in Japan, reinforcing their basic assessment that mainstream Taiwanese object to unification with mainland. The big loss the Nationalist Party suffered at the local elections on November 22, 2014 was interpreted as resulting from a harsh voter evaluation of the Ma administration and a setback for Beijing. On January 9, 2015, President Ma told the Japanese business associations in Taiwan that he hoped to achieve an economic partnership agreement or free trade agreement with Japan in the coming year (*Sankei shimbun* online January 9, 2015). But he then told the Taiwan media on January 14 that Japan's illegal seizure of Tiaoyutai exactly 120 years has no legal standing, which was promptly reported in official Chinese media (China News Agency online January 15, 2015).

Conclusion

Japan's strategic thinking toward Taiwan has been a product of a complex interaction of transformations in Japan, Taiwan, the PRC and the world as well, including the perceived security environment and national objectives. Diverse opinions about the Taiwan issue exist in Japan. In a market of ideas, the salience of a particular view is contingent upon domestic developments and international politics.

---

[22] Chinese experts on Taiwan see Ma, as both hard and soft on Japan, leveraging China's pressure on Japan to gain benefits from Japan while following the U.S. lead and tolerating Japan's conduct (e.g. Hu 2014).

The Japanese public has become increasingly sympathetic to a democratic, pro-Japan Taiwan since 1989. By contrast, the Japanese view of a non-democratic, rising China has declined sharply. While the marginal improvement in views of Taiwan is now leveling, Taiwan benefits from a continuous decline of China's image due to a series of Japan–China disputes in recent years. Public sentiment alone has been insufficient to push Tokyo to change its Taiwan policy dramatically, but it matters. It exerts pressure on the government to take a firmer stand over disputes with China, which creates more room for Taiwan's diplomacy. It explains partly why the Japanese government has slowly but surely upgraded its official exchange with the government in Taiwan. Ultimately, Japan's assessment of the international environment after the Cold War and its desire to become a normal, great power explain why Japan is interested in situating its relations with China in the global context and seeking greater room to engage with the government in Taiwan. While public opinion is not the same as hard-nosed strategic calculations, growing public sympathy for Taiwan and resentment toward China open up public space for discussion on more sensitive security issues. Security discussion is no longer an impolite topic.

Japan's security thinking about Taiwan has become increasingly based on geopolitics. For some defense thinkers, Taiwan's survival in separation from China is central to Japan's future security and prosperity. Thus, Japan shares common security interest in Taiwan as the U.S. Security concerns about China as a military threat have moved from the margin of the policy community in the early 1990s to close to the center at present. Japan's growing security concerns and worsening public view of China have allowed rightwing critics of China to have greater influence in policy debates.

At the same time, guided by mainstream views, Japan is still being defensive in security thinking at this stage. Much of Japanese strategic calculation is contingent upon China's future actions and development. Japan's thinking toward Taiwan shows that Japanese remain cautious in high-stakes issues. It tends to be reactive to the changing environment and takes half measures. However, this pattern of behavior should not be interpreted as Japan's inability to think strategically or to act assertively. Rather, it reflects the fact that the Taiwan issue is extremely complex. Moreover, one can equally question how strategic and smart the three principals, China, Taiwan, and the U.S. have been. In such a fluid situation, it is unproductive or even counterproductive for Japanese to spell out clearly what its strategic objectives and approaches should be.

Japanese care about the security ramifications of the Taiwan issue. It makes a major difference for Japan's security whether Taiwan is taken over by a China hostile or friendly to Japan. If current Japan–China tensions continue, one should expect Japan to become more pro-active and offensive over the Taiwan question. Simply put, Japan has its own strategic reasons to be involved in the Taiwan issue independent of its alliance obligations to the U.S. Territorial disputes with China and its strategic interest in Taiwan's future will increasingly determine its terms for the alliance with the United States.

Chapter 8

Rare Earth: Vulnerability Interdependence?

In the height of the Chinese fishing boat collision incident in September 2010, it was reported in the Japanese and Western media that China had suspended rare earth exports to Japan. Did the Chinese government adopt that strategy and why? Was it successful? More broadly, what does the case reveal about the nature of growing Sino-Japanese economic interdependence? And what does the case show about the Chinese and Japanese styles of diplomacy? This chapter addresses these questions.

China adopted an explicit strategy to dominate the world rare earth metals market. For the past few years, the Chinese have also become openly concerned about what they view as "unfairly" cheap foreign acquisition of their rare earth supplies and adopted policies to streamline the rare earth sector in favor of domestic firms. China used suspension of rare earth exports as a desperate move to achieve a short-term goal of pressuring the Japanese government to release the Chinese captain in its detention. The rare earth suspension was one of China's countermeasures that helped bring about their desired outcome. But it was a highly costly move entailing long-term reputation damage for China. Beijing has lost badly in the public relations battle over the rare earth issue, revealing severe limitation of its economic leverage on other countries. The case highlights Beijing's top–down, disorganized crisis management style and Tokyo's tight government-business-academy cooperation to advance economic goals and dogged persistence in negotiations.

China's Suspension of Rare Earth Exports to Japan

The rare earth export suspension was one of several punitive measures that the Chinese government adopted to force the Japanese government to release the Chinese captain. The collision incident took place on September 7, 2010 near the disputed islands (Diaoyudao by Chinese and Senkaku by Japanese). The Japanese coast guards arrested the Chinese captain for ramming into a Japanese patrol boat. The Chinese government protested that the Japanese authorities have no jurisdiction in what it claims to be Chinese territorial waters. When the Japanese government decided to detain and prosecute the Chinese captain on September 11, the Chinese government began taking retaliatory actions. The Chinese foreign ministry announced that it would postpone the second round of the East China Sea gas field negotiations scheduled for mid September. On September 14, the Chinese government postponed a visit to Japan by a National People's Congress delegation. On the same day, China's nationalistic popular newspaper *Global Times* published an editorial urging the Chinese government to prepare a whole set of countermeasures to ensure the Chinese captain's release (*Huanqiu shibao* online September 14, 2010). On September 16, news broke that China might not agree to a summit between Chinese Premier Wen Jiabao and Japanese Prime Minister Kan Naoto at the United Nations meeting in the following week. In the afternoon of September 19, the Japanese government decided to extend the detention of the Chinese captain. That night the Chinese government stopped provincial-cabinet minister level exchange with Japan. On the same day, the Chinese foreign ministry indicated that China would take strong measures if the Chinese captain was not released. Shortly afterwards, the Chinese government delayed the scheduled visits to the China Expo by some Japanese youth groups two days before their scheduled departure. By September 23, there were about 20 cases of cancellation of Sino-Japanese cultural exchange events. There was also report that the Chinese tourist agencies had "voluntarily" delayed or canceled tours of Japan. The Chinese media interpreted China's actions as the strongest for the past 38 years of Sino-Japanese diplomatic relations.

The rare earth dispute occurred in that context. *The New York Times* broke the story on September 22 that the Chinese government had essentially stopped exports of rare earths to Japan (Bradsher 2010), which was immediately followed by intensive Japanese media coverage. Rare earths refer to 17 mineral elements such as gadolinium, lanthanum, cerium, and europium that are central to high-tech products in strategic sectors like automobile and electronics. The Japanese government announced subsequently that based on reports from several Japanese importers the Chinese customs had stopped procedures for allowing exports of rare earths to Japan since September 21, the day after the detention of the Chinese captain was extended, and the Japanese government was now seriously investigating that allegation. While the Japanese firms have inventory to sustain production for a few months, they would be negatively impacted because China supplies over 90 percent of global rare earths and Japan imports over 90 percent of rare earths from China. Minister of Economics, Trade and Industry (METI) Ōhata Akihiro and Finance Minister Noda Yoshihiko were both quoted as expressing serious concerns.

Did Beijing use rare earths as a weapon? China had already begun restricting export of rare earth metals. Looking back, some Western journalists pointed out that China's exports of rare earth had decreased from 47,000 tons in 2000 to 30,000 tons in 2010 due to export taxes and quotas (*Economist* 2012). The Chinese government announced in July 2010 that China would reduce rare earth export permits by 40 percent from the previous year. Incidentally, some Japanese business leaders were in Beijing urging the Chinese government to abandon that plan on September 7, the day the collision incident took place. With the Japanese government pressuring Beijing to clarify whether rare earth exports were being stopped, the Chinese government responded that their restriction on exports had been adopted since before the incident and was not restricted to Japan. But the Japanese government did not buy the arguments because they had gathered data from the Japanese firms engaged in rare earth imports.[1] The Japanese made a strong case that the Chinese government had stopped rare earth shipment for diplomatic purposes. It is now generally accepted that China did use rare earths as a weapon against Japan.

Why did China stop rare earth exports? As mentioned before, Beijing adopted various measures to put pressure on Tokyo. The central government mobilized various government agencies to think of ways to accomplish a specific goal of forcing the release of the Chinese captain, partly to alleviate domestic criticism of supposedly "weak" government response to Japan. While the Chinese government appeared organized and strategic from outside, looking at its handling of the crisis from inside one saw a high degree of disorganization and confusion.[2] There were two dozen or so recommended countermeasures on the table.[3] Without knowing which measure might actually work, the Chinese government essentially adopted a non-strategy of throwing mud on the wall hoping one would stick.

The rare earth stoppage had a clear shock effect on the Japanese. Some of the other Chinese measures adopted during the crisis such as stopping government to government and cultural exchange were stronger than before but were familiar tactics. By contrast, an explicit use of economic leverage was new. The Japanese had already become concerned about dependence on China for rare earth imports before the collision incident. Noda Yoshihiko (2009, 149–151) who was Japan's finance minister when the collision incident occurred had advocated for a strong space program in his 2009 book, citing one benefit as helping to find rare earth deposits on the ocean bottom and noting that Japan now imports 90 percent of rare earths from China. But the Japanese government, business community and

---

[1] Talk with a senior METI official involved in the issue, Tokyo, February 2012.

[2] China's problem has partly resulted from a pluralization of players in Chinese foreign policy decision making process. See Jakobson and Knox 2010.

[3] Discussion with Chinese analysts knowledgeable about the incident, particularly in Beijing in June 2011 and in Tokyo in January 2012.

media were surprised by the Chinese move. As a senior Japanese official put it, "developed countries just don't do something like that."[4] In fact, the developed countries have often used economic sanctions explicitly for various reasons. But the Japanese have not been on the receiving end that often. Thus, China's use of rare earth weapon was one of the most frequently discussed issues on television programs, mainstream daily newspapers, weeklies and other forms of communications. For a country heavily focused on exports of high-tech products, rare earths were characterized as a matter of life and death.

The Japanese government released the Chinese captain on September 24. The Japanese firms reported that the Chinese government restarted the procedures for customs clearance for exporting rare earths to Japan on September 28. Thus, Beijing's suspension of rare earth supplies lasted for a week, from September 21 to 28. The Japanese government continued to monitor the situation and viewed the stoppage as actually lasting longer. Moreover, the Chinese government has continued to control exports of rare earths, creating a lasting source of tension with Japan, which has also become multilateralized as the United States and the European Union have taken up the issue with China as well.

Vulnerability Interdependence between Japan and China?

Discussion on the rare earth case in Japan or other developed countries has been linked with the danger of China becoming too powerful economically and of other countries such as Japan becoming too dependent on the China market or Chinese supplies. The appropriate theoretical framework for studying this issue is then "vulnerability interdependence." Reflecting on the increasing economic ties in the world, Keohane and Nye (1977) studied the power of interdependence, which refers to reciprocal relationships between states that limit their autonomy. They differentiated

---

[4]Talk with the official, Tokyo, February 2012.

vulnerability independence from "sensitivity interdependence". Sensitivity interdependence is a situation in which developments or events in one country will be felt quickly in another country. But it is costly for a country in a vulnerability independence situation not to adapt to the preferences of the country it depends on.

The world has become even more interdependent since the 1970s and degrees of vulnerability interdependence between various pairs of countries have also increased. But use of economic advantages has produced mixed results (Hufbauer *et al.* 2008). The developed countries, particularly the United States, have resorted to economic sanctions as a less costly way than wars to effect desirable policy changes in other countries, but they have not been always successful. The developing countries have also used resources as weapons against the developed countries since the early 1970s. But they are rarely successful with the Organization of the Petroleum Exporting Countries (OPEC) as an important exception. This limit of economic statecraft does not diminish the importance of interdependence arguments because military power has also shown limitation in the world of ours.

How much vulnerability economic interdependence exists between China and Japan? China has become more important for Japan than vice versa judging by trade patterns. As Figure 8.1 shows, China was far more dependent on the Japan market than the other way around through the 1990s. But the China share for Japanese trade approximated the Japan share for Chinese trade in 2003 and has rapidly exceeded it since 2004, reflecting China's rise as a bigger trading country than Japan and the increasing importance of the China market for the Japanese. The China market became particularly important for Japan for the past few years given slow growth in the developed world. As recognized by the Japan External Trade Organization (JETRO), Japan's trade promoting agency, exports to Japan accounted only for 7.8 percent of China's total exports (18.8 percent to the European Union and 17.1 percent to the United States) in 2011 while exports to China accounted for 19.7 percent of Japan's total exports (15.3 percent to the United States and 11.6 percent to EU) (*Asahi shimbun* September 29, 2012, 13).

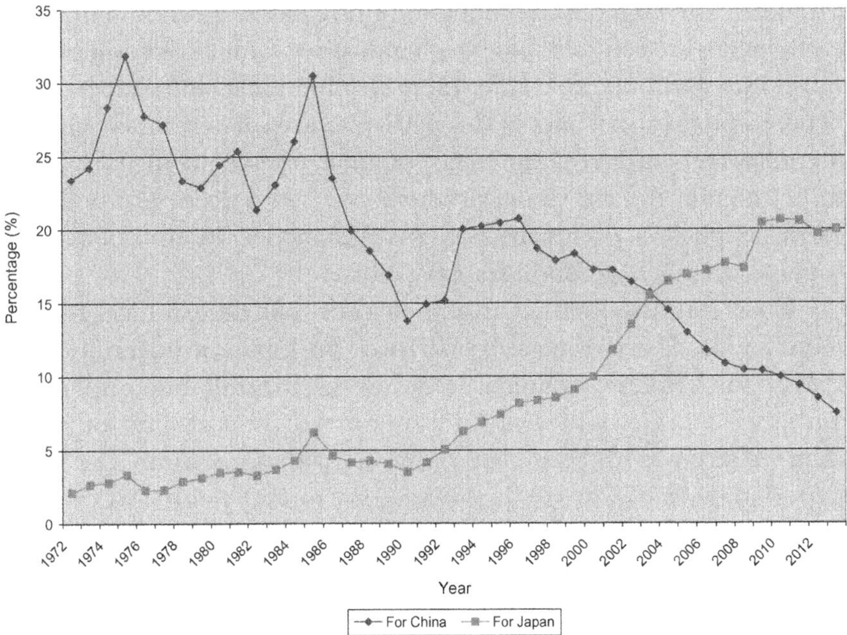

Figure 8.1   Sino-Japanese Trade as Shares of Total Trade, 1972–2013.

Source: International Monetary Fund 1977; 1984; 1991; 1997; 2004; 2011; 2014.

Note: Shares are calculated by the author, the China share for Japan from the Japan pages and the Japan share for China from the China pages.

But the greater importance of the China market does not necessarily mean that the Chinese government can use it to advance its strategic goals because it simply cannot make all the difference. China has become stronger economically because it is being integrated into the global market and China is part of the Asian production network supplying both to the region and the world. China's use of economic leverage would hurt itself as much as Japan. Furthermore, China is now a member of the World Trade Organization, which has been a key factor in expanding Sino-Japanese economic ties despite political and historical tensions (Armstrong 2012).

One may argue that China does not need to start an economic total war and can simply use a specific economic leverage to achieve a specific policy objective. In that regard, rare earths seem to be a good candidate for targeted sanctions for the Chinese government. Rare earth metals are central to high-tech industries. China has cornered the world rare earth market. Thus, there is vulnerability interdependence between Japan and China in this particular area. The Chinese government has recognized that strategic potential, often equating rare earths to petroleum. In fact, China produces over 90 percent of world rare earth supplies, a dominant position unmatched by any petroleum superpowers such as Saudi Arabia or Russia.

It was discussed earlier in the chapter that the Chinese government adopted various measures to force the Japanese government to release the Chinese captain as if they were throwing mud on the wall and hoping one would stick. Did the rare earth mud stick for China then? There was no consensus opinion on that question. The newspaper analyses of why the Japanese government yielded to Chinese pressure eventually did not single out rare earth as the key reason. *Asahi shimbun*'s analysis of the releasing of the captain the next day included the following reasons. While the Japanese government was initially firm, Chinese Premier Wen's stern public demand for an immediate and unconditional release of the Chinese captain in New York on September 21 was viewed as a turning point for Japanese calculations about what to do. Rare earth suspension was cited as a reason because the business community delivered messages to the prime minister's office to resolve the dispute. Then the Chinese government detained four Japanese nationals working for Fujitsu on September 23, interpreted as Chinese retaliation. Prime Minister Kan also wanted to meet with Wen in New York (*Asahi shimbun* September 25, 2010, 2). People have good reasons to say things differently and some may want to avoid giving the adversary any satisfaction. My own evaluation is that the rare earth weapon worked partly, not just because rare earths did matter to the Japanese but more because China's use of rare earth weapons sent a signal that Beijing would continue to escalate.

Even if the rare earth weapon contributed to Beijing's success, the victory was short-lived and costly. China's excessive measures to win release of the captain created their own problems. Moreover, if one examines the real situation, China does not have as strong a position as it appears. It was almost immediately recognized that China would not hold its position for long. Rare earths are not rare. It is just costly to find high concentration of the metals and extract them, which can be detrimental to the environment. Moreover, China controls the production but not the known deposits of rare earth elements. According to the Chinese government estimate, China has about one quarter of world reserves (China State Council Information Office 2012). China gained dominance by beating other countries in prices but some foreign mines are simply shut down. If China becomes successful in raising the price through export control, it would naturally attract newcomers or returnees into the rare earth business, particularly in Australia and the United States. And higher prices will provide greater incentives for unlicensed Chinese rare earth mining operations to engage in smuggling. Foreign customs statistics showed that rare earth imports from China was 2.2 times of Chinese customs statistics for rare earth exports in 2011, meaning that smuggled rare earths were 120 percent of authorized exports (Xinhua News Agency online August 21, 2012). The Chinese smugglers consider smuggling in rare earths as generating heroine-level profits without heroine-level risk (China Non-ferrous Metals Newsweb September 25, 2012). Things have not improved for the Chinese government. According to one estimate, Chinese smuggling of rare earths through Vietnam and Hong Kong amounted to about 40,000 tonnes a year, surpassing Beijing's official export quota of about 31,000 tonnes and suppressing sharply the prices (Els 2014; *Economic Times* 2014). Thus, the Chinese government has revealed weakness about the reach of its regulations, which calls into question how effective it can be in seeking to manipulate market to advance its political and strategic interests. While rare earth prices shot up initially, they subsequently came down and sufficient supplies became available. And China's share of the world market has diminished. Thus, the rare earth case has revealed the power of market forces, which have made the Chinese economic statecraft in this area ineffective (Gholz 2014).

The Japanese Response

The Japanese government responded quickly and effectively over the rare earth issue. Japan had prior experience dealing with foreign stoppage of natural resource. The U.S. stoppage of oil in early 1941 put their country in a difficult position. The Japanese foolishly took a risky move in response. Another prominent example was the first oil crisis. The Japanese government went into a high gear. It shifted its policy to a pro-Arab one. It adopted measures at home to save energy and put a high priority on price stability. It also sought to reduce dependence on the Middle East and on oil by diversifying sources of supply. It became heavily dependent on nuclear power because of its strong desire to achieve energy autonomy.

The Japanese government immediately sought information from the Japanese firms and confronted the Chinese government over the rare earth issue. Since the Chinese government denied use of rare earths as a weapon, the Japanese government wanted to put the Chinese government on the defensive. The Japanese put full court pressure, living up to their reputation as unrelenting negotiators. As one Chinese embassy official complained, the Japanese government would talk about rare earth whatever the formal agenda was. While the Japanese government mishandled the crisis management, it sought to recover losses in other areas. Rare earths became a battle ground. Japan has other plans to ensure supplies of rare earth metals but it continues to pressure China mainly because the Chinese supplies are crucial for the next few years at least and because it is in Japan's interest to have more Chinese supplies in the market to keep the prices down wherever Japan imports rare earth metals.

Japan now became even more worried about overdependence on China, with much discussion of the so-called "China risk". *Daiyamondo* (Diamond), a major Japanese business weekly, used the term for the cover of its October 30, 2010 issue. The Japanese government had already become more concerned in the early 2000s, adopting a China plus one policy. Japan now actively sought alternative sources, making public announcement partly meant to indicate to the domestic audience that it was working hard to reduce Japan's dependence on China. In a tried and true fashion, METI publicly solicited proposals for reducing use of rare earth. To deal with rising rare earth prices, METI announced on June 3, 2011 that it would provide ¥30 billon emergency support for firms engaged in alternative materials or rare earth recycling. The ministry was concerned about the hollowing out of automobile and electronics industries if they did not have sufficient rare earth supplies. By February 2012, the Japanese government had prepared a bill for encouraging recycling of electronic products that contain rare earth or other metals. On February 8, it announced that it would subsidize 49 selected projects with around ¥5 billion of funding. Ten days later, METI Minister Edano visited a TDK Narida factory to support efforts to "leave rare earth." Japanese firms have also taken measures to deal with the problem, in close cooperation with the government. Japan's efforts yielded good results. According to the Japanese statistics, Japan's demand for rare earths had decreased from around 32,000 tonnes in 2007 to about 14,000 tonnes in 2012, which pushed the price down to about one tenth of the peak price in 2011 (*Yomiuri shimbun* online October 26, 2013).

Since it is difficult to find alternatives to rare earths, the Japanese government also seeks to secure supplies of rare earth from non-Chinese sources. The Mountain Path rare earth mine in California reopened in late 2011. Australia's Lynas mining company plans to set up a rare earth plant in Malaysia, producing 11,000 tons of rare earth metals annually by shipping rare earth ores from Australia to Malaysia for processing. But protesters backed by powerful opposition parties are demanding to shut down the operation on environmental grounds. The Japanese government is now also pursuing closer cooperation with those countries that could possibly supply rare earths in places such as Mongolia and Vietnam. Noda and the visiting Mongolian prime minister agreed on March 12, 2012 that the two countries would enter Economic Partnership Agreement (EPA) negotiations, which would be the first FTA for Mongolia. Japan is interested in Mongolia's rich reserves in coal and rare earth and views Mongolia as strategically important being situated between China and Russia. Japan has also been talking with India for rare earth supplies.

Securing supplies of rare earth remains a high diplomatic priority for the Japanese government.

Japan has also become more motivated in finding rare earth deposits on the ocean bottom in its exclusive economic zone (EEZ). A University of Tokyo-led research team found for the first time that there are rare earth metals at the ocean bottom in the Japanese EEZ near Minamitorishima, estimated at 6.8 million tons, which would meet Japan's needs for about 200 years. Japan currently needs 27,000 tons a year. The Japanese government wants to further the research even though it is not yet clear about the technologies required and costs involved in exploration. It does not look practical at this point to extract rare earth metals from the ocean bottom.

Last but not least, Japan has multilateralized the rare earth fight. The Japanese waged a successful public relations campaign. In some way, the Japanese did not have to try that hard since the United States and Europe largely shared Japan's grievance. The Japanese government also indicated that if the Chinese action was confirmed it would be ready to take up the issue with the World Trade Organization (WTO). Japan watched the WTO ruling on China's export controls over other commodities, hoping to build on that and proceed to rare earth. On July 5, 2012, the WTO ruled that China's restrictions on nine raw materials such as bauxite and magnesium violated WTO rules by giving Chinese manufacturers unfair advantages. The Chinese government appealed. On January 31, 2012, the WTO rejected China's appeal. Incidentally, METI officials watched the WTO ruling very closely.[5] China could respond by making sure the national treatment principle is upheld by restricting rare earth supplies to both foreign and domestic users. Rare earth extraction is also more damaging to the environment than the nine minerals in the WTO ruling because of toxic chemicals released in the process, as recognized by some trade experts.[6]

---

[5] Interview with a senior METI official, Tokyo, 30 January 2012.

[6] Gary Hufbauer of the Peterson Institute for International Economics, for example, was quoted in an *Economist* (2012) article as making that argument.

The U.S. government requested consultation on rare earths with China on March 13, 2012.[7] Even though the Japanese sounded more cautious initially, it joined the United States, along with the European Union, on March 22. Canada also joined on March 26. With the April negotiations failing to yield results to their satisfaction, the United States, Japan, and the European Union formally asked the WTO to form a panel over China's rare earth export restrictions on June 27. The Chinese government's response remained largely the same. The Chinese Foreign Ministry spokesman stated the next day that China's rare earth policy was based on concerns for the environment, public health and protection of resources rather than manipulation to protect domestic industry and that it is unfair to expect China that has about one quarter of world reserves to provide over 90 percent of world supplies. China had earlier issued a rare earth white paper to publicize its position (China News Agency online June 20, 2012). China wanted rare earth-rich countries to explore and produce rare earth metals.

The WTO expert panel ruled on March 26, 2014 that while it accepts China's overall policy toward resource management and environmental protect it found the Chinese government's export duties and export quotas to be in violation of WTO rules. The United States declared victory (USTR online March 26, 2014). The Chinese side expressed regret over the WTO ruling but interpreted the ruling as accepting the Chinese government's intent to protect exhaustible resources and the environment (China News Agency online March 26 and 27, 2014). Thus, the Chinese felt that they could adopt different measures to accomplish their goals as long as these measures do not discriminate against foreign firms. On April 25, China decided to appeal the ruling within the 60-day period allowed, focusing on specific issues related to protection of exhaustible resources and the environment and to other WTO agreements rather than the final findings

---

[7]For the basic timeline, arguments and decisions, see World Trade Organization 2014.

of the panel. On August 7, the Appellate Body upheld the panel report.[8] On August 29, the WTO's Dispute Settlement Body (DSB) accepted the Appellate Body report. China informed the DSB on September 26 that it would implement the DSB recommendations but would need reasonable time to do so.[9] In fact, China's export of rare earths had already seen a 30 percent increase in August in the aftermath of the WTO Appellate Body ruling (*Economic Times* 2014). While letting the United States do the heavy lifting, the Japanese followed and cheered on the WTO case against China. In fact, Japanese media leaked in October 2013 that the WTO panel would rule against China and viewed the Chinese control of rare earth as a "complete failure" (*Yomiuri shimbun* online October 26, 2013). The Japanese media stories were duly noticed by the Chinese side. After the WTO panel ruling in March, an official from the Chinese Department of Commerce was quoted in Chinese media that as a plaintiff Japan had leaked the information to talk down the rare earth prices to make unfair economic gains and the Chinese had already complained to the WTO (China News Agency online March 26, 2014). In the end Chinese media reported on January 5, 2015 that the Chinese government had decided to remove rare earth quotas and export taxes were expected to be removed shortly as well. China appears to be complying with the WTO ruling.

It is recognized both in and outside China that the Chinese government could still protect its rare earth supplies by focusing on production control rather than export control. The Chinese government was already making that shift before the WTO ruling. However, that is easier said than done in China. Restriction of rare earth export or production leads to higher prices, which entice illegal mining and smuggling. As discussed before, massive smuggling of rare earths has undermined the Chinese government's ability to influence the supply and pricing of rare earths.

---

[8] USTR (August 7, 2014) again declared victory.
[9] There has been legal dissent (e.g. Qin 2014), but the case has been decided.

Chinese Decision Making Style

The rare earth case highlights the difference between the Chinese and Japanese decision making styles. The Japanese would not let go of the issue. By contrast, China did not do much follow-up after its temporary halt of rare earth supplies to Japan. Thus, the case offers a good opportunity to observe how the Chinese operate. China seemed strategic in seeking dominance in the rare earth sector (Ting and Seaman 2013). Deng Xiaoping was frequently quoted as saying early on that rare earths would be for China what oil is for the Middle East oil producing countries. With government support and strong private investment entering the market, China indeed came to corner the world rare earths market, increasing its annual output from 16,000 tons in 1990 to 73,000 tons in 2000 and peaking in 2009 with 129,000 tons that accounted for 97 percent of world production. China exported a bit less than half of production (Ma 2012).

If China indeed wanted to control the world market, it should act like Saudi Arabia to raise prices enough to maximize gains while avoiding its clients from diversifying. It would be such a waste to squander its dominance in the market, which took decades to build. But it was clear even before the fishing boat incident that the Chinese government came to emphasize other objectives. Rather than seeking complete dominance, they now worried about depletion of valuable natural resources and the environmental damage. The government also sought to consolidate its rare earth sector to achieve better economic results and to make foreign firms transfer technologies. That process started long before the collision incident. In August 2009, the Ministry of Industry and Information Technology (MIIT) announced a strategic plan for rare earth industry for 2015 to restrict production in order to push up the price and used China's dominance in rare earths production as an opportunity to upgrade Chinese high-tech industries for a bigger share of profits in the global production network (Ma 2012). Thus, China was behaving more like a strategic trader than a strategic geopolitical player.

The rare earth case also revealed Beijing's weakness in public relations. China was more likely to lose the rare earth public relations battle because sympathy would naturally go to Japan that was subjected to a punitive active by an overreacting Chinese government. But Beijing did not have to lose so badly. The Chinese government did not say that much over the case in public, allowing the Japanese to frame the issue successfully in the international community. Much of the discussion outside China has been that China wants to convert its domination in the rare earth market to policy advantages. But does Beijing really want to dominate in this area? There has certainly been such suggestion in China, but the dominant concern is more self-centered than global conquering. If Beijing wants to monopolize, it should actively discourage diversification of supplies. In contrary, the Chinese government apparently wanted more supplies. When some Japanese business leaders urged the Chinese government to drop its plan to reduce exports of rare earths, the Chinese officials asked the Japanese to seek other sources of supplies such as the United States, Canada, and Australia, arguing that China produces 90 percent of the rare earths on the market while having only half of the world reserves (*Japan Times* 2010d). The theme that China "unfairly" supplies most of rare earths has become more and more prominent. This of course contradicts earlier Chinese emphasis on achieving a dominant market position in the rare earth sector.

The rare earth case also highlights a broad difference in styles between China and Japan. The Japanese side sees close cooperation between the government and the industry and there is dogged persistence in pursuing issues of concern. In negotiations, the Japanese demonstrate their persistence to the extent that it irritates the Chinese side. The Chinese officials complained that the Japanese could not talk about anything else and focused almost exclusively on rare earths no matter what the official agenda was supposed to be. After March 11, an added issue was to persuade the Chinese government to remove restrictions on imports of Japanese food items. For the Chinese, high-level government meetings became almost like non-stop petition occasions by the Japanese on rare earths and food export to China. It was even reported in Japanese media that the Chinese government had become wary of Japan's detail-oriented petitions in high level meeting prior to the Japan–China cabinet level economic exchange scheduled for mid March 2012 in Tokyo (*Asahi shimbun* February 22, 2012, 5). Conversely, the Japanese officials complained that the Chinese side talked too much about "strategic" issues without solving concrete problems.

China's Japan policy has basically failed because of rising tension with its neighbor. Success or failure is defined here based on what China wants to achieve. If Beijing wishes a tense relationship with Tokyo, it would have succeeded. However, I do judge the Chinese government as wanting to have a close relationship with Japan, albeit on its terms. China has largely failed because the opposite is happening. The rare earth case is a good exhibit of unwise Chinese decision making. The Chinese government does internally reflect on its Japan policy and make policy adjustment from time to time. At the same time, one major flaw in the Chinese system is that the government typically does not take responsibility for domestic or foreign policy failures. All governments have a hard time admitting their failures, but non-democracies have a far more serious problem since no one at home is in a position to hold the government accountable. It is still the case that China's official media and analysts focus on what is wrong with Japan as the root cause of China's growing tension with Japan without looking at its own fault.

In retrospect, Beijing's move on rare earths looked more like a desperate policy measure than a calculated strategy. While the rare earth suspension might have contributed to a short term policy goal, it backfired on China. As a result, China should think twice to use economic leverage so explicitly again. However, there are signs that Beijing may use economic sanctions explicitly or implicitly more often in the future. During the China–Philippines standoff over a disputed reef in May–June, 2012, the Chinese government effectively stopped importing Filipino bananas. China has become a major importer of Filipino bananas. China has become more powerful economically and has incentive to use economic means as better than threat of force given its rising tension with some neighboring countries. With a new round of Sino-Japanese tension over Prime

Minister Noda's nationalization of the disputed Senkakus announced on September 10, 2012, the Chinese reacted strongly and many called for economic retaliation including using the rare earth weapon again. Japan's exports to China suffered.

Conclusion

During the Chinese fishing boat collision incident in September 2010, the Chinese government temporarily halted shipment of rare earths to Japan as a retaliatory measure. Rather than demonstrating Japan's vulnerable dependence on China, the case shows that it is difficult to use trade advantage to advance security interest in a globalizing economy. Rare earths represent a rare case where China is dominant but even there it shows that China cannot hope to exert long-term influence. The Chinese government did not act that strategically because it used rare earth for policy expediency and largely failed at that. In the long run, determined efforts and profit motives will end China's monopoly.

The Japanese government has demonstrated their famed dedication to the issues they consider important. They adopt dogged diplomatic approach to negotiate with the Chinese government, seeking to achieve results. They recognize that China is the largest supplier and will continue to be important. They also seek allies among other developed countries in a multilateral approach. The Japanese are seeking alternative sources and encouraging technical innovation to reduce use of rare earths or better recycling.

By contrast, the Chinese government has not thought through the implication of their policy moves, reflecting on a larger problem of insufficiently examining their policy failure and making quick adjustment. Despite its limited success this time around, with bigger economic clout and growing security tension with some countries, Beijing may not be able to resist the temptation to use economic means as less costly than threat or use of force in the near future. The rare earth case is an indication of things to come.

Chapter 9

China and Japan's ODA Program

Japan's Official Development Assistance (ODA) does not attract that much attention these days, in sharp contrast to the heydays of Japanese largeness in the late 1980s and the early 1990s.[1] This is partly because Japan's ODA budget is sharply shrinking, dropping the country from the world's largest ODA donor (in net disbursement) in 2000 to number five since 2007, trailing the United States, Great Britain, France, and Germany among the 23 member states of the Development Assistance Committee (DAC) of the Organization for Economic Co-operation and Development (OECD). Japan's net ODA disbursement decreased again in 2012, keeping the country in the fifth place (*Asahi shimbun* online February 13, 2014). Japan ranks even lower in terms of ODA as share of gross national income, at twentieth in 2010 (*Kokusai kaihatsu jannaru* 2012). Japan maintained that low ranking in 2012 and its ODA per capita ranked

---

[1] As an exception, after Prime Minister Abe Shinzō announced a $200 million aid package for countries fighting the Islamic State during his trip to the Middle East on January 17, 2015, the Islamic State militants released a video on January 20, threatening to behead two Japanese hostages within 72 hours unless the Japanese government pays up $200 million, emphasizing specifically that this was a retaliation for Abe's aid pledge against them. The two Japanese nationals were subsequently killed. But the world attention was focused on the brutality of the Islamic State rater than Japan's ODA policy.

eighteenth in 2012 (Japan Ministry of Foreign Affairs 2014). And Japan has experienced two decades of economic slowdown, which have taken away the shine from the much touted Japanese model of development. But away from spotlight, Japan's ODA program has gone through major transformation in the past decade, with China factoring in heavily in the process.

For those who remember the old debate outside Japan about the extraordinary caution the Japanese government exercised in implementing its ODA policy, it would be a shock to hear that Japan began considering use of ODA funds for providing military equipment to countries in security conflict. At the end of April 2012, the Japanese government made it clear that it would use ODA money for strategic purposes (*Asahi shimbun* April 25, 2012, 1). As an *Asahi shimbun* editorial (May 2, 2012, 10) questioned immediately, wouldn't using ODA money to provide weapons contradict Japan's Official Development Assistance Charter (ODA Charter) that does not allow ODA for military purpose? Despite some concerns such as the one expressed in the *Asahi* editorial just mentioned, it is also telling that there has been little public discussion, let alone criticism, of Japan's rapidly shrinking ODA budget and changing policy. It appears almost like it is only natural to make a 180 degree shift in ODA policy. By 2014, a case was being made to relax the ban on military use for ODA and to allow ODA to go to middle-income countries or countries that have already graduated from ODA in a new ODA Charter under consideration. The Cabinet approved a new "Development Cooperation Charter" to replace the old ODA Charter on February 10, 2015. The new charter allows assistance to foreign military for "non-military purposes." This change in Japanese ODA policy sheds light on previous Japanese ODA programs as well as continuity and change in Japanese foreign policy. Going deeper than rational calculations of pros and cons of a particular policy, vested interests of the organizations in charge or development philosophy, Japanese public sentiment combined with group-oriented decision making style have played a crucial role in shifting Japanese ODA policy.

China has been a major factor in Japan's changing thinking and practice of ODA. Japan wants to compete with China that has used its rapidly expanding foreign aid program to advance its political and economic interest around the world. Feeling threatened by China's growing military capability, Japan is thinking of using ODA to provide patrol boats to countries like the Philippines that are in territorial disputes with China in the South China Sea. Underlying all these calculations is an emerging consensus in the Japanese policy community and the public that a rising China is more a menace than an opportunity for Japan. Thus, while Japan seeks as much economic gain from the China market as possible it wants to check on China's growing international influence. In that context, ODA is perceived as an obvious diplomatic instrument to advance Japan's security, political and economic interests.

At the same time, the Japanese ODA program and the expanding Chinese foreign aid program share some similarities despite their different origins and the two countries' different situations in the international foreign aid regime. To be exact, the Chinese foreign aid program now looks similar to the Japanese ODA program through the 1970s in terms of emphasis on infrastructure projects, adherence to non-interference in internal affairs and no political conditionals. In fact, Japan's ODA projects in China, particularly in the early stage, showed the way for the Chinese. While Japan sought to move closer to the Western ODA standards in the 1980s and the 1990s, they are going back to their mercantilist roots in ODA projects. Thus, despite growing bilateral tension there is actually much room for collaboration between the two countries, potentially beneficial to them as well as recipient countries.

China and Japan's ODA Program through the 2000s

Japan started its ODA program in the mid 1950s, to repair relations with the Asian countries it had invaded and to advance its economic and political interest in re-entering the Asian markets. Japan's ODA went through several stages after that, shifting to securing energy supplies and enhancing its influence in the United Nations in the 1970s and coordinating with other developed donors to demonstrate its international responsibilities in the 1980s. Japan became an

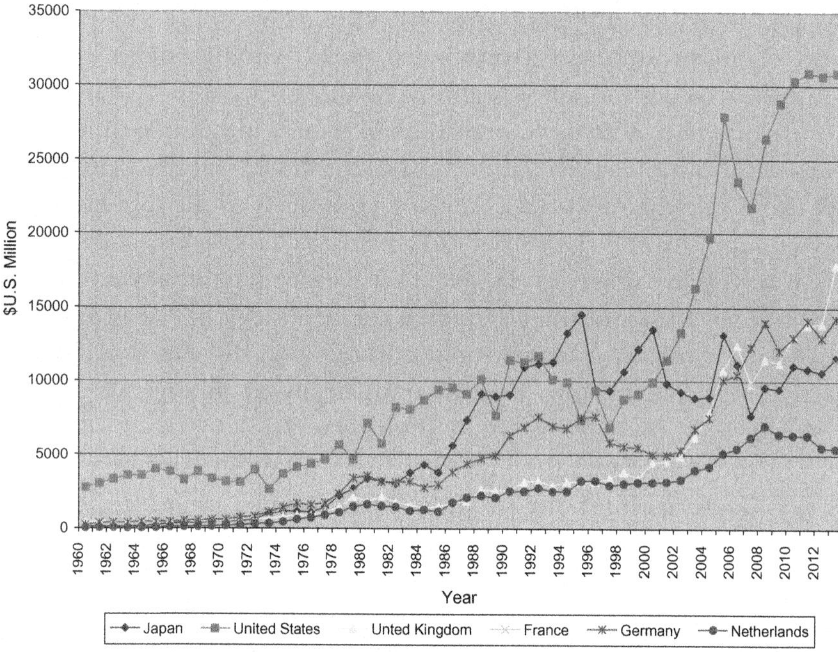

Figure 9.1   Japan's ODA versus Other Major Donor Countries.
Source: OECD 2014a.

aid superpower in the late 1980s and was the world largest ODA
donor in net disbursements in most of the 1990s, as shown in
Figure 9.1.[2] But Japan retreated in the 2000s, which will be discussed
in detail later in the chapter.

China was not a recipient of Japanese ODA until the end of the
1970s. The Cold War prevented Tokyo from establishing diplomatic
ties with Beijing. Japan normalized diplomatic relations with China
in 1972. But China was in the middle of the Cultural Revolution and
had only limited economic exchange with the outside world. Once
Deng Xiaoping started economic reform in 1978, the Japanese government initiated discussion of providing ODA to China. In fact, the
Japanese explained to the Chinese government how ODA works.

---

[2] For early studies of Japanese ODA, see Rix 1980; Yasutomo 1986; Orr 1990; Arase
1995.

Japan was the very first foreign country to provide bilateral ODA to China.

Japan had several motives for providing ODA to China. First, Japan needed to improve relations with China to move beyond the war. The Chinese government gave up on war compensation in the 1972 diplomatic normalization joint communiqué. Thus, ODA was viewed as a substitute for war compensation. This is an important reason that China quickly became one of Japan's largest ODA recipients and the Japanese government provided ODA for five years, which corresponded to the Chinese government's five-year plans. As shown in Figure 9.2, Japan's ODA to China increased drastically in the 1980s and peaked in the early 1990s. Japan's net disbursement partly reflects previous Japanese decision on yen loans. Japan offered its first yen loan of ¥330.9 billion for 1979–1983, second yen loan of ¥470 billion for 1984–1990, third yen loan of ¥810 billion for 1990–1995 and fourth yen loan of ¥970 billion divided in two periods.

Second, Japan wanted to promote its economic and commercial interests. After the First Oil crisis in the early 1970s, energy security

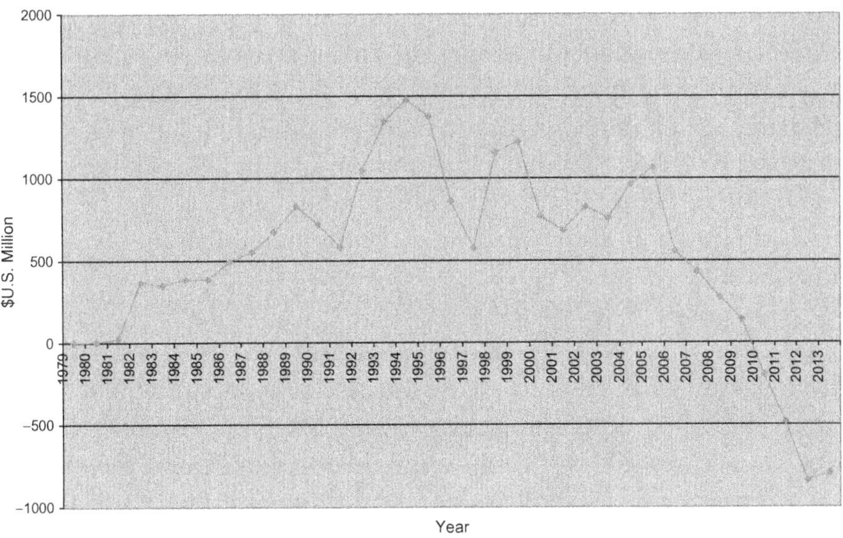

Figure 9.2　Japan's ODA Net Disbursement to China.
Source: OECD 2014b.

became a top priority for Japan. Thus, Japan's first major ODA projects in China were all infrastructure projects in transportation and ports aimed at facilitating Chinese exports of petroleum and coal to Japan. As Japan needed to coordinate more with other donor countries that were moving away from infrastructure, Japan expanded its aid program to other purposes. But Japan's ODA program in China remained heavily focused on infrastructure projects. Japan's ODA program facilitated China's modernization drive. But it was also in Japan's own interest to use ODA as a catalyst for economic interaction with China. Similar to Japanese ODA elsewhere, there was a close connection between ODA and private investment flows. Conducting a conditional logit analysis using Chinese province level statistics in 1980–1999, Séverine Blaise (2005) has shown that Japanese ODA had a significant positive impact on Japanese private investors' location choices. Yen loans were more generous than market-term loans but they were not charities. Japan's ODA to China was mutually beneficial and served its intended purpose.

Japan's expanding ODA program in China took place when political leaders with war experience in both countries had a strong political will to improve the bilateral relationship and often viewed the bilateral relationship as special. This is reflected in Japan's relatively quick resumption of yen loans to China after the 1989 Tiananmen Incident. Moreover, there was not much Japanese public criticism of ODA to China. China was popular in Japan in the 1980s, as shown in Figure 1.1 in Chapter 1. China's popularity began to drop sharply only after Tiananmen, but remained about 50 percent in the 1990s.

Japan shifted its stance on ODA for China in 2001, reducing ODA budget by about a quarter for Fiscal Year 2001 and shifting from a multi-year basis to a case-by-case basis. Japan actually froze grant aid to Beijing over nuclear tests in Fiscal Year 1995. But Tokyo's serious effort for adjusting aid to China came a few years later. Several reasons explain Japan's shifting attitudes toward ODA for China. Tokyo's adjustment started with recognition that Japan was now facing fiscal difficulties and China was becoming stronger economically. But there was also much criticism in Japan that

Japanese largeness had not improved the Chinese image of Japan, often blamed on the Chinese government not publicizing enough the Japanese contributions to Chinese economic development. The bilateral relationship began to experience some serious tension in the mid 1990s. The two sides patched things up but the foundation of the relationship became increasingly weakened. The two countries suffered sustained tension in 2002–2006 mainly over Prime Minister Koizumi Junichirō's annual visits to Yasukuni Shinto Shrine that honors some class-A war criminals. In that context, Japan's ODA to China became more controversial. As Figure 1.1 shows, Japanese view of China worsened rapidly in the 2000s, which put pressure on the Japanese government. The Japanese also noticed China's own expanding aid programs for developing countries and double-digit annual increase in military spending. And Japan saw Chinese exploration of natural gas and oil in the East China Sea as stealing oil and natural gas from its side of the Economic Exclusive Zone. The Japanese government decided in 2005 to end yen loans to China by 2008, the year in which Beijing would host the Olympics (Wan 2006, 262–282). In December 2007, the two governments signed an agreement on Japan's last yen loan to China. Although Japan still provides some technical assistance and grant aid to China (around ¥5 billion a year), the era of Japanese ODA to China was over. In fact, since China needs to repay the past loans, Japan's net disbursement of ODA dropped sharply after the mid 2000s and became negative in 2010, as shown in Figure 9.2.

Those in China and Japan who wanted to maintain good bilateral relations hoped in the mid 2000s for Japan's ODA program in China to end well. With a small amount of grant aid and technical assistance, proponents of bilateral cooperation hoped to achieve better mutual understanding through Japanese non-government personnel participating in grassroots projects in China and Chinese trainees in Japan and improving software to enhance economic exchange by training Chinese officials about international rules (Cai 2011).

Indeed, the Japanese government was careful not to interpret phasing out of yen loans as a punishment for Chinese behavior, which would have invited a stronger backlash. The Japanese could justify their reduction of yen loans to China by the simple fact that Japan had experienced economic difficulties for over a decade, which was visible to all. Japan's overall ODA has decreased sharply since 2000 as shown in Figure 9.1. In fact, the Chinese knew that Japan really began to reduce ODA in the late 1990s but the Japan's special yen loans to help deal with the Asian Financial Crisis in 1997–1998 gave Japan a temporary boost in ODA disbursement (Feng 2008; Lin and Sun 2005).

At the same time, the Chinese analysts also noticed that Japan's ODA to India and then Vietnam dramatically increased despite fiscal difficulties (Song 2010; Liao 2011). As Figure 9.3 shows, India became a large Japanese ODA recipient. India is similar to China in population. One may suggest that it makes sense since India is trailing China in economic development, thus more deserving. But that

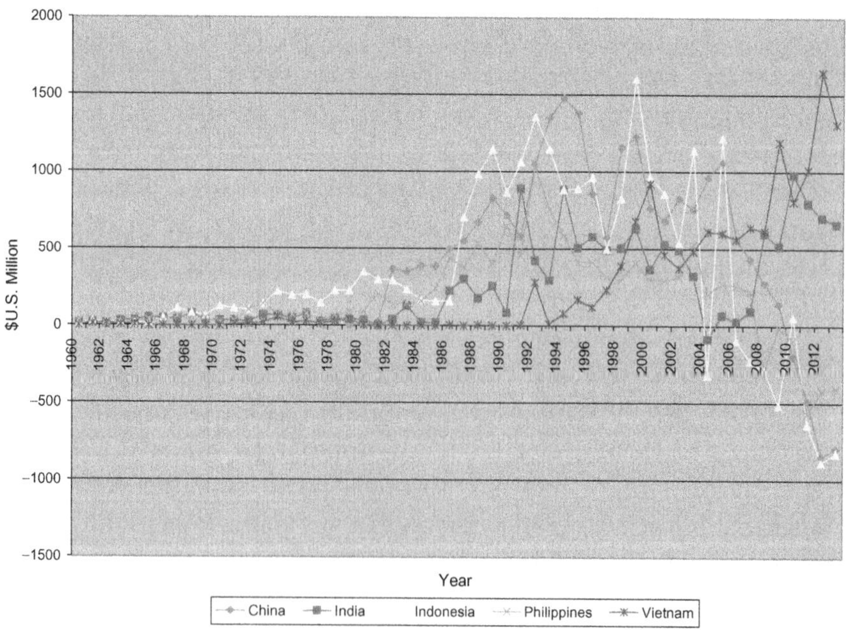

Figure 9.3   Japan's ODA to Select Asian Countries.
Source: OECD 2014b.

argument did not prevent Japan from focusing on China rather than India in the 1980s and the early 1990s. What had changed is Japan's new assessment of a friendlier India as a counterweight to a rising China. Vietnam has seen an even sharper increase in ODA in recent years. Vietnam is viewed as a potential ally checking on China's influence in Southeast Asia, which is important for Japanese interest. Having higher GDP per capita than Vietnam, both Indonesia and the Philippines have seen their share of Japanese ODA money decreasing. But it is likely that the Philippines will receive more ODA money now since the country, like Japan, is in a maritime territorial dispute with China.

While choosing words carefully in public, the Japanese government began to use ODA as an instrument for competing with a rising China in the diplomatic and economic realms in the 2000s. China was an important factor causing a more strategic and activist Japanese foreign economic policy in trade and ODA (Solís and Urata 2007). Japan now viewed China as a rival, combining both efforts to improve bilateral relations and strategic moves to shore up its own position in the regions considered important for its national interests. This was the case for Japan's greater efforts to support the integration of the Association of Southeast Asian Nations (ASEAN), to enhance its economic linkage with the region while decreasing ASEAN dependence on China. Japan's ODA to Southeast Asia was part of that overall strategic calculation (Yoshimatsu and Trinidad 2010). Japan also increased diplomatic and ODA efforts in Africa, which it viewed as important for natural resources and for votes to support its bid to become a permanent member of the United Nations Security Council. China factored in heavily in that area. China's growing political and economic influence in Africa in recent years was viewed in Japan as a crucial reason why African nations, large in numbers, did not actively support Japan's UNSC bid in the mid 2000s when China came out opposing Japan (Song 2010). In another case, Japan viewed Central Asia as strategically important since it is between China and Russia. In recognition of the China factor in Japanese ODA for Central Asia, the Japan International Cooperation Agency (JICA) handles Central Asia in its

East Asian department, unlike most other organizations that lump Central Asia with Russia.

The Chinese noticed Japan's shifting ODA strategy partly to compete more effectively with China, but they did not raise any open objection. They could not object to Japan exercising its sovereign right to decide which developing country to help more. Moreover, the Chinese government sought to stabilize the relationship with Japan after a tumultuous period when Koizumi was prime minister. With three more LDP prime ministers after Koizumi, there seemed to have emerged a consensus between the Chinese and Japanese governments not to rock the boat. As a senior Japanese ODA official pointed out in July 2009, the phasing out of Japanese yen loans to China was not going badly. It was also helpful that Japan still has existing yen loan projects in China.[3] The situation would change drastically in the next decade.

China and Japan's ODA Program in the 2010s

With the Democratic Party of Japan (DPJ)'s landslide electoral victory in August 2009, Japan entered a new phase of party politics. However, Japanese diplomacy suffered under the inexperienced DPJ government. Hatoyama Yukio, the first DPJ prime minister, complicated Japan's relations with the United States when he announced his vision for an East Asian community that seemed to exclude the United States and to move U.S. marine air station Futenma out of Okinawa despite a binding agreement with the United States to move the base to another location within the prefecture. Hatoyama did not improve relations with East Asia either since there was no substance to his East Asian community vision. It was conceivable that Japan's ODA could have become part of that plan but Hatoyama did not serve long enough to create a plan for realizing his vision. The backlash in Japan against Hatoyama also did damage to Japanese enthusiasm for Asian regionalism, which would have implications for Japan's ODA policy. Hatoyama was followed by

---

[3] Interview, Tokyo, July 2009.

fellow DPJ leaders Kan Naoto (June 8, 2010–September 2, 2011) and Noda Yoshihiko (September 2, 2011–December 26, 2012).

The ODA budget suffered further under the DPJ rule. Japan's ODA budget in general account for 2012 decreased by two percent from the previous year, the thirteenth reduction in a row since 2000. Ogata Sadako, the JICA president from October 2003 to March 2012, commented that Japan's ODA budget had decreased since the LDP days because Japan was turning inward. She also commented that while she was hoping that Japan would change with the end of LDP domination but was surprised that ODA became a target and those in charge of budget distribution cared little about aid to developing countries and talked only about cutting aid money (*Asahi shimbun* March 5, 2012, 4).

After the Cold War ended, Japanese ODA policy incorporated more political and market principles, including governance and environmental protection, resulting in an ODA charter adopted in 1992 and revised in 2003. But the DPJ government went back to the roots of mercantilism. The cabinet decided in June 2010 that Japan's new growth strategy should focus on exports of infrastructure projects such as nuclear plants to the emerging countries. Japan's ODA policy was adjusted to support that basic strategy.

The mega disasters of March 11, 2011 had a major impact on Japan's infrastructure-focused export strategy. The Kan cabinet decided on May 10, 2011 that the government would need to re-examine its strategy to export nuclear plants (*Asahi shimbun* May 11, 2011, 5). But the successive Noda cabinet made it clear in October 2011 that Japan would continue the plan to export nuclear plants to Vietnam facilitated by ODA money (*Asahi shimbun* October 28, 2011, 4). More broadly, the Japanese government decided in June 2011 that it would use ODA to facilitate reconstruction in Japan's disaster area, namely purchasing processed seafood from the disaster areas in the Tohoku region as food aid to developing countries. The Japanese Foreign Ministry also wanted to support trainees for the disaster areas and to market Japan's earthquake-resistant technology (*Japan Times* 2011a). The ministry planned to provide ¥4 billion for 15 developing countries in the year of 2012. The Japanese officials saw this approach as "killing two birds with one stone." The first such aid program was initiated on February 22, 2012, ¥250 million of products for the Federal States of Micronesia (*Asahi shimbun* February 23, 2012, 4). Given the magnitude of the disasters, few can blame the Japanese government for seeking to recover whichever way it could.

As discussed before, the LDP government had begun to use ODA to compete with China. That trend became far more pronounced under the DPJ government. The DPJ government was more explicit in seeking to check on China, reacting to and adding to the worsening nature of the bilateral relationship. One frequently reads Japanese media stories of Japanese offering ODA to various countries with China in mind. For example, Japan was quick to reopen yen loans to Myanmar, which it had suspended since 1988. The Noda government reportedly planned to indicate its intention to restart the yen loans in April when the Myanmar president visits Japan (*Asahi shimbun* February 23, 2012, 4). And it did. The Japanese enterprises were eager to re-enter Myanmar for natural resources, labor, and market. The Japanese government also wanted to enhance its influence to counter China's strong presence in the country. In another case, Japan hosted the sixth Japan–Pacific Islands Forum summit in Okinawa on May 26–27, 2012. Japan had viewed the forum as important for winning votes for its UN Security Council permanent seat. But China's rising influence and maritime expansion was a growing concern. The United States joined for the first time. Noda pledged about $500 million of aid for the next three years. But its aid budget actually decreased on the yen-basis from ¥50 billion last time to ¥40 this time, reflecting Japan's fiscal challenges. China provided about $600 million to the region in 2005–2009 (*Asahi shimbun* May 27, 2012, 3). When Japanese worry about Japan's declining presence, they mainly discuss that in contrast to China's perceived rising presence in the region rather than other major players, which is a reflection of Japan's stronger sense of rivalry with China.

Since the Chinese fishing boat collision incident in September 2010, the Japanese government has also been using ODA to secure supplies of rare earth from different countries. During the incident, the Chinese government stopped shipment of rare earth to Japan, which led to much discussion of Japan's vulnerable dependence on China that is now supplying about 90 percent of rare earth in the world market. Rare earth is a crucial material for high-tech sectors such as electronics and automobile. Avoiding dependence on Chinese rare earth supplies is one of the frequently discussed themes in the Japanese media. Vietnam, India, Myanmar, and some Central Asian countries are often discussed with ODA, rare earth and check on Chinese influence in the same breadth.

The Japanese media sometimes exaggerates the China factor in often far more complex stories, in contrast to the Japanese government that has been more cautious in characterizing its ODA policy as aiming at China. But the China narrative in the Japanese media matters because it shapes the public opinion that affects Japan's diplomacy, particularly its ODA policy. The narrative in Japan is that ODA money comes from Japanese taxes and taxpayers therefore have a strong interest in how their money is being spent. Thus, since the Japanese public worries about China, a China angle helps justify Japan's ODA budgets. That sense of being threatened has not led to any push for even greater ODA budget. As revealed in Figure 9.4, the Japanese public seems to mostly want to maintain the current level of ODA. But as Figure 9.1 shows, Japan's "current level" is declining. Thus, the Japanese public basically accepts the declining level of Japanese ODA and how the money is used partly to balance against Beijing.

As an even more drastic change in Japanese ODA program, it was reported in March 2012 that the Japanese government now wanted to offer an antipiracy boat to Yemen as part of ODA for the country. Foreign Minister Genba Kōichirō said that Japan intended to provide patrol boats to coastal countries to enhance sea lane security by using ODA money. Such a policy was made possible by the government's relaxation on arms export in December 2011 (*Japan Times* 2012c). It was reported in April 2012 that Prime Minister Noda would indicate in his meeting with Obama on April 30 that Japan would now use ODA for providing weapons to Japan's neighboring countries (*Asahi shimbun* April 25, 2012, 1). Unlike in the late

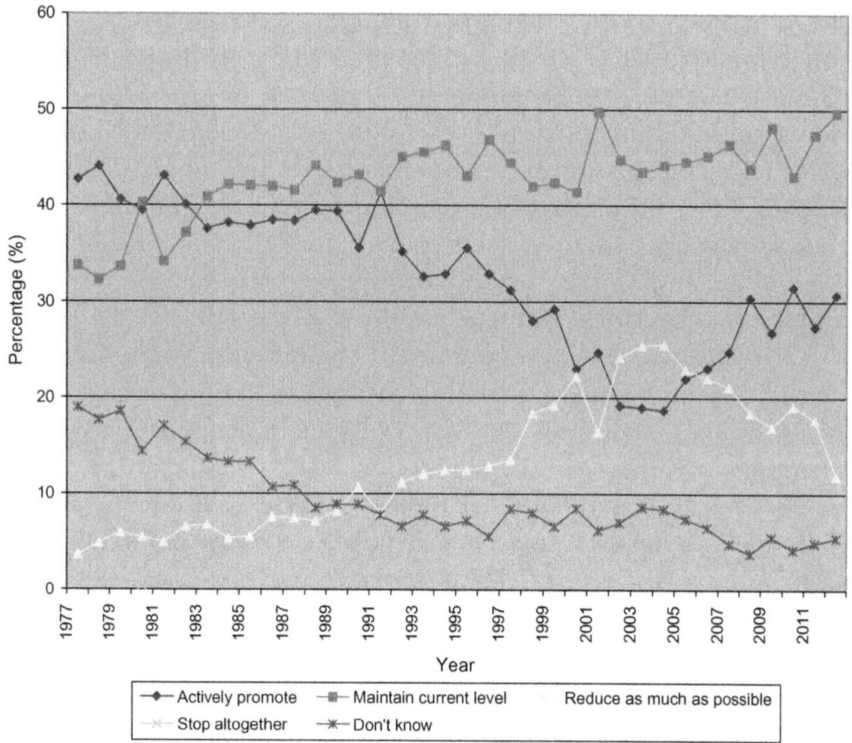

Figure 9.4   Japanese Public Support for ODA.

Source: Japan Prime Minister's Cabinet Office 2014.

Note: The polls did not ask the same question in 2012 and 2013.

1980s when Japan tried to substitute economic cooperation for burden sharing, Japan was now directly using money for security cooperation (*Asahi shimbun* April 25, 2012, 3). Patrol boats are weapons if we follow Japan's trade management ordinance (bōeki kanrirei). Japan's 2003 ODA Charter says clearly that Japan cannot provide aid for military purposes. The Japanese government did make an exception in 2006 to provide patrol boats to Indonesia to combat piracy (*Asahi shimbun* May 16, 2012, 2). But the current Japanese thinking was to make offer of patrol boats a new norm.

The DPJ suffered a major loss in the Lower House election in December 2012 mainly because the voters had become disillusioned with the party's poor performance in governance and economic challenges. The DPJ government's perceived weakness in handling China was also a major factor. Abe's LDP government has been actively using ODA money or promise of ODA money to compete with China. The Japanese Ministry of Foreign Affairs announced the establishment of a consultation council on revising the ODA Charter on March 28, 2014, based on Abe's new national security strategy formulated in the previous year. Abe called his strategy "proactive pacifism," which was apparently based on collective defense, strategic use of ODA and arms export (*Asahi shimbun* online January 9, 2015). The Japanese government might now lift the ban on use of ODA money for foreign militaries for non-combat missions (*Japan Times* 2014). Another thrust of the discussion has been to resume aid to the countries that have already "graduated" from the ODA recipient list because of their strategic and commercial importance for Japan. The Abe government basically decided on January 8, 2015 that a new charter would be adopted to allow support for foreign militaries in non-military areas such as disaster relief (*Asahi shimbun* online January 9, 2015).

Japan's new ODA strategy is drastically different from its approach in the late 1980s and the early 1990s. At that time, the Japanese government was trying to demonstrate its contributions to the alliance with the United States and to the international community by providing money for international development and for dealing with international financial crises. It was a sort of "side payment" or "substitution" for direct defense assistance to the United States (Wan 2001b). That strategy was criticized as "checkbook diplomacy" by the United States, particularly during the Gulf War. Now that Japan has become far more willing to provide direct assistance to the United States to strengthen the alliance, which it values more than before because of China's rise. In that context, there has been little American criticism of how much or for what purpose Japan is spending its aid money.

It is striking that there has been little public discussion whether this new ODA approach is consistent with the international norm. Use of money for military use is inconsistent with the criteria of

ODA by the OECD's Development Co-operation Directorate (DAC), the international organization for ODA. The DAC definition is as follows (OECD 2014c):

> The DAC defines ODA as "those flows to countries and territories on the DAC List of ODA Recipients and to multilateral institutions which are:
>
> i. *Provided by official agencies*, including state and local governments, or by their executive agencies; and
> ii. Each transaction of which:
>
>> (a) Is administered with the promotion of the *economic development and welfare of developing countries* as its main objective; and
>> (b) Is *concessional in character* and conveys a grant element of at least 25 percent (calculated at a rate of discount of 10 percent)."

To avoid confusion, the DAC has also clarified what is and what is not considered to be ODA, as follows. One may indeed justify aid to military so long as it is used for humanitarian assistance. The danger lies in how one actually defines what humanitarian aid is and in the possibility that a foreign military will be able to use "saved" funds or ODA equipment for military use.

- "Military aid: No military equipment or services are reportable as ODA. Anti-terrorism activities are also excluded. However, the cost of using donors' armed forces to deliver humanitarian aid is eligible.
- Peacekeeping: Most peacekeeping expenditures are excluded in line with the exclusion of military costs. However, some closely-defined developmentally relevant activities within peacekeeping operations are included.
- Nuclear energy: Reportable as ODA, provided it is for civilian purposes."

A drastic shift in Japanese ODA programs raises a question about what the Japanese ODA has been all about. There used to be a debate over the purpose of Japanese ODA with some non-Japanese analysts trying desperately to probe what economic and security interests Japan had in its ODA while the Japanese officials apparently had difficulty in explaining the benign nature of Japanese ODA program.[4] However, the fact that the Japanese government now has a different take on ODA should not mean that Japan's earlier emphasis on peace and development was disingenuous. That was a different time and different players were in charge. There has been a changing guard in the Japanese government and changing domestic and international environment. Many of those working in the Japanese ODA programs were genuinely interested in international development and worked tirelessly for the effort, which was made possible by public acceptance and political support. Nevertheless, it is in Japan's own interest to use different institutions to handle security-driven projects rather than using the ODA institution to make such a drastic policy shift contrary to its legal mission, which may also diminish the value of its past efforts for those who have a short-term memory. Indeed, the Japanese government is currently considering the establishment of a "military version of ODA" based on the cabinet decision on weapons transfer in April 2014. A proposed law is expected in Fall 2015 (*Sankei shimbun* online February 10, 2015). This parallel discussion partly explains why the February 10, 2015 cabinet decision on a new "Development Cooperation Charter" to replace the old ODA Charter did not go as far as earlier decision would suggest. The new charter aims at advancing Japan's strategic interest and allows use of ODA for assisting foreign military for non-military purposes (Kameda 2015). But one would have expected more if one had followed the Japanese discussion before October 2014.

The Japanese and Chinese Foreign Aid Systems

As discussed before, Japan is adjusting its ODA program partly to compete with China that has an expanding foreign aid program. There is now strong interest in comparing the Japanese and Chinese

---

[4] For a past critical analysis of Japan's ODA, see Ensign 1992.

aid programs mainly because the size of the Chinese program has grown dramatically. Such a comparison would not be necessary a decade earlier.

The Japanese and Chinese aid programs came from different origins. The Japanese mainly drew from their earlier development experience in Hokkaido and then its colonies or semi-colonies in Taiwan, Korea, and Manchuria. The Chinese started their aid program supporting communist and independence insurgency movements. While a developing country, China started its foreign aid program in the early 1950s, about the same time as Japan did. Different from Japan, China began its aid program to advance its ideological and political agenda. However, China and Japan converged later in terms of attitude toward the sovereignty of the recipient countries. Japan emphasized self-help and request-based operational principles, with few political conditions (Shimomura, Nakagawa and Saitō 1999). The Chinese government emphasized a non-interference in domestic affairs principle and intense consultation with the recipient countries based on their needs (Chinese Ministry of Foreign Economics and Trade 1985, 6–9; Zhou 2008). Moreover, China's aid program after 1978 came to resemble Japan's during the Cold War, both exhibiting mercantilist elements. After all, China essentially adopted a developmental state approach with its reform and opening. In that context, the Japanese ODA program in China had a clear impact on China's post-revolution aid program (Wan 2014, 79).

For the past decade, China has expanded its aid program while Japan has shrunk its ODA budget, resulting in its status as the world's largest donor country in the 1990s to only number five by 2008. Detailed and systemic information on China's foreign aid is harder to come by than Japan's. Some 20 non-DAC countries report their aid to DAC, but China is not one of them. China's *China Statistical Yearbook* and the yearbook of the Chinese Ministry of Commerce contain some information on Chinese aid but China's actual aid is believed to be much bigger (Maeda 2009). Chinese newspapers reveal various numbers about Chinese foreign aid from time to time. The Chinese State Council Information Office issued China's foreign aid white paper in April 2011. It is reported in the white paper that China's foreign aid includes grant aid, interest-free loans and low interest loans (typically 2–3 percent interest rate for 15–20 years). By end of 2009, China offered 256.29 billion of yuan in foreign aid, including 106.2 billion in grant aid, 76.54 billion in interest-free loans and 73.55 billion in low interest loans. In 2009, 45.7 percent of Chinese foreign aid funds went to Africa and 32.8 percent went to Asia. China is not yet as big a donor as Japan, but it is growing rapidly.

One major difference between the Japanese and Chinese foreign aid systems is that Japan is a member of the international ODA regime while China is not. In fact, I use the term "foreign aid" in the section title due to this difference. If we study Japan alone, we would normally use the term ODA rather than foreign aid. But China's aid program is not termed ODA. To qualify as ODA, one has to participate in the international aid regime. As mentioned before, Japan expanded its ODA program in the 1980s to demonstrate its contribution to the United States-led world order. It was partly a burden sharing for the alliance. China does not think that way.

Japan now almost stands alone from the reformist trend since the mid 1990s to emphasize development coordination among donor countries in an aid recipient country, principally in Africa, because of its historically informed self-help philosophy and weak institutional setup for policy coordination with the European donors countries strongly interested in the new approach (Takahashi 2010a, 58–66). Unlike the European donors, Japan has been hesitant to grant debt cancellation because it believes that external credit is crucial for economic development, based on its own experience (Hasegawa 2010). Different or not, Japan still has to adhere to certain international rules. In particular, Japan has to be transparent in its ODA projects.

By contrast, China is outside the international ODA regime. The West has been interested in having China participate in the existing system but Beijing has been reluctant. China and several other emerging powers were invited to attend the Fourth High-Level Forum on Aid Effectiveness (HLF-4) in Busan, Korea on November 29–December 1, 2011. China participated in the drafting of a multilateral agreement on transparency and global coordination but did not sign it despite persuasion from the United States, Australia and others that want to see a more transparent Chinese aid program. Beijing simply does not want to be bound by the existing international aid regime that is based on Western values. Besides China, Brazil, and India did not sign the agreement either. Moreover, China is tentatively moving to create its own international aid institutions and rules. For the past few years, Beijing has created a development bank with the other four members of the so-called BRICS (Brazil, Russia, India, China and South Africa), which reflects the growing influence of the emerging powers. In Asia, China has created the Asian Infrastructure Investment Bank (AIIB), which the United States and Japan have so far shown little interest in joining.

It is on balance a good development that the emerging powers are increasing aid to less developed countries, which compensates the decreasing ODA budgets from the developed countries. One may also argue that the development experience of more recently succeeding countries is more appropriate for those less successful. From a strategic perspective, it is more advantageous for recipient countries to have more options, which give them greater bargaining leverage. And whoever finances infrastructure projects, they are beneficial for all. At the same time, there are prices to be paid with new money from the emerging powers. In particular, a lack of transparency in Chinese aid program raises questions whether the China-funded projects would have negative impact on the environment, labor standards and good governance.

Experiencing China's tougher challenge, Japan now faces a choice of becoming more coordinated with the European donors in the new development agenda or reverting back to its previous infrastructure-based ODA approach and becoming more like China (Takahashi 2010b). As discussed before, the DPJ government decided in June 2010 on a new growth strategy based on exports of infrastructure projects such as nuclear plans and bullet trains to the emerging countries. Japan's ODA policy has been adjusted accordingly to facilitate its overall economic diplomacy by using aid money as incentives for foreign governments to accept Japanese bids against competitors from China and elsewhere.[5] The Japanese government feels that Japan has trailed behind China and South Korea in exporting infrastructure project such as railways and power plants (*Asahi shimbun* April 6, 2012, 8). Similar to China, Japan demands few political conditions. Cambodians, for example see Chinese aid and Japanese aid programs as similar in not imposing preconditions and different from the United States and other Western powers that tie aid to human rights and democracy (Kea 2011).

Due to China's rise, some in Japan also argue whether it is still in Japan's interest to stay within the DAC that has put so much pressure on Japan to untie its aid projects, which has been a source of resentment among the Japanese companies for a while now, dating before China's rise. But the rise of emerging donor countries such as China that are not bound by the DAC rules means for some Japanese observers that Japan should not constrain itself by the DAC rules. Rather, the Japanese government needs to use its aid money to support its companies more strongly (Araki 2012).

While Japan and China are now competing with each other for economic and political influence in Asia and the world, there is room for cooperation in the foreign aid area. Ogata, the previous JICA president, thought it was possible for Japan to cooperate with China. She recalled that when she met Chinese Vice Premier Li Keqiang in 2010, Li suggested that it would be good to exchange information about aid to Africa with Japan (*Asahi shimbun* March 5, 2012, 4). Ogata was viewed as having a strong belief in cooperating with China. Her successor Tanaka Akihiko also adopted concrete measures to cooperate with the Chinese aid agencies (*Asahi shimbun* May 19, 2012, 4).[6] He talked about cooperation with China that shares experience of Japanese ODA in another interview with *Asahi shimbun* on June 3, 2012 (*Asahi shimbun* June 5, 2012, 12). The Chinese side has been thinking along this line for several years as well (Cai 2011).

---

[5] A senior Japanese ODA official familiar with Japanese ODA to China agreed that the Japanese government is now focused on economic growth in its aid projects and China is one of the factors affecting that change. Talk with the official, Tokyo, February 2011.

[6] Also see Tanaka's interview with *Kokusai kaihatsu jannaru*, April 2012, pp. 8–11.

There is a basis for Sino-Japanese aid cooperation if the governments have the will to do so. As mentioned earlier, the two countries have some shared experience of foreign aid and considerable experience of achieving economic development. Moreover, the Chinese and Japanese officials handling ODA often know each other due to past experience of cooperating over Japanese ODA projects in China. The Japanese have also done much research on Chinese foreign aid program, both specifically and as part of a broader theme of China's rising influence (e.g. Maeda 2009). In fact, the Japanese ODA officials often know what the Chinese are doing in foreign aid areas better than the Chinese themselves due to the diverse organizational structure of the Chinese foreign aid decision making and implementation structure. As a senior Japanese ODA official told me in July 2009, when he went to China to discuss the structure of the Chinese foreign aid programs to various Chinese agencies, the Chinese officials often asked him to say more about what the other Chinese agencies were doing.[7] As the Chinese themselves have recognized, Japan has a far more experienced and institutionalized system of selecting, implementing and assessing ODA projects (Huang and Meng 2011).

It is difficult to cooperate on aid projects between two countries. It was difficult for Japan and the United States to cooperate over ODA projects in the earlier years even though the two countries were close allies. At the same time, it might actually be easier for China and Japan to collaborate since both countries focus on infrastructure projects, which by nature are large and suitable for a multinational consortium to combine different advantages and diversify the risks. The Chinese side is familiar with Japanese ODA projects in China. And some Chinese firms have won contracts for the Japanese ODA-funded projects. According to Japanese statistics, in 2005–2009 Chinese firms won 19 percent of the yen loan contracts for companies from a single country and seven percent of the contract amount, compared to 17 percent and 26 percent for Japanese firms (*Kokusai kaihatsu jannaru* Editorial Office 2012).

---

[7] Interview, Tokyo, July 2009.

Furthermore, China has borrowed the Japanese assistance practice learned from the early years of Chinese opening. Indeed, a senior Japanese ODA official agreed that China partly borrowed the Japanese practice such as quality control in implementing Chinese aid projects in third countries.[8] More broadly, China has learned from how Japan practiced ODA in China in the early years of reform. As observed by Deborah Brautigam (2009, 13), a noted scholar on Chinese aid to Africa, "China's engagement with Africa often repeats patterns established by the West, and especially Japan *in China*." She is right that the Chinese government learned that aid can be combined with other forms of economic exchange such as direct investment that aid is often designed to benefit both the donors and recipients and that such an approach can facilitate development. A hallmark of Chinese aid program in places like Africa is offering packaged deals exchanging infrastructure projects for natural resources, which is not too different from Japan's packaged ODA projects exchanging infrastructure projects for supplies of natural resources in China in the 1980s.

While the current tension between Japan and China makes it difficult for bilateral cooperation, it is not impossible for them to collaborate as long as the joint projects are clearly mutually beneficial. With joint Japanese and Chinese expertise, such joint projects should be beneficial for recipient countries as well. It would be unrealistic to expect for such joint projects to help improve the overall relations, but they would surely help to make the bilateral relationship more mature and nuanced as it should be.

Conclusion

China has been a crucial reason for Japan's changing thinking and practice of ODA. Japan used ODA as a major policy instrument to improve relations with China and advance its economic and commercial interest in China through the early 1990s, which was beneficial for both countries. But China's rise has caused much

---

[8] Talk by the official, Tokyo, February 2011.

anxiety in Japan since the early 2000s and Japan stopped yen loans to China in 2008. Even before that decision to end yen loans, Japan had already made a strategic shift in using ODA to compete with China for political influence and supply of natural resources. With China's more assertive security and economic policy since around 2008, the Japanese government has begun using ODA even more explicitly as a tool to balance against Beijing. At the same time, the two countries share some similarities in their foreign aid programs, in terms of emphasis on infrastructure projects and avoidance of interference in domestic affairs. China's current foreign aid practice has been partially influenced by their experience with the Japanese ODA projects in China in the early years. Thus, there is room for the two countries to cooperate, which could be beneficial to the two countries and recipient countries.

Chapter 10

The Trans-Pacific Partnership Agreement

No free trade agreements (FTAs) are devoid of security concerns. European integration, the golden standard for regionalism, started with a strong strategic interest in preventing repeat of wars through economic cooperation. Even when states try not to touch upon sensitive security issues in free trade negotiations, security provides the necessary stable environment for such an endeavor. And commercial liberals often argue that FTAs have a moderating effect on security tension among member states. The Trans-Pacific Partnership Agreement (TPP) is a contemporary example of a strategic economic arrangement to serve a larger purpose of keeping the United States in East Asia and a rising China in check (possibly allowed in later on American terms).

This chapter examines how Japan's approach toward this ambitious on-going regional ordering project in the context of its relations with China. It is widely recognized that cooperation between France and Germany has been central to success of European integration and an absence of similar collaboration between Beijing and Tokyo partly explains slow progress in East Asian regionalism. Through the TPP, the United States seeks to dominate in East Asian regional order with Japan's help, facing a rising China. The TPP is a strong American strategic move based on its strengths and past investment in relationships in Asia. A more confident China's own strategic confusion has contributed to America's diplomatic success in this area.

Japan–China relations experienced a serious downturn in 2010, after the Chinese fishing boat collision incident in September. The Japanese government actively sought multilateral support for its intensifying rivalry with China. The Kan Naoto government's subsequent decision to consider joining the TPP talks constituted a Japanese strategic choice for a U.S.-centered Asian international order and a clear rejection of Japan–China cooperation if that means distancing from the United States. On March 15, 2013, Prime Minister Abe declared that Japan would join the TPP negotiations. But the TPP has turned out to be far more complicated than a simple strategic game among great powers due to the nature of the TPP, the market fundamentals and the always messy domestic politics. While Japan has a strong strategic interest in strengthening its U.S. alliance, the government was unable for a long time to formally join the TPP talks and has been unable so far to strike a deal with the United States because it finds it almost impossible to balance between fierce domestic opposition and strong American pressure. And Japan can and is supporting the United States more directly in security, which ironically makes what Tokyo would view as trade concessions less necessary for alliance maintenance. Thus, while the TPP constitutes a key pillar of American strategy of rebalancing with Asia and it is stealing the show at present, its ultimate success remains uncertain although there have been clear signs since the start of 2015 that Japan and the United States might be able to strike a deal after all. The United States is likely to maintain its leadership role in Asia based on security while economic gravity steadily but surely shifts to China. Such a likely scenario does not mean victory for Beijing though since Japan and some other Asian countries are directly assisting the United States in the now higher politics of international security.

This chapter includes six sections. The first section relates the TPP question to studies of Asian regionalism. The second section discusses the strategic dimension of the TPP and what that means for students of East Asian regionalism and Sino-Japanese relations. The next three sections flesh out the tension between strategic calculations and domestic politics in the administrations of Prime Minister Kan Naoto (June 8, 2010–September 2, 2011), Prime Minister Noda Yoshihiko (September 2, 2011–December 26, 2012), and Prime Minister Abe Shinzō (December 26, 2012–present). The last section concludes the chapter.

The TPP and Asian Regionalism

Asian regionalism is a well studied subject matter, with virtually all possible analytical angles examined.[1] We see a general tendency for academic research to follow the real world developments, from networked, open regionalism to more institutionalized and competitive types at the turn of the new century (e.g. Ravenhill 2000; Stubbs 2002; Terada 2003; Munakata 2006; Aggarwal and Koo 2005).

The TPP represents a major development in Asian regionalism, introducing more powerfully the strategic and national security factor into the equation. Students of Asian regionalism in the 1990s tended to focus on economic rationale, politics, culture, and identity to explain why competing regional projects had emerged (Higgott and Stubbs 1995). Security was also understood as an underlying factor, but most often framed broadly to incorporate economic development. The security-economics nexus has been studied for the past decade and half (e.g. Harris and Mack 1997; Shirk and Twomey 1997). In fact, Ravenhill (2009), a noted economist and longtime student of Asian regionalism, has observed that East Asians have sought diplomatic and strategic gains through FTAs, resulting in limited aggregate economic benefits. In fact, awareness of the inefficiency of the "noodle bow" of FTAs is a crucial

---

[1] See for examples Garnaut tand Drysdale (1994); Katzenstein and Shiraishi (1997); Pempel (2005); Aggarwal and Urata (2006); Aggarwal and Lee (2011); Solís, Stallings and Katada (2009); Lincoln (2004); Acharya and Johnston (2007); Wigen (1999); Cho and Park (2014).

reason for broader arrangement such as the TPP (Chapling and Ravenhill 2011). Different from before, traditional security is now asserting itself in the academic discourse, reflecting sea changes in Asia (e.g. Pempel 2010; Aggarwal and Govella 2012).

China's rise has affected Japan's approach toward Asian regionalism and growing tension between the two countries both limits the prospect of Asian regionalism and creates different preferences for it, with Japan wanting more outside powers in and China wishing to start from a closer club among East Asians (Terada 2010; Chung 2013; Zhang 2014). It is recognized widely how rivalries and suspicions, particular that between China and Japan, have stunted Asian regionalism (Rozman 2004; Lee 2012). The United States has an overall role in Asian regionalism, providing a security structure to ensure prosperity from early on and now more fully engaging in regional integration projects after years of seemingly disinterest or distraction by events elsewhere in the world (e.g. Calder 2004; Rapkin 2001; Bergsten 2001; Schott 2004; Aggarwal 2012). Some analysts have highlighted America's securitization of FTAs, namely using FTAs to reward its strategic partners, particularly since the September 11, 2001 terrorist attacks (Higgott 2004a and 2004b; Sohn and Koo 2011).

While one may see the TPP project as evolving from the developments discussed so far, it is still puzzling that Japan took a long time to formally join the TPP talks and is now dragging them out with so much perceived strategic and economic advantage. This case shows that an international political economy approach focusing on domestic-international interaction remains central for studies of regional FTAs even when strategic and security factors have become far more prominent.[2] Domestic political economy still trumps. Moreover, securitization of economic organizations has its natural limits. A government may choose among different FTAs to maximize its security and economic gains, a task made difficult when geopolitics and geoeconomics do not overlap neatly. Ironically,

---

[2] For the domestic–international relations as a central concern for the field of international political economy, see a field survey article by Frieden and Martin 2002.

when security becomes really important, a country can engage it more directly rather than through economic integration.

The TPP as a Strategic Game

The TPP started as an obscure regional free trade agreement (FTA), called initially as P-4, with New Zealand, Singapore, Brunei, and Chile reaching an agreement in 2006 to remove in principle tariffs on all merchandize items within 10 years. The United States, Australia, Malaysia, Peru, and Vietnam later joined the TPP talks. Besides Japan, Canada, Mexico, and some other countries became interested as well. Starting around the same time as Japan did, Mexico and Canada accepted invitation to join the TPP talks in June 2012 and formally joined in October 2012.

The Bush administration joined the TPP negotiations in 2008, which did not attract much attention. Some Asian regionalism research projects hardly mentioned the TPP even when they included chapters on U.S. policy toward Asian regionalism. But once the Obama administration decided to treat the TPP as the central piece of its Asian economic strategy, the initiative was suddenly the hottest regional order project, a reflection of the power of the United States as the world's only superpower and its strong appeal in East Asia. When Obama visited Asia in late 2009, he indicated that the United States would restart exploratory talks on the TPP. Under U.S. leadership, the TPP was expanded to include 24 areas such as financial service, investment, the environment, labor, and government procurement in March 2010. Obama became fully committed to the TPP during the APEC summit held in Honolulu in November 2011.

America's TPP push has all the hallmarks of a U.S. strategic move, decisive, and ambitious. Secretary of State Hillary Clinton (2011) announced in a November 2011 *Foreign Policy* article that the Obama administration views "harnessing Asia's growth and dynamism" as "central to American economic and strategic interests". She touted the TPP as a crucial component of America's pivot to the Asia-Pacific. While the United States has strong self-interest in striking trade deals with a growing East Asia, it also sees itself as the guarantor and creator of strong international rules for the common good. As Clinton put it in her *Foreign Policy* article, "a TPP agreement with high standards can serve as a benchmark for future agreements — and grow to serve as a platform for broader regional interaction and eventually a free trade area of the Asia-Pacific." The United States is being strategic, utilizing its existing influence to lock in its advantage by placing itself at the center of an Asian regional order to counter what they view as Beijing's success in recent years to conclude trade agreements with other Asian nations while the United States was distracted by war on terror. More recently, in his state of the union address on January 20, 2015, President Obama made the following remarks. He was of course selling to the American public the strategic rationale for the TPP.

> "As we speak, China wants to write the rules for the world's fastest-growing region. That would put our workers and businesses at a disadvantage. Why would we let that happen? We should write those rules. We should level the playing field. That's why I'm asking both parties to give me trade promotion authority to protect American workers, with strong new trade deals from Asia to Europe that aren't just free, but fair."

To accomplish America's strategic objectives, the TPP needs to include large economies. In her *Foreign Policy* article, Secretary of State Clinton recognized China, India, and Indonesia as the emerging powers in Asia, none of which was participating in the TPP talks at that time. As the third largest economy in the world and most advanced Asian economy, Japan would thus be crucial. In fact, one concern behind America's pivot to Asia was that China had gained much ground in economic influence among America's traditional allies in Asia and may create an East Asian regional order that excludes the United States. The United States needs Japan to be on its side not only as a security ally but also as an economic partner. Thus, the office of the U.S. Trade Representative (USTR) urged Japan to participate in the TPP in September 2009 (Sakuradani 2012, 103).

The United States was concerned where Japan was headed when the Democratic Party of Japan (DPJ) won a landslide electoral victory in 2009. DPJ Prime Minister Hatoyama Yukio advocated an East Asian community, highlighting his vision in a United Nations speech on September 24. That notion did not include the United States, at least not initially. To make things worse, the DPJ government wanted to move the U.S. marine air station Futenma to at least outside Okinawa Prefecture. The United States and Japan agreed to return Futenma to Japan in April 1996 and it took ten years for the two governments to reach an agreement to move 8,000 marines and their dependents to Guam upon completion of a replacement airbase in Henoko of Nago in Okinawa by 2014 (yet to be accomplished). The Hatoyama government's position on the East Asian community and Futenma caused tension with the United States. On top of that, DPJ strongman Ozawa Ichirō, a close ally of Hatoyama, led a large delegation to China while having not visited the United States for some time. Many in the U.S. policy community felt the DPJ was dangerously turning to China, which would undercut America's strategic position in East Asia.

Tension with Washington helped mobilize the dominant pro-U.S. forces in Japanese domestic politics to attack the Hatoyama policy. The mainstream Japanese media was largely critical of Hatoyama. Hatoyama was forced to resign. The DPJ government under Kan and then Noda moved Japan's foreign policy back to focusing on a strong alliance with the United States. Washington particularly welcomed Noda's steady hand and strong support for the alliance, hoping he would stay longer to be effective.

A warmer relationship with the United States meant greater distance with China given the dominant view in Japan that it had to choose. But China helped the U.S. pivot to Asia with its own strategic confusion. Beijing did not respond quickly and positively to the Hatoyama initiative, which would have given him some benefits to show for. More broadly, China's increasingly pluralized bureaucratic decision making process under group leadership led to an expansion of "core national interests", causing conflicts with some neighboring countries. The Chinese fishing boat collision incident that occurred on September 7, 2010 seriously damaged the bilateral relationship. All these developments contributed to an emerging consensus among Japan's establishment that Japan needed to be firmly allied with the United States against a rising China.

Even though the TPP is a multilateral FTA, Japanese view it as a bilateral FTA with the United States in disguise. As it is often pointed out in Japan, the United States and Japan account for 90 percent of the total TPP economic size. The TPP is thus fundamentally about Japan–U.S. relations for Tokyo, which explains why the Japanese government has scheduled TPP decision making around Japan–U.S. summits.

It took a long time for Japan to join the TPP negotiations. Kan and Noda wanted to join the TPP and used much political capital for the initiative. But both leaders were constrained by what they could say and do. Even after Abe made the decision, the negotiations have dragged on, mainly between Japan and the United States. The Japanese government has to play a two-level game, managing a strategic triangle with the United States and China on the international level and handling a fierce clash of liberalization versus protectionism on the domestic level.

There is support from various countries around the Pacific for the U.S.-led TPP. Some countries view the TPP from a strategic angle. Vietnam in particular is moving closer to the United States in both security and economic areas based on shared concerns over China's assertiveness in the South China Sea. Vietnam was welcomed into the TPP negotiations in November 2010 (Burghardt 2012). But for some other states, the TPP gives them more free trade options, a particularly large noodle in their already overflowing spaghetti bowls of FTAs. They compete for access to the U.S. market, as always. But they are also not ignoring the growing China market. Some TPP partners have FTAs with China already although not as liberalizing and wide-ranging as the TPP. The TPP is different from a security alliance because it is far less a zero-sum game.

China is rising precisely because its growing economy is tied closely to other Asian economies. China is thus different from the Soviet Union. The United States cannot keep China out in the market place. At the same time, the United States remains important for East Asia, as a final market for much of Asian manufacturing products.

Some East Asian countries such as Singapore and South Korea have concluded FTAs with the United States. There is limit to how strategic a FTA is in contrast to a security alliance. In fact, if one concludes FTAs with virtually everyone, there is also less strategic meaning for any individual one and that country is strategic mainly in that it has chosen to open up its market for global competition.

How China responds to America's pivot or rebalancing affects the environment in which Japan decides on the TPP. The Chinese government's response has been measured even though hardliners view the U.S.-led project as revealing a strong intent to encircle China and urge stronger Chinese response. Beijing is moderate because it recognizes that the United States still has greater power and some Asian countries prefer the United States to China and that it is still desirable and possible to manage the relationship with the United States. It has thus toned down the significance of the American rebalance. At the same time, the likelihood of further friction has increased due to strong mistrust between the two countries (Lieberthal and Wang 2012).

In that context, the Chinese government has not openly criticized the TPP initiative. In fact, Beijing has shown interest in joining the negotiations from time to time. The Japanese media followed Chinese response to Japan's decision to join the TPP closely but could come up with few negative Chinese comments. Chinese President Hu Jintao expressed some understanding of Japan's decision at a press conference at the APEC summit in Hawaii on November 12, 2011. But Hu made it clear that China welcomed all channels to promote Asian regionalism. He basically stated the same position at the APEC summit in Vladivostok on September 8, 2012. For some time now, China's basic approach has been not to openly oppose the regionalism projects it does not like while actively promoting the ones it prefers (Wan 2010 and 2011). The Chinese commerce minister was quoted in Japanese media on March 7, 2012 as saying that Japan's participation in the TPP should not affect East Asian regional cooperation and expressing hope to start negotiations on a China–Japan–Republic of Korea (ROK) FTA at the trilateral summit in May 2012 (*Asahi shimbun* March 8, 2012, 6).

If one reads Chinese analysis of the TPP, one gets a mixed message. Most view the TPP without too much alarm, seeing it mainly as America's signaling rather than something that is achievable. Some even see the United States as mainly a "spoiler" in Asian regionalism (e.g. Shen 2010; Du 2011). Similarly, the Chinese analysts summarize what they have heard from their Japanese counterparts or media stories why Japan wants to join but also highlight domestic difficulties the Japanese government faces (e.g. Gao 2011; Liu 2011). Chinese thinkers worry about the TPP more in private conversations but still consider it too difficult to realize. I also argue in this chapter that the TPP will be difficult to achieve. But the Chinese analysts generally under-appreciate America's pivot and the power of institutions reflecting China's own weak institutionalization. Whether the TPP itself will be successful, the United States can make a lasting impact through institution-building in Asia. But the point here is that Chinese calculations have left room for Japan to maneuver, which ironically makes it more possible for Japan not to ignore the China market.

Different from the United States, Japan has other options for FTAs in East Asia, including the ASEAN Plus Six, the ASEAN Plus Three and the Japan–China–ROK FTA. Even strongest Japanese proponents for the TPP do not argue to exclude China in a strict sense. Japanese cannot exclude China for the simple fact that China is Japan's largest trading partner and is growing. Moreover, when Japanese debate over the TPP, particularly from the business side, they focus on South Korea rather than China. South Korea has become increasingly competitive and has been pro-active and achieved FTAs with major economies in the world, which is deeply threatening to Japan as an export-oriented trading state. It is South Korea rather than China that competes with Japan head on in the automobile and home electronics sectors.

Japan is being strategic mainly in sequencing of various FTA schemes and degree of efforts put into them. Sequencing matters because it is believed that whichever scheme is established first decides on the rules for Asian regional cooperation and gives the creators the founder advantages. Some Japanese proponents of the

TPP essentially want to participate in rulemaking with the United States and then possibly include China in a more entrenched institutional structure. It makes sense for declining states to lock in institutionally what is currently advantageous to them. But Japan's government is constrained in policy making and implementation.

Prime Minister Kan's TPP Policy

Shortly after forming his new cabinet on September 17, 2010, Prime Minister Kan announced his intention for Japan to join the TPP in his policy speech on October 1. He was aiming to make it formal when hosting the APEC meeting in Yokohama on November 13–14. Kan himself did not focus on the China factor. He called participation in FTAs such as the TPP as Japan's third opening, after the Meiji Restoration and the American Occupation. At the same time, Japan's rivalry with China played a part in the government thinking about the TPP. Japanese commentators generally viewed the DPJ government's decision in the context of growing tension with China. Some Japanese political leaders said as much. Genba Kōichirō (2010), then state minister for national policy and later foreign minister, argued that Japan's declining economy was a crucial reason why the country was facing territorial disputes with Russia and China. Japan needed to strengthen its economic and diplomatic power, with the TPP as a crucial pathway.

For many Japanese, the TPP represented a different path from Hatoyama's East Asian community concept. Yachi (2011a), the administrative vice foreign minister in 2005–2008, saw Japan joining the TPP as a breakthrough path to reviving Japan that had been in decline since the early 1990s. The TPP would benefit Japan economically. Japan could also participate in rulemaking for China to abide by if it wants to join. Yachi (2011b), who later became Abe's key foreign policy advisor, made it even more explicit in a different paper that the TPP is a strategic necessity for Japan. Japan's loss in World War II shows that Japan alone cannot dominate in East Asia and needs to put itself firmly in the Western camp that has facilitated Japan's post-war economic miracle. Japan needs to abandon the illusion of Asianism given the geopolitical reality of a rising China. As a retired diplomat at the time, Yachi could say what serving officials cannot express openly.

The Kan government announced a week before the APEC summit in Yokohama in November 2010 that it needed to prepare the domestic environment for participating and would postpone the participation decision to mid 2011. Kan could not deliver on formal entry in the TPP talks mainly due to domestic opposition that was immediate and intense.[3] As usual, the Central Union of Agricultural Cooperatives (JA) and their politician supporters in both the LDP and the DPJ rose against the TPP, mobilized through study groups, gathering and protests. On October 21, 110 DPJ Diet members held an anti-TPP study group led by Hatoyama. Hatoyama was allied with Ozawa whose largest faction in the DPJ was opposed to the TPP. In fact, the Kan cabinet was divided over the TPP. While Foreign Minister Maehara Seiji was actively supportive, Agriculture, Forestry and Fisheries (MAFF) Minister Kano Michihiko was vehemently opposed. Even Economy, Trade and Industry (METI) Minister Ōhata Akihiro was cautious. The DPJ's small coalition party Kokumin Shinto (People's New Party) was also opposed to the TPP. The largest opposition party Liberal Democratic Party (LDP) was divided over the TPP and was in no hurry to make up its mind. The Japanese local governments were largely opposed to the TPP. By January 2011, 70 percent of the prefectural and major city assemblies had adopted statements critical of the TPP (*Japan Times* 2011b).

Not surprisingly, Nippon Keidanren (the Japan Business Federation) supported the TPP strongly and pressured the government to announce participation in the TPP talks at the APEC meeting. On November 1, 2010, the Keidanren and two other major business associations, the Japan Association of Corporate Executives and the Japan Chamber of Commerce and Industry, held a joint

---

[3] As an indication of strong public interest, there were volumes of books criticizing TPP and a smaller number of books supporting it (e.g. Nakano 2011; Hiromiya and Aoki 2011; Watanabe 2011). Journal articles also carry much writing on the TPP debates.

gathering to urge the Japanese government to join the TPP talks. The Japanese business community did not support the TPP exclusively. They were also supportive of other FTA deals, including ones involving China. In fact, some strong supporters for the TPP hoped to promote liberalization of Japanese economy to make it more competitive rather than for an impossible strategy of encircling China (Hasegawa 2012). Furthermore, the threat for the Japanese business community came mainly from South Korea that competes directly with Japan in the automobile and home electronics sectors.

In such a complex domestic political economy, those who supported the TPP were not necessarily anti-China. METI had been interested in free trade deals of all kinds.[4] Kaieda Banri who became METI minister partly because of his enthusiasm for the TPP was also widely viewed as a moderate on China. Conversely, a strong critic of China, Kobayashi Yoshinori (2012) published a highly critical cartoon book against the TPP, seeing it as surrendering to the United States and inevitably enlarging the wealth gap and increasing poverty in Japan. After all, Japan's political economy challenge for regionalism preceded China's rise and continues to be important.

The TPP is ambitious institutionally as intended by the United States to set the standard for other FTAs in the Asia-Pacific. It involves a high degree of liberalization and covers so much more than merchandize trade. The demanding nature of the TPP makes it too advanced for the stage of development in Asia (Gresser 2012).

Supporters for free trade in Japan believed that Japan needed to open its door wider to the international community. But is the TPP the right way to do it? By January 2011, the Japanese Foreign Ministry realized that since the TPP is led by the United States, the U.S. standards for FTAs would apply, which means that the TPP would have a minimal liberalization degree of 96 percent. By contrast, Japan's bilateral economic partnership agreements (EPAs) had liberalization degree ranging from 80 to 86 percent. And the TPP would not exempt agricultural products (*Asahi shimbun* January 28, 2011, 6).

---

[4] Interview with a senior METI official dealing with China. Tokyo, January 2012.

How much can Japan gain from the TPP? Three government estimates emerged, respectively by METI, MAFF and the Cabinet Office. The Cabinet Office announced on October 22, 2010 that Japan's membership in the TPP that includes the agricultural sector would see an annual increase of ¥2.5–3.4 trillion to its GDP, representing 0.48–0.64 GDP annual growth. METI estimated that if its main competitor South Korea establishes FTAs with the United States, the European Union and China but Japan does not, Japan would see a decrease of ¥8.6 trillion in exports and ¥20.7 trillion in production a year, focusing on the automobile and home electronics sectors. As the METI assumption reveals, South Korea loomed large as the main economic reason for Japan to join the TPP. Based on different assumptions, MAFF calculated in 2007 that if tariffs on agricultural products are completely removed, Japan would lose ¥3.6 trillion or 40 percent of its agricultural production. The ministry announced on October 22, 2010 that Japan would lose ¥4.1 trillion in agricultural production if it joins the TPP. The Japanese government eventually decided that the Cabinet Office estimate would be the official one.[5]

Japan could gain more from a regional free trade agreement that includes China. China was now Japan's largest trading partner and it was actually growing. Moreover, the United States was seeking to export out of its economic problems and China was slowly adjusting its growth strategy to a more balanced one with greater import and domestic consumption. There was simply more room to increase export to China than to the United States at this point. According to the estimates of the Research Institute of Economy, Trade and Industry (RIETI), an independent entity funded mainly by METI, Japan would gain more from any FTA that involves China than from the TPP that does not include China. Japan would see its real GDP increase by 0.66 percent 10 years after entering a bilateral FTA with China, 0.74 percent from a trilateral FTA with China and

---

⁵ Interview with a senior METI official, Tokyo, January 2012. For the cabinet office calculation as well as the METI and MAFF estimates, see Japan Prime Minister's Cabinet Office 2010.

South Korea, and 1.1 percent from the ASEAN Plus Six. By contrast, Japan would gain 0.54 percent from the TPP that does not include China (*Asahi shimbun* May 13, 2012, 3). And Japanese recognized increasingly that the hurdles to the TPP are high while those to the China-included FTAs are low.

On January 4, 2011, Kan reiterated his intent to reach a decision on the TPP by June. Japan and the United States held their first discussion on the TPP in mid January. The U.S. trade officials told the Japanese that the TPP has higher goals than those in their past trade agreements (*Japan Times* 2011c). By late February, the Kan government's push for the TPP was losing momentum. On March 11, *Japan Times* reported that "the Kan administration is facing head winds in pushing for joining negotiations for the Trans-Pacific Partnership as concerns spread among the public that participation in the free-trade pact would adversely affect not only the farm sector but other, wide-reaching areas as well" (Tanaka 2011). *Asahi shimbun* carried a lengthy debate on the same day among Diet members on both sides of the TPP issue from both the DPJ and LDP. That afternoon, the triple disasters of earthquake, tsunami, and Fukushima nuclear accident would affect Japan profoundly and push back other issues including the TPP. Understandably, the Kan cabinet decided on May 17 that a TPP decision would now be postponed.

Prime Minister Noda's TPP Policy

Kan was forced to resign on August 26. Three days later Noda won a tough party election as a dark horse. The Kano faction's support was crucial for Noda's win. As a reward, Kano was kept as the farm minister. Within days, Kano told journalists that the government should be cautious on participating in the TPP. But Noda told Obama in their summit on September 21 that he would seek an early conclusion on the TPP.

Noda was a strong supporter of the alliance with the United States. He hoped to make a favorable TPP decision when meeting Obama at the APEC meeting in Hawaii in November 2011, which would send a signal of Japan treating its alliance with the United

States as central. Noda calculated that he needed to deliver on TPP participation to prevent a worsening of Japan–U.S. relations since he could not move on the Futenma issue. Okinawan opposition to the Futenma move had stiffened.

However, similar to Kan a year earlier, Noda could not realize his plan. Noda announced on November 11 that Japan would participate in talks toward deciding to join or not. The key reason for Noda's hesitation was again domestic opposition, which had become stronger over time. The Japanese opponents watched the government decision making process closely and were extremely motivated to thwart the government plan. They often forced Diet members to express public opposition to the trade accord and threatened negative electoral consequences for those supporting the TPP. JA (Central Union of Agricultural Cooperatives), for example, put pressure on Diet members to attend anti-TPP rallies. According to their count prior to Noda's decision, JA claimed that at least 350 of the 722 Diet members supported their petition not to join the TPP (*Japan Times* 2011d).

Since the TPP is broader than a typical FTA, it also invites stronger pushback. The Japan Medical Association (JMA) came out strongly against the TPP and was also critical of the Noda government in fall 2011. Other medical associations such as those for dentists, pharmacists, and nurses were also opposed to the TPP.

Opposition to Noda's plan to move forward with the TPP was intense. On October 21, about 110 Diet members participated in an anti-TPP rally. They were members of a group of more than 200 Diet members from the DPJ, its junior coalition partner Kokumin Shinto and the Social Democratic Party, led by former farm minister Yamada Masahiko. Yamada was a member of the powerful Ozawa faction opposed to the TPP. Noda had introduced a system for the DPJ to review policy. The DPJ's project team on economic cooperation recommended caution for joining the TPP. While not taking a clear position before, the LDP decided by early November 2011 to oppose an early decision on the TPP based on the argument that Noda had not adequately explained his TPP policy. The LDP was more interested in dethroning the DPJ than supporting DPJ policies even if they might have similar policy preferences.

Similar to the LDP, the third largest political party New Komeito was also divided. On October 24, 2011, JA counted over 60 percent of Komeito Diet members and over 80 percent of LDP members as opposed to the TPP (*Asahi shimbun* October 25, 2011, 4). A few days later New Komeito announced its decision to oppose the TPP based on concern that the agreement would put pressure on agriculture and industry and that the Noda government had not explained its TPP policy clearly.

The Japanese public was divided evenly. A poll showed that 38.7 percent supported the TPP while 36.1 percent opposed. It also showed that 78.1 percent of the polled believed that the government had not explained sufficiently the effect of trade negotiations (*Japan Times* 2011e). A poll conducted before Noda's decision in November 2011 showed that only six of the 47 prefectural governors favored the TPP while 14 were opposed. The remaining 27 governors were neutral (*Japan Times* 2011f).

Noda then began thinking about formally joining the TPP talks during his visit to the United States on April 30, 2012. Yet again, Noda decided to postpone decision to join the TPP because his policy to raise consumption tax hike and join the TPP encountered stiff resistance even from within the DPJ and preliminary talks with the United States had turned out to be difficult.

Noda faced strong opposition from the opposition parties. Playing electoral politics, the LDP expressed opposition to complete removal of tariffs on March 7. The LDP's draft election manifesto released on April 9 said the party would oppose the TPP if Japan has to remove "sacred tariffs" as a precondition for joining it, which of course refers to protection of the agricultural sector. With Noda's later effort to push for consumption tax increase and an electoral reform that would put it at a disadvantage, New Komeito was increasingly anti-DPJ.

Noda also faced strong dissent within the DPJ. The opposition within the project team argued strongly that the government needed the party understanding before making its final decision on the TPP even though Maehara, the pro-TPP party policy chief, argued that such a step was not necessary. Even members of the Noda cabinet remained cautious over the TPP. The powerful Ozawa group was firmly against the TPP. The situation became tougher for Noda when Ozawa was acquitted by the Tokyo District Court on April 26 of political fund conspiracy. Similar to Kan, Noda had used Ozawa's indictment as an opportunity to purge his influence within the DPJ. Ozawa was expected to be reinstated for his DPJ party membership and mount a leadership challenge to Noda at the DPJ presidential election scheduled for September.

Besides the TPP, Noda announced in his policy speech at the Diet on October 28 that he wanted a consumption tax increase. He staked his own political life on the issue. There was expectation among the Japanese observers that the Noda administration could be doomed over consumption tax hike and the TPP, both highly controversial in domestic politics. A Kyodo News poll right before Noda's visit to Washington showed that the Noda cabinet's popularity rating had fallen to a record low of 26.4 percent (*Japan Times* 2012d). While having a similar policy preference, the LDP opposed consumption tax hike to force an election to win back parliamentary control. The Ozawa faction was strongly opposed to consumption tax increase on the ground that it violated the DPJ manifesto. To make life tougher, Noda also faced strong resistance to restarting the Oi nuclear power plant in Fukui Prefecture. METI Minister Edano Yukio announced on April 9 that the Oi plant was ready to restart, touching off a political storm.

Noda now focused more on consumption tax hike than the TPP. By early 2012, the Japanese public interest was also far more focused on consumption tax than the TPP. The TPP remained on the Noda government agenda since the Japanese bureaucrats now engaged in preliminary diplomatic talks. But the Noda government faced challenges on that front as well, part of the reason for postponing a final decision until much later. With tenacity rare among current Japanese leaders and shrew maneuvering to build a pro-tax coalition with the heads of the LDP and the New Komeito, Noda won his tax increase on August 10, 2012. Brutalized by the consumption tax fight and suffering defection of Ozawa and dozens of other Diet members, Noda was in no position to start another fight right before the DPJ presidential election scheduled for September. Thus, he let the world know at the APEC summit in Vladivostok on September 8 that he would postpone Japan's formal participation in the TPP talks.

Whether Japan could join the TPP also depended on the consent from the existing nine TPP member states. Japan engaged in preliminary talks in 2012. With its final round of preliminary talks ending on February 23, only six countries approved Japan's participation in formal TPP talks. Australia did not declare support for Japan's participation. Australia had been negotiating with Japan for the past five years over a bilateral FTA. Canberra wanted Japan to remove tariffs on beef, dairy products, and sugar. New Zealand also focused on increasing agricultural exports to Japan.

As the Japanese had recognized, the United States was the biggest obstacle to Japan's TPP membership. Unlike with the other countries, Japan engaged in two rounds of preliminary talks with the United States. On February 21–22, Japan and the United States agreed to continue talks scheduled for March and April. U.S. Trade Representative Ron Kirk told the Senate Finance Committee on March 8 that Japan must address all the American concerns and put everything on the table. In fact, he said that the United States would press Japan to "fully open their market and meet their international obligations with respect to opening their agriculture and on insurance" whether Japan joins the TPP or not. The United States intended to make as much progress in negotiations as possible before new participants complicate things. No decision on Japan's formal participation in negotiations would be made before September (*Japan Times* 2012e). With pressure from the business community, the U.S. government paid particular attention to postal service, automobile and agriculture. As President Obama was facing a tough re-election year, he was unwilling to appear compromising to Japan over trade issues. Indeed, Obama raised the issues of automobile, insurance, and beef in his April 30 summit with Noda.

It became increasingly clear by early 2012 that Japan could not participate in rulemaking as advocates argued. A DPJ delegation visiting the USTR in early April 2012 walked away with a clear message from the U.S. officials that even if Japan participates, it would have no voice over the rules that had already been made and that the U.S. would treat automobile, beef, and insurance are important topics. By mid May the USTR had prepared a list of ten non-tariff auto barriers for negotiations with Japan. On September 9, 2012, the American Automotive Policy Council (AAPC) that represents Chrysler, Ford and General Motor called on the government to conclude the TPP without Japan on the ground that the Japanese government had used currency manipulation to subsidize the Japanese auto industry (*Asahi shimbun* online September 10, 2012).

Opponents to the TPP in Japan sometimes argued that the TPP is simply a most recent U.S. attempt to spread its institutions to the Asia Pacific and to facilitate its firms in the Japanese and Asian market (e.g. Sakuradani 2012). The TPP covers 24 areas such as medical care, financial service, and government procurement. Thus, those who are familiar with the United States know that Japan's institutions have to be "Americanized" to a large extent to join the TPP. For example, Sakakibara Eisuke (2012, 204), a former senior Ministry of Finance official with extensive exchange with American officials, argued that the TPP would Americanize the Japanese system because Japan would have to allow mixed medical care and remove preferences for local construction companies.

Japan's domestic political economy indeed came into direct conflict with the United States over the TPP. After the DPJ, the LDP, and New Komeito submitted a postal privatization amendment bill to roll back Koizumi's privatization postal reform, USTR Carter told Genba on April 10 that the U.S. insurance industry and Congress were strongly concerned about the amendment bill, seeing it as giving the two postal financial institutions advantages that make it impossible to compete in the Japanese market. A few hours later, the bill cleared the Diet postal reform special committee. It was now clearly understood in Japan that the postal reform bill would impede Japan's participation in the TPP. In fact, the U.S. officials told some visiting DPJ Diet members that Japan needed to address American concerns before joining TPP talks. But the bill became law on April 27. Domestic politics trumped diplomacy. With a nod to American concerns, The Japan Post Insurance Co. announced on May 8 that it would delay entry into the cancer insurance field in which the American insurance firms had a 70 percent share of the Japan market.

Regardless of Japan's participation, TPP negotiations would be difficult. There was much suggestion in the Japanese media why Japan needed to get on the TPP bus because it was believed that Obama was aiming at concluding the negotiation by the APEC meeting to be held in Hawaii in November 2011. That was too optimistic. One difficulty was that the United States wanted a level playing field for state and private firms, which received negative reaction from Vietnam and Malaysia. Indeed, the nine TPP negotiating countries decided at the APEC summit in Vladivostok in early September 2012 that they would not seek to conclude the TPP negotiations by the end of the year due to major differences among the member countries.

Common security concerns have never been sufficient for achieving FTAs. It should not surprise people then that Japan had wandering eyes. After the March 11 disaster, Chinese Premier Wen Jiabao and South Korean President Lee Myung-bak came to Japan and gave a boost to trilateral cooperation. When Noda visited China at the end of 2011, he agreed with Chinese President Hu Jintao to make a serious effort to achieve a Japan–China–ROK investment agreement and then an early start of a trilateral FTA. At their meeting held in Ningbo, China on April 8, 2012, the foreign ministers from the three countries confirmed that their governments were now ready to sign the investment agreement at the May summit.

But the South Korean government hesitated to set a starting date for the trilateral FTA negotiations due to their concern about

Japanese industrial products pressuring Korean firms.[6] As a result, the Japanese government began considering a bilateral FTA with China if Seoul formally opposed to the trilateral FTA at the May summit. On May 2 China and South Korea decided to launch FTA negotiations, to formally start on May 14. Seoul was interested in FTA with China as its largest trading partner and the only country with leverage on North Korea.[7] If a FTA with China is concluded, Korea would become a hub for virtually all major economies in the world. Seoul was interested in concluding a FTA with China before a trilateral FTA. Concerned with Japan's trade surplus, non-trade barriers and direct competition in strategic sectors, Seoul made no moves on its stalled bilateral FTA with Japan. As for China, progress in FTA negotiations with South Korea would also put pressure on Japan to move faster. But Beijing was interested in starting the trilateral talks for political reasons. In the end, the trilateral summit held in Beijing on May 13 signed the trilateral investment agreement as expected and agreed to start FTA negotiations by the end of year. The Chinese and Japanese persuaded the Koreans to go along with the plan. China and Japan had hoped to launch the negotiations immediately. South Korea's disinterest remained a main hurdle for realizing the trilateral FTA.

Japan and China engaged in more cooperation in the financial area than in their overall bilateral relations. China, Japan, and South Korea agreed to purchase each other's national bonds at a trilateral finance minister meeting held on May 3, 2012 on the side of the ASEAN Plus Three finance minister and central banker meeting held in Manila. That meeting also doubled the currency swap funds available for the Chiang Mai Initiative to $240 billion and to strengthen institutionally the initiative.

Japan remained interested in FTAs involving China because those who were familiar with the business issues in Japan knew that

---

[6]A senior METI official characterized South Korea as focusing on relative gains from its self image of a small country between two great powers and moving in any direction unpredictably. Interview. Tokyo, January 2012.

[7]Talk with a Korean specialist on Asian regionalism, Seoul, March 16, 2012.

Japan needed to put some of its eggs in the China basket, which was more important than the U.S. basket in economic terms at this point. Niwa Uichirō (2012, 49), the business man-turned Japanese ambassador to China, pointed out in an interview in early 2012 that China's economic growth was Japan's biggest chance since the combined trade volumes of China and Japan was bigger than that of the United States and the TPP would fail if China did not join in ten years.

While there was much discussion of the China risk shortly after the Chinese fishing boat collision incident and much excitement about alternative places such as Vietnam and Myanmar, the Japanese business news still revealed a strong interest in the China market. The key sectors supporting the TPP were Japan's automobile and home electronics sectors. But they were not shunning the China market. The chiefs of the Japanese automobile firms such as Toyota Motor Corp. President Toyota Akio flocked to the Auto China 2012 show in April 2012 and there was regret that the Japanese had come to the China market late compared to the American, European, and South Korean competitors. China had become the world largest automobile market. It was recognized in Japan that China that had been hesitant about the investment agreement showed more flexibility with Japan's intention to join the TPP.

In another move, Japan stated at the Japan–ASEAN economic minister meeting held in Tokyo on April 28, 2012, right before the Noda–Obama summit, that it was interested in moving the ASEAN Plus Six FTA forward. The Japanese government would follow a timetable: Consultations with the ASEAN Plus Six senior officials in May, prepare for negotiations at the ASEAN Plus Six economic minister meeting in August and reach an agreement to start negotiations at the East Asia Summit in November. METI officials were quoted in media as reasoning that when Japan moves on the TPP, the Japan–European Union FTA, the Japan–China–Korea FTA and, the ASEAN

Plus Six FTA in parallel, progress in one would put pressure on others, which would put Japan in a favorable position.[8] Japan was indeed leveraging its unique position as a major economic player in both the U.S.-centered TPP and Asian regional projects. In his talk with Obama, Noda characterized the TPP as one of the paths toward a broader Free Trade Area of the Asia-Pacific (FTAAP). Noda indicated again at the APEC summit in Vladivostok on September 8, 2012 that Japan wanted to pursue the TPP, the Japan–China–South Korea FTA and ASEAN-centered broad FTAs in parallel. However, to take advantage of that position, Japan needed domestic adjustment, which is lacking. No wonder Japan's main business newspaper *Nihon keizai shimbun* noted the day after the Japan–China–Korea summit on May 13 that with Korea going over Japan to start a bilateral FTA with China Japan may lose on both fronts.

On August 3, 2012, Noda expressed caution about Japan's early participation in the TPP negotiations. But by the end of August, Noda told the Diet it was in Japan's national interest to join the TPP negotiations and he subsequently indicated that the TPP would be on the DPJ's electoral platform. On November 16, Noda dissolved the Diet's lower house. The TPP became an electoral issue. Noda pushed for Japan's participation. LDP's president Abe argued that he would make a decision based on whether removal of the protection of sacred areas would be a precondition for joining the negotiations. As discussed earlier, the LDP had expressed reservation about the TPP. The other party leaders had different views about the wisdom of TPP membership.

Prime Minister Abe's TPP Policy

Abe led the LDP to a landslide victory in the December election. It was widely believed by observers and politicians alike that the Japanese voters had voted against the DPJ rather than for the LDP.

---

[8] *Asahi shimbun*, April 29, 2012, 3. As a senior METI official told me, METI was interested in pushing for all free trade deals to maximize Japan's economic interests. Interview, Tokyo, January 2012.

Nevertheless, a victory was a victory. Abe was determined to provide decisive leadership that the Japanese citizens were yearning for. He promised economic reforms and a tougher stand on China. A TPP membership would facilitate economic structural reforms and strengthen Japan's position in the Asia-Pacific. Therefore, even though Abe had not sounded enthusiastic before the LDP came back to power, as prime minister he moved fast on the TPP front. He started the consultation process almost immediately. By late February 2013, the ruling LDP party decided to entrust Abe with the TPP decision. On February 22, Abe and Obama met in the White House and announced a joint statement that Japan did not have to commit to a promise to remove all tariffs before joining the negotiations. Despite resistance, Abe announced on March 15 that Japan would join the TPP negotiations. Abe surely took far less time than the DPJ prime ministers over the TPP issue.

The LDP prides itself as a guardian of the Japan–U.S. alliance and blames the DPJ for a worsening tie with Washington. The TPP is a crucial component in the Japan–U.S. strategic relationship. At the same time, the LDP has also been tough in trade negotiations with the United States. One could thus predict that Japan's participation would also complicate the TPP negotiations and the Japanese would push hard for what they view as Japan's national interests. The Abe government formed a strong TPP negotiation team. Japan was prepared to negotiate tough. Moreover, unlike the previous LDP administrations, the Abe administration is seeking direct security cooperation with the United States, which ironically makes it less necessary to make what Japan views as concessions on the economic front as a side payment for U.S. military protection. And Japan sees a rising nationalist tide. Conservative Japanese politicians may recognize the need for U.S. security cooperation, but they have pride in their own country. As a case in point, Japan's lead negotiator Amari Akira was quoted with approval in the conservative *Sankei shimbun* as angrily telling the American negotiator Michael Froman that "Japan is not a subordinate to the United States!" in a tense exchange (*Sankei shimbun* online December 23, 2014).

With several rounds of tough negotiations and missed deadlines, the Japan–U.S. negotiations continue. Japan wants to protect its sacred areas as much as possible and presses the United States to make concessions. An argument one often hears from the Japanese is that the United States should be more flexible to make the TPP a reality to prevent China from forming a China-centered East Asian international order. For obvious domestic reasons, the Obama administration is also negotiating hard. With the Republican victory in the midterm election in November 2014, the Japanese government hopes that a more free-trade friendly Republican Congress might facilitate the TPP negotiations.

The TPP faces a tough situation in the United States. The Democrats have been more suspicious of new multilateral FTAs. The Republic victory in the midterm election in November 2014 could indeed pave the way for the United States to move forward on the TPP. Obama needs the fast track authorization. But the opposition remains strong. Sen. Elizabeth Warren, for example, sent a letter, co-signed by two other Democratic senators, to the USTR expressing concern that the TPP might erode U.S. financial regulations and the ability to protect the American economy (Nakamura 2014a). The midterm electoral defeat ironically energized the Obama administration to take more decisive actions in foreign policy. By Christmas time, Obama was reported as, preparing for an all-out push for the conclusion of the TPP, counting on Republican support (Nakamura 2014b). Obama apparently sees the TPP as his legacy. As discussed earlier, he urged Congress to pass legislation on fast track authority to facilitate FTA negotiations such as the TPP.

Calling a surprising general election on December 14, 2014, Abe won a re-election that potentially could give him four years as prime minister and therefore make him one of the longest-serving prime ministers since the end of the war. Abe made a calculated political gamble given the economic challenges he was facing and declining popularity. His gamble paid well handsomely. Of the things he promised to do was speedy conclusion of the TPP negotiations. The Abe government has indeed made greater efforts since the start of 2015, reportedly making concessions over beef, pork, and rice and weakening JA's power to introduce some needed reform in the agricultural sector.

The Chinese government has become even more active in forming regional organizations on its own term. While the TPP negotiations had stalled, China presented the FTAAP proposal and concluded the China–South Korea FTA and the China–Australia FTA in principle during the APEC summit in Beijing and after the G-20 summit in Australia. Beijing had also established development banks such as the Shanghai Cooperation Organization Development Bank and the Asian Infrastructure Investment Bank (AIIB). A BRICS (Brazil, Russia, India, China, and South Africa) Development Bank is also being created. Thus, the Japanese government has become even more alarmed about China's growing influence than before.[9] Since the start of the New Year, there have been positive movements signaling that the two sides might indeed be pushing for conclusion of the TPP in the first half of 2015. It is recognized that there is not much time left with the American presidential election and the Japanese senate election in 2016 (*Nikkei shimbun* online January 16, 2015). *Asahi shimbun* (online February 10, 2015) quoted a senior American TPP negotiator as saying that an agreement was near. Abe himself considered the TPP negotiations entering their final stage at his policy speech given at Diet on February 12, 2015.

Conclusion

The TPP is strategic in the sense that the United States as the lead country has a clear strategic vision to structure East Asian international relations on the economic front to complement its extensive alliances. Some other TPP member countries are also interested in keeping the United States in East Asia to balance against a rising China. Similarly, concern about Beijing's strategic intention toward Japan contributed to the Japanese government's decision to consider

---

[9]The American policy community also sees the Chinese creating rival institutions but they are generally more confident and accommodating than the Japanese. See for example Frost 2014.

joining the TPP. Some in Japan have thought strategically. However, a trade deal has to stand on its own for cost-benefit merits. Strategic thinking underlying the TPP has been insufficient so far to offset domestic political economy calculations in Japan's case. Japan's divided TPP politics is fully predictable. Moreover, Japan may utilize its unique position between Asia and the West to great advantage. Japan is at the same time cooperating directly with the United States in the security realm, which puts far great pressure on Beijing's regional foreign policy. In conclusion, the TPP case shows that an international political economy approach toward regional FTAs remains sound even when a regional integration project becomes more strategic.

Bibliography

Abe, Shinzō (2006), *Utsukushii Kuni E* [*Toward a Beautiful Country*], Tokyo: Bungei shunjū.

Acharya, Amitav and Alastair Iain Johnston, eds. (2007), *Crafting Cooperation: Regional International Institutions in Comparative Perspective*, New York: Cambridge University Press.

Aggarwal, Vinod K. (2012), "Linking Traditional and Human Security to Trade: The U.S. Approach," in Vinod K. Aggarwal and Kristi Govella, eds., *Linking Trade and Security: Evolving Institutions and Strategies in Asia, Europe and the United States*, New York: Springer, 1–22.

Aggarwal, Vinod K. and Kristi Govella, eds. (2012), *Linking Trade and Security: Evolving Institutions and Strategies in Asia, Europe and the United States*, New York: Springer.

Aggarwal, Vinod K. and Mingyo Koo (2005), "Beyond Network Power? The Dynamics of Formal Economic Integration in Northeast Asia," *The Pacific Review* 18 (2), 189–216.

Aggarwal, Vinod K. and Seungjoo Lee, eds. (2011), *Trade Policy in the Asia-Pacific: The Role of Ideas, Interests, and Domestic Institutions*, New York: Springer.

Aggarwal, Vinod K. and Shujiro Urata, eds. (2006), *Bilateral Trade Agreements in the Asia-Pacific: Origins, Evolution, and Implications*, London: Routledge.

Amako, Satoshi (2003), *Tōshindai No Chūgoku* [*China that is the Same Size*], Tokyo: Keisōshobō.

Andrade, Tonio (2005), "Pirates, Pelts, and Promises: The Sino-Dutch Colony of Seventeenth-Century Taiwan and the Aboriginal Village of Favorolang," *The Journal of Asian Studies* 64 (2), 295–321.

Araki, Mitsuya (2012), "Sangiin ODA Tokubetsu Iinkai De No Ronten" [The Points Made at the Senate Oda Special Committee], *Kokusai Kaihatsu Jannaru* [*International Development Journal*] April, 6–7.

Arase, David (1995), *Buying Power: The Political Economy of Japan's Foreign Aid*, Boulder, CO: Lynne Rienner Publishers.

Armitage, Richard L. and Joseph S. Nye (2007), "The U.S.–Japan Alliance: Getting Asia Right through 2020," Center for Strategic and International Studies Report, available online at http://csis.org/files/media/csis/pubs/070216_asia2020.pdf.

Armstrong, Shiro P. (2012), "The Politics of Japan–China Trade and the Role of the World Trade System," *The World Economy* 35 (9), 1102–1120.

Asahi shimbun (2004), "China Syndrome: Tensions Rise," December 29.

Asō, Tarō (2007a), *Jiyū to Hanei No Ko* [*Arc of Freedom and Prosperity*], Tokyo: Gentosha.

Asō, Tarō (2007b), *Totetsumonai Nihon* [*Tremendous Japan*], Tokyo: Shinchosha.

Authers, John (2006), "Making Good Again: German Compensation for Forced and Slave Laborers," in Pablo De Greiff, ed., *The Handbook of Reparations*, New York: Oxford University Press, 420–448.

Baerwald, Hans H. (1977), "The Diet and Foreign Policy," in Robert A. Scalapino, ed., *The Foreign Policy of Modern Japan*, Berkeley: University of California Press, 37–54.

Befu, Harumi, ed. (1993), *Cultural Nationalism in East Asia: Representation and Identity*, Berkeley: Institute of East Asian Studies, University of California.

Bergsten, C. Fred (2001), "America's Two-Front Economic Conflict," *Foreign Affairs* 80 (2), 16–27.

Blaise, Séverine (2005), "On the Link between Japanese ODA and FDI in China: A Microeconomic Evaluation Using Conditional Logit Analysis," *Applied Economics* 37 (1), 51–55.

Bradsher, Keith (2010), "In Dispute, China Blocks Rare Earth Exports to Japan," *New York Times*, September 23, B1.

Brautigam, Deborah (2009), *The Dragon's Gift: The Real Story of China in Africa*, New York: Oxford University.

Brysk, Alison, ed. (2002), *Globalization and Human Rights*, Berkeley: University of California Press.

Burghardt, Raymond (2012), "U.S.–Vietnam: New Strategic Partners Begin Tough Trade Talks," *Asia Pacific Bulletin* 153, February 29.

Cai, Liang (2011), "Houriyuan Daikuan Shidai Riben Duihua ODA De Tezheng Yingxiang Ji Zoushi" [The Characteristics, Impact and Trends of Japan's ODA to China in the Post Yen Credit Era], *Guoji Luntan* [*International Forum*] 13 (5), 31–37.

Calder, Kent E. (2004), "Securing Security through Prosperity: The San Francisco System in Comparative Perspective," *The Pacific Review* 17 (1), 135–157.

Chao, Chien-min and Ho Szu-shen (2004), "Riben Waijiao Zhong Youguan Zhongguo Huo Meiguo Youxian Zhi Zhenglun" [Japanese Debate Over Whether China Or The United States Should Take Priority], *Wenti Yu Yanjiu* [*Issues and Studies*] 43 (1), 83–104.

Chapling, Ann and John Ravenhill (2011), "Multilarising Regionalism: What Role for the Trans-Pacific Partnership Agreement?" *Pacific Review* 24 (5), 553–575.

Chen, Liu (2014), "Lun Woguo Fayuan Duiri Minjian Suopei De Guanxiaquan" [Our Country Courts' Jurisdiction over Private Suits for Compensation against Japan], *Zhishi jingji* [*Knowledge economy*] 10, 29.

Chin, Chōhin (Chen Zhao-bin) (2000), *Sengo Nihon No Chūgoku Seisaku: 1950-Nendai Higashi Ajia Kokusai Seiji No Bunmyaku* [*Japan's Postwar China Policy: The Context of East Asian International Politics in the 1950sw*], Tokyo: Tokyo Daigaku shuppankai.

China Customs (2015), January 13, available online at http://www.customs.gov.cn/publish/portal0/tab49666/ (accessed January 13, 2015).

China State Council Information Office (2012), "Zhongguo De Xitu Yu Zhengce" [China's Rare Earth Situation and Policy], June 20, available online at http://finance.chinanews.com/cj/2012/06-20/3975858.shtml (accessed June 20, 2012).

Chinese Foreign Ministry (2002), May 8, available online at http://www.fmprc.gov.cn/mfa_eng/wjb_663304/zzjg_663340/yzs_663350/gjlb_663354/2721_663446/2722_663448/t15974.shtml (accessed February 13, 2007).

Chinese Ministry of Foreign Economics and Trade (1985), *Zhongguo Duiwai Jingji Jishu Yuanzhu* [*China's Foreign Economic and Technical Assistance*], internal publication, Beijing: Zhongguo duiwai jingji maoyu chubanshe.

Cho, IL Hyun and Seo Hyun Park (2014), "Domestic Legitimacy Politics and Varieties of Regionalism in East Asia," *Review of International Studies* 40 (3), 583–606.

Chung, Chien-peng (2013), "China and Japan in "ASEAN Plus" Multilateral Arrangement," *Asian Survey* 53 (5), 801–824.

Clinton, Hilary (2011), "America's Pacific Century," *Foreign Policy*, November, available online at http://www.foreignpolicy.com/articles/2011/10/11/americas_pacific_century.

Cohen, Richard (2014), "Japan's Facts and Fictions," *The Washington Post*, December 9, A19.

Coicaud, Jean-Marc, Michael W. Doyle and Anne-Marie Gardner, eds. (2003), *The Globalization of Human Rights*, Tokyo: United Nations University Press.

Curtis, Gerald L. (1988), *The Japanese Way of Politics*, New York: Columbia University Press.

Curtis, Gerald L. (1999), *The Logic of Japanese Politics: Leaders, Institutions, and the Limits of Change*, New York: Columbia University Press.

Daly, Erin and Jeremy Sarkin (2006), *Reconciliation in Divided Societies: Finding Common Ground*, Philadelphia: University of Pennsylvania Press.

De Greiff, Pablo, ed. (2006), *The Handbook of Reparations*, New York: Oxford University Press.

Delamotte, Guibourg (2011), "China and the United States as Alternatives', in the Diplomacy of the Democratic Party of Japan," in Bert Edström, ed., *Japan's Foreign Policy in Transition: The Way Forward for Japan as an International Actor in a World in Flux*, Stockholm: Institute for Security & Development Policy, 2011, 21–31.

Deng, Yong (2008), *China's Struggle for Status: The Realignment of International Relations*, New York: Cambridge University Press.

Diamond, Jared (1999), *Guns, Germs, and Steel: The Fates of Human Societies*, New York: W.W. Norton.

Dittmer, Lowell and Samuel S. Kim, eds. (1993), *China's Quest for National Identity*, Ithaca, NY: Cornell University Press.

Doi, Ayako (2008), "In Japan, the Picture Isn't Quite So Bright," *Washington Post*, November 16, B3.

Dower, John W. (1986), *War without Mercy: Race and Power in the Pacific War*, New York: Pantheon Books.

Du, Lan (2011), "Meiguo Litui Taipingyang Huoban Guanxi Zhanlue Lunxi" [Analyzing America's Strategy for Pushing the Trans-Pacific Partnership Agreement], *Guoji Wenti Yanjiu* [*Journal of International Studies*] 1, 45–51.

Dueck, Colin (2010), *Hardline: The Republican Party and U.S. Foreign Policy since World War II*, Princeton: Princeton University Press.

Easley, Leif-Eric, Tetsuo Kotani and Aki Mori (2010), "Electing a New Japanese Security Policy? Examining Foreign Policy Visions within the Democratic Party of Japan," *Asia Policy* 9, 45–66.

East Asian Network of Cultural Studies (2001), *Kobayashi Yoshinori Taiwanron Wo Koete* [*Beyond Kobayashi Yoshinori's Taiwan Theory*], Tokyo: Sakuhinsha.

Economic Times (2014), "China's Rare Earth Export Jumps by 31% after WTO Ruling," September 8, available online at http://articles.economictimes.indiatimes.com/2014-09-08/news/53691273_1_rare-earths-export-duties-wto-rules.

Economist (2012), "China and Rare Earths: Of Metals and Market Forces," February 4, 75.

Economist (2013a), "Japan's New Cabinet: Back to the Future," January 5, 29.

Economist (2013b), "Japanese Foreign Policy: Down-turn Abe," January 5, 8.

Els, Frik (2014), "China's rare earth industry will look very different in 5 months," Mining.com, August 8, available online at http://www.mining.com/chinas-rare-earth-industry-will-look-very-different-at-the-end-of-the-year-53315/.

Ensign, Margee (1992), *Doing Good or Doing Well? Japan's Foreign Aid Program*, New York: Columbia University Press.

Feng, Jian (2008), "Guoji Bijiao Kuangjia Zhong De Riben ODA Quanqiu Zhanlue Fenxi" [Japan's Global ODA Strategy: An International Comparative Analysis], *Shijie Jingji Yu Zhengzhi* [*World Economics and Politics*] 6, 50–58.

Ferencz, Benjamin B. (2002), *Less Than Slaves: Jewish Forced Labor and the Quest for Compensation*, Bloomington: Indiana University Press.

Fogel, Joshua A. (2009), *Articulating the Sinosphere: Sino-Japanese Relations in Space and Time*, Cambridge, Mass.: Harvard University Press.

Frieden, Jeffry and Lisa L. Martin (2002), "International Political Economy: Global and Domestic Interactions," in Ira Katznelson and Helen Milner, eds., *Political Science: The State of the Discipline*, New York: W.W. Norton, 118–146.

Frost, Ellen L. (2014), "Rival Regionalisms and Regional Order: A Slow Crisis of Legitimacy," *NBR Special Report* #48, December, 1–24.

Fujiwara, Daisuke (2008), *Chūgoku Shinshikō Genekitokuhain Ga Mitaminjitsu No Chūgoku Senhappyaknichi* [*New Thinking about China: Real China Seen by Active Correspondent in 1,800 days*], Tokyo: Nippon kyōhōsha.

Fukuda, Madoka (2012), "Nicchu kōkū kyōtei kōshoō" [The Japan–China aviation agreement negotiation], in Takahara Akio and Hattori Ryuji, eds., *Nicchu kankeishi 1972–2012; 1: seiji.* [*A History of Japan–China Relations, 1972–2012.* Vol. 1], Tokyo: University of Tokyo Press, 71–98.

Fukui, Haruhiro (1977), "Policy-Making in the Japanese Foreign Ministry," in Robert A. Scalapino, ed., *The Foreign Policy of Modern Japan,* Berkeley: University of California Press, 3–36.

Fukushima, Glen S. (2012), "Japan's Role in America's Asia Pivot," *The Washington Post,* December 21, A27.

Funabashi, Yoichi (1999), *Alliance Adrift,* New York: Council on Foreign Relations Press.

Furusawa, Tadahiko (2001), "The Chinese and the Sea," Defense Research Center (DRC) (Japan), *DRC Annual Report 2001,* available online at http://www.drc-jpn.org/AR-5E/furusawa_t-e.htm (accessed April 17, 2005).

Furusawa, Tadahiko (2004), "Nihon no kokueiki to Taiwan" [Japan's national interest and Taiwan], Defense Research Center (DRC) (Japan), *DRC Annual Report 2004,* October 15, available online at http://www.drc-jpn.org/AR-8/furusawa-04j.htm (accessed April 18, 2005).

Gao, Lan (2011), "Riben Teipipi Zhanlue De Fazhan Tezheng Jiqi Yingxiang" [The Development of Japan's Tpp Strategy and its Impact], *Shijie Jingji Yanjiu* [*World Economy Study*] 6, 75–80.

Garnaut, Ross and Peter Drysdale, eds. (1994), *Asia Pacific Regionalism: Readings in International Economic Relations,* Pymble, Australia: HarperEducational.

Genba, Koichiro (2010), "Free Trade Agreements: An Urgent Part of Japan's Agenda," JapanEchoWeb 4, available online at http://www.japanechoweb.jp/diplomacy-politics/jew0414 (accessed February 28, 2012).

Genron NPO (2012), June 20, available online at http://www.genron-npo.net/world/genre/cat119/2012-a.html (accessed August 8, 2012).

Genron NPO (2014a), *Nicchu Kyōdō Yoron Chōsa Nicchu Hikaku Shiryō* [*Japan–China Joint Survey Research: Japan–China Comparative Materials*], available online at http://www.genron-npo.net/pdf/2014forum_d.pdf (accessed January 2, 2015).

Genron NPO (2014b), September 9, available online at http://www.genron-npo.net/pdf/2014forum.pdf (accessed December 20, 2014).

Gholz, Eugene (2014), "Rare Earth Elements and National Security," Council on Foreign Relations, October.

Gomi, Matsuyoshi (2004), "Chūgoku No Kaiyō Shishutsu" [The Japanese maritime expansion], Defense Research Center (DRC) (Japan), *DRC Annual Report 2004*, October 15, available online at http://www.drc-jpn.org/AR-8/gomi-04j.htm (accessed April 18, 2005).

Gresser, Edward (2012), "Does U.S. Pacific Policy Need a Trade Policy?" NBR, Engaging Asia 2012, March.

Harris, Stuart and Andrew Mack. eds. (1997), *Asia-Pacific Security: The Economics-Politics Nexus*, Sydney: Allen & Unwin.

Harris, Tobias (2010), "How Will the DPJ Change Japan?" *Naval War College Review* 63 (1), 77–96.

Hasegawa, Keitarō and Nakajima Mineo (2001), *Iatsu No Chūgoku Nihon No Hikutsu* [*China's Overreaction and Japan's Humility*], Tokyo: Bijinesusha.

Hasegawa, Yukihiro (2012) "Teipipi Sanka Sanseiha Kara No Keikoku" [Warning from Supporters for Joining TPP], *Voice*, January, 146–152.

Hasegawa, Junichi (2010), "International Debt Management: Japan's Policy toward Africa," in Howard P. Lehman, ed., *Japan and Africa: Globalization and Foreign Aid in the 21st Century*, New York: Routledge, 71–92.

Hasegawa, Tsuyoshi and Kazuhiko Togo, eds. (2008), *East Asia's Haunted Present: Historical Memories and the Resurgence of Nationalism*, Westport, Conn.: Praeger.

He, Yinan (2009), *The Search for Reconciliation: Sino-Japanese and German-Polish Relations since World War II*, New York: Cambridge University Press.

Hellmann, Donald C. (1969), *Japanese Domestic Politics and Foreign Policy*, Berkeley: University of California Press.

Higgott, Richard (2004a), "After Neoliberal Globalization: The 'Securitization' of U.S. Foreign Economic Policy in East Asia," *Critical Asian Studies* 36 (3), 425–444.

Higgott, Richard (2004b), "US Foreign Economic Policy and the Securitisation of Globalisation," *International Politics* 41 (2), 147–175.

Higgott, Richard and Richard Stubbs (1995), "Competing Conceptions of Economic Regionalism: APEC versus EAEC in the Asia Pacific," *Review of International Political Economy* 2 (3), 516–535.

Hiramatsu, Shigeo (1991), *Yomigaeru Chūgoku Kaigun* [*Awakening Chinese navy*], Tokyo: Keisōshobō.

Hiramatsu, Shigeo (1993), *Chūgoku No Kaiyō Senryaku* [*China's Maritime Strategy*], Tokyo: Keisōshobō.

Hiromiya, Yoshinobu and Aoki Fumitaka, (2011), *Teipipi Ga Nihon Wo Kowasu* [*TPP Destroys Japan*], Tokyo: Furosha.

Holmes, Linda Goetz (2001), *Unjust Enrichment: How Japan's Companies Built Postwar Fortunes Using American POWs*, Mechanicsburg, Penn.: Stackpole Books.

Hosoya, Yuichi (2012), "Japan's National Identity in Postwar Diplomacy: The Three Basic Principles," in Gilbert Rozman, ed., *East Asian National Identities: Common Roots and Chinese Exceptionalism*, Washington, DC and Stanford, CA: Woodrow Wilson Center Press and Stanford University Press, 169–195.

Hotta, Eri (2007), *Pan-Asianism and Japan's War, 1931–1945*, New York: Palgrave Macmillan.

Hu, Benliang (2014), "Ma Yingjiu Dui Riben Wehe Yingzhong Dairan" [Why is Ma Ying-jeou both Strong and Weak on Japan?], *Shijie Zhishi* [*World Affairs*] (15), 58–59.

Huang, Meibo and Meng Tingfeng (2011), "Xinshiji Riben De Duiwai Yuanzhu Jiqi Guanli" [Japan's Foreign Aid and its Management in the New Century], *Fazhan yu yuanzhu* [*Development and Aid*] 2, 39–46.

Hufbauer, Gary Clyde, Jeffrey J. Schott, Kimberly Ann Elliott and Barbara Oegg (2008), *Economic Sanctions Reconsidered*, 3rd edn., Washington, DC: Peterson Institute for International Economics.

Hughes, Christopher R. (2008), "Japan in the Politics of Chinese Leadership Legitimacy: Recent Developments in Historical Perspective," *Japan Forum* 20 (2), 245–266.

Huntington, Samuel P. (2004), *Who Are We? The Challenges to America's National Identity*, New York: Simon & Schuster.

Ijiri, Hidenori, ed. (1997), *Chūtai Kiki No Kōzō Taiwan Kaikyō Kuraishishisu No Imisurumono* [*The Framework of the China–Taiwan crisis: The Meaning of the Taiwan Strait Clashes*], Tokyo: Keisōshobō.

Ikenberry, G. John (2006), "Japan's History Problem," *The Washington Post*, August 17, A25.

Inoue, Masaya (2012), "Kokkō seijōka" [Diplomatic normalization], in Takahara Akio and Hattori Ryuji, eds., *Nicchu kankeishi* 1972–2012; 1: seiji. [*A History of Japan–China Relations, 1972–2012. Vol. 1*], Tokyo: University of Tokyo Press, 41–69.

Institute of International Education (2014), "International Students: Leading Places of Origin," available online at http://www.iie.org/Research-and-Publications/Open-Doors/Data/International-Students/Leading-Places-of-Origin (accessed January 9, 2015).

International Monetary Fund (1977), *Direction of Trade Statistics Yearbook*, Washington, DC: International Monetary Fund.

International Monetary Fund (1984), *Direction of Trade Statistics Yearbook*, Washington, DC: International Monetary Fund.

International Monetary Fund (1991), *Direction of Trade Statistics Yearbook*, Washington, DC: International Monetary Fund.

International Monetary Fund (1997), *Direction of Trade Statistics Yearbook*, Washington, DC: International Monetary Fund.

International Monetary Fund (2004), *Direction of Trade Statistics Yearbook*, Washington, DC: International Monetary Fund.

International Monetary Fund (2011), *Direction of Trade Statistics Yearbook*, Washington, DC: International Monetary Fund.

International Monetary Fund (2014), *Direction of Trade Statistics Yearbook*, Washington, DC: International Monetary Fund.

Iriye, Akira (1992), *China and Japan in the Global Setting*, Cambridge: Harvard University Press.

Ishizuka, Isao (2000), "21 Seiki Wagakuni No Anzen Hoshō Kankyō" [The Security Environment of Our Country in the 21st Century], Defense Research Center (DRC) (Japan), *DRC Annual Report 2000.*

Izumi, Tarō (1998), *Nichibeitai Sangoku No Jidai Beichū Reisen No Ajia Shūdan Ampo Taisei* [*The Era of a Japan–U.S.–Taiwan "Trilateral Alliance": The Asian Collective Security System under a U.S.–China Cold War*], Tokyo: Tendensha.

Jacobsen, Gene S. (2004), *We Refused to Die*: *My Time as a Prisoner of War in Bataan and Japan, 1942–1945*, Salt Lake City: The University of Utah Press.

Jakobson, Linda and Dean Knox (2010), *New Foreign Policy Actors in China*, SIPRI Paper 26, September, available online at http://books.sipri.org/product_info?c_product_id=410.

Japan Institute of International Affairs (2012), "The Senkakus: Actions to Keep The Situation Under Control," September 24.

Japan Ministry of Finance, trade statistics, available online at http://www.customs.go.jp/toukei/srch/index.htm?M=23&P=1,,,,,,,,,,5,1,2004, 0,0,0,,,,,,,,,,5,106,105,108,304,,,,,,,,,,,,,20 (accessed January 14, 2015).

Japan Ministry of Foreign Affairs (2013), First and Second China and Mongolia Divisions, "Recent Japan–Taiwan Relations and the Taiwan Situation," July, available online at http://www.mofa.go.jp/region/asia-paci/taiwan/pdfs/japan-taiwan_relations.pdf (accessed January 2, 2015).

Japan Ministry of Foreign Affairs (2014), available online at http://www. mofa.go.jp/mofaj/gaiko/oda/about/oda/oda_jisseki.html (accessed December 24, 2014).

Japan Prime Minister's Cabinet Office (2010), "Nihon No Keizai Renkei No Shinchoku" [Progress in Japan's Economic Cooperation], October 27, available online at http://www.mofa.go.jp/mofaj/gaiko/fta/pdfs/ siryou20101106.pdf (accessed February 11, 2012).

Japan Prime Minister's Cabinet Office (2014), "Gaikō Ni Kansuru Yoron Chōsa" [Opinion Polls on Diplomacy], available online at http://survey. gov-online.go.jp/h26/h26-gaiko/index.html (accessed December 29, 2014).

Japan Times (2006), "Koizumi U.S. Can't Stop Yasukuni Visits," January 22, available online at http://www.japantimes.co.jp/cgi-bin/getarticle. pl5?nn20060122a4.htm (accessed August 8, 2009).

Japan Times (2010a), "China, Japan Stick to Negative Views," August 16, 2.

Japan Times (2010b), "Risks of a More Active Defense," September 6, 14.

Japan Times (2010c), "China Edges Japan as No. 2 Economy," August 17, 1.

Japan Times (2010d), "Business Leaders Urge China to Cancel Rare-earth Export Curbs," September 9, 7.

Japan Times (2011a), "ODA Funds Redirected," June 29, 2.

Japan Times (2011b), "TPP Jitters Spur Protest Statements," January 17, 1.

Japan Times (2011c), "U.S. Warns Japan that TPP Goals Exceed Those in Past Trade Pacts," January 16, 2.

Japan Times (2011d), "Farm Co-ops Plan Petition Drive against TPP," October 25, 7.

Japan Times (2011e), "Poll Finds Predictable Split on TPP Dialogue," November 7, 1.

Japan Times (2011f), "Survey: Only Six Governors Favor Joining TPP Trade Talks," October 30, 2.

Japan Times (2012a), "Ad in Wall Street Journal Seeks U.S. Support for Senkaku Purchase Plan," July 29, 1.

Japan Times (2012b), "California City Proclaims Korean Comfort Women Day," August 4, 3.

Japan Times (2012c), "Patrol Boat for Yemen in Works via Eased Arms Ban," March 13, 1.

Japan Times (2012d), "Cabinet Polling at New Record Low of 26%," April 30, 1.

Japan Times (2012e), "U.S. to Push regardless of TPP talks," March 9, 7.

Japan Times (2014), "ODA for Foreign Armies Mulled," May 24.

Jinghua Shibao [Beijing China Times] (2006), "Minjian Duiri Susong Huojuan Erbailiushiwuwanyuan Guanfangjigou Biaoshizhichi" [Private Lawsuits Received Donations worth 2.56 Million Yuan, Official Agencies Expressed Support], February 26, available online at http://news.sina.com.cn/c/2006-02-26/02078302274s.shtml.

Kabashima, Ikuo and Gill Steel (2007), "The Koizumi Revolution," *PS: Political Science & Politics* 40 (1), 79–84.

Kameda, Masaaki (2015), "Japan Adopts New Aid Policy, May Aid Foreign Militaries," February 10, available online at http://http://www.japantimes.co.jp/news/2015/02/10/national/politics-diplomacy/japan-adopts-new-aid-policy-may-aid-foreign-militaries/#.VNoRzCjOCwA (accessed February 10, 2015).

Kang, David C. (2010), *East Asia before the West: Five Centuries of Trade and Tribute*, New York: Columbia University Press.

Katzenstein, Peter J. and Takahi Shiraishi, eds. (1997), *Network Power: Japan and Asia*, Ithaca: Cornell University Press.

Kawashima, Kōzō (1990), *Gekido suru To Shohei go no Chugoku* [*Turbulent China after Deng Xiaoping*], Tokyo: Daiichi kikaku shuppan.

Kayahara, Ikeo, ed. (2008), *Chūgoku No Gunjiryoku Nisenniji Yūnen No Shōrai Yotsuku* [*China's Military Power: Forecasting the Year 2020*], Tokyo: Tsūtsūsha.

Kea, Puy (2011), "Japan in Cambodia Has China Aid Rival," *Japan Times*, February 9, 3.

Keck, Margaret E. and Kathryn Sikkink (1998), *Activists beyond Borders: Advocacy Networks in International Politics*, Ithaca: Cornell University Press.

Kelly, Robert E. (2012), "A 'Confucian Long Peace' in Pre-Western East Asia?" *European Journal of International Relations* 18 (3), 407–430.

Keohane, Robert O. and Joseph S. Nye, Jr. (1977), *Power and Interdependence*, Boston: Little, Brown.

Kin, Birei and Shu Eimei (2001), *Nihon yo Taiwan yo* [*Japan, Taiwan*], Tokyo: Fusosha.

Kirby, William C. (1994), "Traditions of Centrality, Authority, and Management in Modern China's Foreign Relations," in Thomas W. Robinson and David Shambaugh, eds., *Chinese Foreign Policy: Theory and Practice*, Oxford: Clarendon Press, 13–29.

Kishi, Toshihiko, ed. (2009), *Mosakusuru Kindai Nicchū Kankai Taiwa To Kyōzun No Jidai* [*Modern Japan–China Relations: The Era of Dialogue and Competition*], Tokyo: Tōkyō daigaku shuppankai.

Kissinger, Henry (2011), *On China*, New York: Penguin.

Kō, Bunyū (2001), *Taiwan Wa Nihonjin Ga Tsukutta* [*Taiwan made by Japanese*], Tokyo: Tokuma shoten.

Kobayashi, Yoshinori (2000), *Taiwanron* [*Theory of Taiwan*], Tokyo: Shōgakukan.

Kobayashi, Yoshinori (2012), *Hantipipiron* [*Anti-TPP view*], Tokyo: Gentosha.

Kojima, Kazuko (2012), "Kōkaryō mondai" [The Kōkaryō Hostel issue], in Takahara Akio and Hattori Ryuji, eds., *Nicchu Kankeishi* 1972–2012; 1: seiji. [*A History of Japan–China Relations, 1972–2012. Vol. 1*], Tokyo: University of Tokyo Press, 197–227.

Kojima, Tomoyuki (1997), *Chūgoku No Yukue* [*China's Whereabouts*], Tokyo: Jiji tsūshinsha.

Kokubun, Ryōsei (2001), "Reisen Shūketsugo No Nitchū Kankei 72 Taisei No Tenkan" [Japan–China Relations after the End of the Cold war: Transformation of the 1972 System], *Kokusai Mondai*, January, 42–56.

Kokusai kaihatsu jannaru [*International development journal*] (2012), "2012 Nendo ODA Yosan Shohō" [Detailed ODA Budget for 2012], May, 13–24.

Kokusai kaihatsu jannaru Editorial Office (2012), "Enshakkan Juchū Toppu Wa Chūgokusei" [The Chinese are Top Receivers of Yen Loan Orders], *Kokusai Kaihatsu Jannaru*, May, 8–9.

Kratoska, Paul H., ed. (2005), *Asian Labor in the Wartime Japanese Empire: Unknown Histories*, Armonk, NY: M.E. Sharpe.

Krauss, Ellis S. and Robert J. Pekkanen (2011), *The Rise and Fall of Japan's LDP: Political Party Organizations as Historical Institutions*, Ithaca: Cornell University Press.

Kyodo News Agency (2014), "55% Do not Support Abe's Security Policies, Poll Shows," December 16, available online at http://www.japantimes.co.jp/news/2014/12/16/national/politics-diplomacy/55-do-not-support-abes-security-policies-poll-shows/#.VJB8U03wtdg (accessed December 16, 2014).

Lai, Yew Meng (2013), *Nationalism and Power Politics in Japan's Relations with China: A Neoclassical Realist Interpretation*, London: Routledge, 2013.

Lam, Peng Er, ed. (2006), *Japan's Relations with China: Facing a Rising Power*, London: Routledge.

Laskai, Lorand C. (2014), "History and the Possibility of Taiwan–Japan Relations," *The Diplomat*, September 12, available online at http://thediplomat.com/2014/09/history-and-the-possibility-of-taiwan-japan-relations/802 (accessed May 8, 2015).

Lee, Chae-Jin (1984), *China and Japan: New Economic Diplomacy*, Stanford, Calif.: Hoover Institution Press.

Lee, Seungjoo (2012), "The Economy-Security Nexus in East Asian FTAs," in Vinod K. Aggarwal and Kristi Govella, eds., *Linking Trade and Security: Evolving Institutions and Strategies in Asia, Europe and the United States*, New York: Springer, 135–156.

Li, Xiushi (2010), *Riben Xinbaoshouzhuyi Zhanlue Yanjiu* [*Strategic Study of Japan's New Conservatism*], Beijing: Shishi chubanshe.

Liao, Peiling (2011), "Qianxi Riben Dui Yuenan De Zhengfu Kaifa Yuanzhu" [Japan's ODA to Vietnam], *Dongnanya Zongheng* [*Around Southeast Asia*], September, 17–21.

Lieberthal, Kenneth G. and Wang Jisi (2012), *Addressing U.S.–China Strategic Distrust*, Washington, DC: John L. Thornton China Center at Brookings Institution.

Lin, Xiaoguang and Sun Hui (2005), "Riben Zhengfu Duihua Kaifa Yuanzhu Yu Zhongri Guanxi" [Japan's ODA and Sino-Japanese Relations], *Xiandai Riben Jingji* [*Contemporary Economy of Japan*] 3, 7–12.

Lincoln, Edward J. (2004), *East Asian Economic Regionalism*, Washington, DC: Brookings Institution Press.

Liu, Changli (2011), "Riben Canjia Teipipi Tanpan De Dongyin Zhiyue Yinsu Yu Zhengce Cuoshi [The Reasons, Constraints and Policy Measures for Japan's Participating in TPP Negotiations], *Riben Xuekan* [*Japanese Studies*] 1, 65–78.

Liu, Jiangyong (2000), *Panghuang Zhong De Riben* [*Japan in Hesitation*], Tianjin: Tianjin Renmin Chubanshe.

Ma, Damien (2012), "China Digs It: How Beijing Cornered the Rare Earths Market," *Foreign Affairs*, April 25, available online at http://www.foreign affairs.com/articles/137602/damien-ma/china-digs-it?cid=nlc-this_week_on_foreignaffairs_co-042612-china_digs_it_3-042612 (accessed May 5, 2012).

MacArthur, Brian (2005), *Surviving the Sword: Prisoners of the Japanese in the Far East, 1942–45*, New York: Random House.

Maeda, Hiroko (2009), "Chūgoku No Taigai Enjo" [China's Foreign Aid], *PHP Policy Review* 3 (13), 6–7.

Manicom, James (2014), *Bridging Troubled Waters: China, Japan, and Maritime Order in the East China Sea*, Washington, DC: Georgetown University Press.

Martin, Alex (2011), "1953 Records on Handling U.S. Forces Released," *Japan Times*, August 27, 2.

Martin, Alex and Eric Johnston (2011), "Noda Po-U.S. but Past Remarks May Haunt Asia Ties," *Japan Times*, August 30, 2.

Matsubara, Hiroshi (2012), "Tokyo Governor Ishihara Calls out his Enemies at FCCJ," *The Asahi shimbun*, May 29.

Mitani, Hiroshi (2006), *Meiji Ishin Wo Kangaeru* [*Thoughts about Meiji Restoration*], New York: Yushisha.

Mitani, Hiromi and Kimu Teichan, eds. (2007), *Higashi Ajia Rekishi Taiwa Kokkyō to Sedai O Koete* [*East Asia Historical Dialogue: Beyond Borders and Generations*], Tokyo: Tokyo daigaku shuppankai.

Mizutani, Naoko (2006), *Hannichi Izen Chūgoku Tainichi Kōsakusha Tachi No Kaisō* [*Before "anti-Japan": Memoirs of China's officials dealing with Japan*], Tokyo: Bungei shunjū.

Mochizuki, Mike M. (2007), "Dealing with a Rising China," in Thomas U. Berger, Mike M. Mochizuki and Jitsuo Tsuchiyama, eds., *Japan in International Politics: The Foreign Policies of an Adaptive State*, Boulder, CO: Lynne Rienner, 229–255.

Moriki, Akira (2009), *Nichibei Dōji Hasan Chūgoku Haken Ni Yoru Otsuroshii Jidaiga Yatteguru* [*Simultaneous Bankruptcy for Japan and America: The Scary Era of Chinese Hegemony is Coming*], Tokyo: Daiyamondo.

Munakata, Naoko (2006), *Transforming East Asia: The Evolution of Regional Economic Integration*, Washington, DC: Brookings Institution and Research Institute of Economy, Trade and Industry.

Mutsu, Munemitsu (1982), *Kenkenroku* [*A Diplomatic Record of the Sino-Japanese War, 1894–1895*], translated by Gordon Mark Berger, ed., Princeton, NJ: Princeton University Press.

Najita, Tetsuo (1974), *Japan: The Intellectual Foundations of Modern Japanese Politics*, Chicago: University of Chicago Press.

Nakai, Yoshifumi (2000), "*Nitchū kankei*" [*Japan–China relations*], in Takagi Sciichirō, ed., *Datsu Reisenki No Chūgoku Gaikō to Ajia Taiheiyō* [*Chinese Foreign Policy and Asia Pacific in the post-Cold War Period*], Tokyo: Japan Institute of International Affairs, 105–133.

Nakajima, Mineo and Komori Yoshihisa (2004), *Chūgoku Bōhatsu* [*China's Accidental Gun Discharge*], Tokyo: Bijinesusha.

Nakamura, Katsunori (1998), *Unmei Kyōdōtai to Shite No Nichi-Bei Soshite Taiwan: Nijūisseiki No Kokka Senryaku* [*Japan–U.S. and Taiwan as a Community of Destiny: A State Strategy for the 21ˢᵗ Century*], Tokyo: Tendensha.

Nakamura, Katsunori, Yō Gōgi and Akino Kazuo (2003), *Nichibei Dōmei to Taiwan* [*The Japan–U.S. Alliance and Taiwan*], Tokyo: Waseda shuppan.

Nakamura, David (2014a), "Democrats Raise their Trade-Pact Concerns," *The Washington Post*, December 18, A6.

Nakamura, David (2014b), "Obama to Seek GOP's Help: Prepares Push for Free-Trade Pact," *The Washington Post*, December 27, A1.

Nakanishi, Terumasa (2009), *Nippon No Jiryoku* [*Japan's Strength*], Tokyo: Kairyūsha.

Nakano, Takeshi (2011), *Teipipi Bōkokuron* [*TPP Ends the Country*], Tokyo: Shueisha.

Nakano, Koichi (1998), "Nationalism and Localism in Japan's Political Debate of the 1990s," *Pacific Review* 11 (4), 505–524.

Niwa, Uichirō (2012), "Nicchū No Shōtotsu Wa Shintai Wo Hatte Soshi Suru" [Stop Japan–China Collision With Own Body], *Voice*, March, 44–51.

Noda, Yoshihiko (2009), *Minshu No Teki* [*Democracy's Enemy*], Tokyo: Shinchosha.

Odum, Eugene P. (1997), *Ecology: A Bridge between Science and Society*, 3rd edn., Sunderland, Mass.: Sinauer Associates.

Ogata, Sadako (1988), *Normalization with China: A Comparative Study of U.S. and Japanese Processes*, Berkeley: Institute of East Asian Studies, University of California.

Okada, Takashi (2003), *Chūgoku to Taiwan: Tairitsu to Kyōzon No Ryōgan Kankei* [*China and Taiwan: Rivalry and Co-existence*], Tokyo: Kodansha gendai shinsho.

Okazaki, Hisahiko and Nishimura Shigeki (2012), "Higashiajia No Jiyū No Toride Taiwan wo Nichibei Kyōryoku De Shishuseyo" ["East Asia's Freedom Fortress": Japan and the U.S. Should Defend Taiwan to the Death], *Voice*, August, 70–77.

Organization for Economic Co-operation and Development (2014a), OECD International Development Statistics online, last updated December 19, available online at http://stats.oecd.org/Index.aspx?datasetcode=TABLE1# (accessed December 29, 2014).

Organization for Economic Co-operation and Development (2014b), "Net official development assistance (ODA): Development aid," September 22, available online at http://stats.oecd.org/qwids (accessed December 30, 2014).

Organization for Economic Co-operation and Development (2014c), "Official Development Assistance — Definition and Coverage," available online at http://www.oecd.org/dac/stats/officialdevelopmentassistance-definitionandcoverage.htm (accessed December 28, 2014).

Orr, Robert M., Jr. (1990), *The Emergence of Japan's Foreign Aid Power*, New York: Columbia University Press.

Paine, S. C. M. (2003), *The Sino-Japanese War of 1894–1895: Perceptions, Power, and Primacy*, New York: Cambridge University Press.

Pan, Min (2006), *1937–1945 Jiangsu Riwei Jiceng Zhengquan Yanjiu* [*Study of the Local Japanese and Puppet Governments in Jiangsu 1937–1945*], Shanghai: Shanghai renmin chubanshe.

Peattie, Mark R. (1975), *Ishiwara Kanji and Japan's Confrontation with the West*, Princeton, NJ: Princeton University Press.

Pempel, T.J. (2010), "Soft Balancing, Hedging, and Institutional Darwinism: The Economic-Security Nexus and East Asian Regionalism," *Journal of East Asian Studies* 10, 209–238.

Pempel, T.J., ed. (2005), *Remapping East Asia: The Construction of a Region*, Ithaca: Cornell University Press.

Perdue, Peter C. (2005), *China Marches West: The Qing Conquest of Central Eurasia*, Cambridge, Mass.: Harvard University Press.

Pew Research Center (2012), The Pew Forum on Religion & Public Life, "A Report on the Size and Distribution of the World's Major Religious Groups as of 2010," December 18, available online at http://www.pewforum.org/global-religious-landscape-exec.aspx (accessed December 24, 2012).

Pyle, Kenneth B. (2007), *Japan Rising: The Resurgence of Japanese Power and Purpose*, New York: Public Affairs.

Qin, Julia Y. (2014), "Judicial Authority in WTO Law: A Commentary on the Appellate Body's Decision in China-Rare earths," *Chinese Journal of Law* 13 (4), 639–651.

Rapkin, David P. (2001), "The United States, Japan, and the Power to Block: The APEC and AMF Cases," *The Pacific Review* 14 (3), 373–410.

Ravenhill, John (2000), "APEC Adrift: Implications for Economic Regionalism in Asia and the Pacific," *The Pacific Review* 13 (2), 319–333.

Ravenhill, John (2009), "East Asian Regionalism. Much Ado about Nothing?" *Review of International Studies* 35, 215–235.

Reischauer, Edwin O. (1977), "Foreword," in Robert A. Scalapino, ed., *The Foreign Policy of Modern Japan*, Berkeley: University of California Press, xi–xix.

Remembrance and Future Fund (2007), available online at http://www.stiftung-evz.de/eng/payments_to_former_forced_labourers/ (accessed November 30, 2007).

Rix, Alan (1980), *Japan's Economic Aid: Policy-Making and Politics*, New York: St. Martin's Press.

Rose, Caroline (2004), *Sino-Japanese Relations: Towards a Future-Oriented Diplomacy*, New York: RoutledgeCurzon.

Rozman, Gilbert (1999), "China's Quest for Great Power Identity," *Orbis* 43 (3), 383–402.

Rozman, Gilbert (2002), "Japan's Quest for Great Power Identity," *Orbis* 46 (1), 73–91.

Rozman, Gilbert (2004), *Northeast Asia's Stunted Regionalism*, Cambridge: Cambridge University Press.

Rozman, Gilbert (2008), "Internationalism and Asianism in Japanese Strategic Thought from Meiji to Heisei," *Japanese Journal of Political Science* 9 (2), 209–232.

Rozman, Gilbert (2012a), "Introduction," in Gilbert Rozman, ed., *East Asian National Identities: Common Roots and Chinese Exceptionalism*, Stanford: Woodrow Wilson Center Press and Stanford University Press, 1–16.

Rozman, Gilbert (2012b), "Japanese National Identity: A Six-Dimensional Analysis," in Gilbert Rozman, ed., *East Asian National Identities: Common Roots and Chinese Exceptionalism*, Washington, DC and Stanford, CA: Woodrow Wilson Center Press and Stanford University Press, 17–45.

Rozman, Gilbert, ed. (2013), *National Identities and Bilateral Relations: Widening Gaps in East Asia and Chinese Demonization of the United States*, Washington, DC and Stanford, CA: Woodrow Wilson Center Press and Stanford University Press.

Ryū, Ketsu (Liu Jie) and Kawashima Shin, eds. (2009), *Senkyūhyakuyonjūgonen No Rekishi Ninshiki Shūsen O Meguru Nicchuū Taiwa No Kokoromi* [*History of 1945: Discuss the End of War through a Japan–China Dialogue*], Tokyo: Tōkyō daigaku shuppankai.

Ryū, Ketsu (Liu Jie), Mitani Hiromi and Daqing Yang, eds. (2006), *Kokkyō to Sedai O Koeru Rekishi Ninshiki Nicchuū Taiwa No Kokoromi* [*History beyond Border: A Japan–China Dialogue*], Tokyo: Tokyo daigaku shuppankai.

Sakaki, Atsuko (2006), *Obsessions with the Sino-Japanese Polarity in Japanese Literature*, Honolulu: University of Hawaii Press.

Sakakibara, Eisuke (2007), *Keizai No Sekai Seiriyokuzu* [*The World Economic Power Distribution*], Tokyo: Bungei shunjū.

Sakakibara, Eisuke (2012), *Naze Nihon No Seiji Wa Kko Made Daraku Shita No Ka Matsushida Seikeijuku No Taizai* [*Why has Japanese politics degraded to this place? The big crime of matsushida political economy school*], Tokyo: Asahi shimbun shuppan.

Sakuradani, Katsumi (2012), "Amerika No Tainichi Taiajia Seisaku to Teipipi" [America's Policy toward Japan, Asia and TPP], *Keizai* [*Economics*] January, 94–108.

Satō, Seizaburō and Matsuzaki Tetsuhisa (1986), *Jimintō seiken* [*LDP Regime*], Tokyo: Chūō kōronsha.

Scalapino, Robert A. ed. (1977), *The Foreign Policy of Modern Japan*, Berkeley: University of California Press.

Schaller, Michael (1997), *Altered States: The United States and Japan since the Occupation*, New York: Oxford University Press.

Schott, Jeffrey J., ed. (2004), *Free Trade Agreements: U.S. Strategies and Priorities*, Washington, DC: Institute for International Economics.

Shen, Minghui (2010), "Dongya Hezuo Zhong De Meiguo Yinsu" [The U.S. Factor in East Asian Cooperation], *Taipingyang Xuebao* [*Pacific Journal*] 18 (6), 57–63.

Shimomura, Yasutami, Nakagawa Junji and Saitō Atsushi (1999), *ODA Taikō No Seiji Keizaigaku: Unyō To Enjo Rinen* [*The Political Economy of the ODA Charter: Implementation and Aid Philosophy*], Tokyo: Yūhikaku.

Shirk, Susan L. and Christopher Twomey, eds. (1997), *Power and Prosperity: Economics and Security Linkages in the Asia-Pacific*, New Brunswick: Transaction.

Soeya, Yoshihide (1998), *Japan's Economic Diplomacy with China, 1945–1978*, Oxford: Oxford University Press.

Sohn, Yul and Min Gyo Koo (2011), "Securitizing Trade: The Case of the Korea–U.S. Free Trade Agreement," *International Relations of the Asia-Pacific* 11 (3), 433–460.

Solís, Mireya and Shujiro Urata (2007), "Japan's New Foreign Economic Policy: A Shift toward a Strategic and Activist Model?" *Asian Economic Policy Review* 2 (2), 227–245.

Solís, Mireya, Barbara Stallings and Saori N. Katada, eds. (2009), *Competitive Regionalism: FTA Diffusion in the Pacific Rim*, New York: Palgrave Macmillan.

Song, Shuangshuang (2010), "Riben ODA Diqu Jiegou Bianqian De Zhongguo Yinsu" [The China Factor in Shifting Regional Distribution of Japanese ODA], *Riben Yanjiu* [*Japan Studies*] 3, 69–73.

State Statistical Bureau of China (1983), *Statistical Yearbook of China 1982*, Hong Kong: Economic Information Agency.

Stubbs, Richard (2002), "ASEAN Plus Three: Emerging East Asian Regionalism?" *Asian Survey* 42 (3), 440–455.

Sun, Jing (2012), *Japan and China as Charm Rivals: Soft Power in Regional Diplomacy*, University of Michigan.

Suzuki, Shogo (2007), "The Importance of 'Othering' in China's National Identity: Sino-Japanese Relations as a Stage of Identity Conflicts," *Pacific Review* 20 (1), 23–47.

Suzuki, Shogo (2009), *Civilization and Empire: China and Japan's Encounter with European International Society*, London: Routledge.

Swaine, Michael D. (1995), *China: Domestic Change and Foreign Policy*, Santa Monica, Calif.: RAND Corporation.

Taipei Times (2004), "Chen Claims Taipei Told Japan about Chinese Submarine," November 20, 3.

Taipei Times (2011), "Poll Shows Most Japanese Feel Affection for Taiwan," June 3. *Taiwan News.com* (2004), "Taiwan, Japan Ties Need More Realism," October 5.

Takagi, Seiichirō (2006), "The Taiwan Factor in Japan–China Relations," in Lam Peng Er, ed., *Japan's Relations with China: Facing a Rising Power*, London: Routledge, 107–127.

Takahashi, Motoki (2010a), "The Ambiguous Japan: Aid Experience and the Notion of Self-Help," in Howard P. Lehman, ed., *Japan and Africa: Globalization and Foreign Aid in the 21st Century*, New York: Routledge, 39–70.

Takahashi, Motoki (2010b), "Japan and the Poverty Reduction Aid Regime: Challenges and Opportunities in Assistance for Africa," in Howard P. Lehman, ed., *Japan and Africa: Globalization and Foreign Aid in the 21st Century*, New York: Routledge, 117–148.

Tanaka, Hiroshi and Matsuzawa Tessei, eds. (1995), *Chūgokujin Kyōsei Renkō Shiryō:Gaimushō Hōkokusho Zen Gobunsatsu Hoka [Materials of Chinese Forced Labor: Five volumes of the Foreign Ministry Report]*, Tokyo: Gendai Shokan.

Tanaka, Miya (2011), "Pitching TPP a Tough Nut to Crack," *Japan Times*, March 11, 3.

Tanaka, Stefan (1993), *Japan's Orient: Rendering Pasts into History*, Berkeley: University of California Press.

Task Force on Foreign Relations for the Prime Minister (2002), *21 Seiki Nihon Gaiko No Kihon Senryaku—Aratana Jidai, Aratana Bijon, Aratana Gaiko [Basic Strategies for Japan's Foreign Policy in the 21st Century: New era, New vision, New diplomacy]*, November 28.

Teow, See Heng (1999), *Japan's Cultural Policy toward China, 1918–1931*, Cambridge: Harvard University Asia Center, Harvard University Press.

Terada, Takashi (2003), "Constructing an 'East Asian' Concept and Growing Regional Identity: From EAEC to ASEAN+3," *The Pacific Review* 16 (2), 251–277.

Terada, Takashi (2010), "The Origins of ASEAN+6 and Japan's Initiatives: China's Rise and the Agent-Structure Analysis," *The Pacific Review* 23 (1), 71–92.

Thayer, Nathaniel B. (1969), *How the Conservatives Rule Japan*, Princeton: Princeton University Press.

Thompson, John N. (1982), *Interaction and Coevolution*, New York: Wiley.

Thompson, John N. (2005), *The Geographic Mosaic of Coevolution*, Chicago: University of Chicago Press.

Thompson, John N. (2013), *Relentless Evolution*, Chicago: University of Chicago Press.

Ting, Ming Hwa and John Seaman (2013), "Rare Earths: Future Elements of Conflict in Asia?" *Asian Studies Review* 37 (2), 234–252.

Togo, Kazuhiko (2012), "Japanese National Identity: Evolution and Prospects," in Gilbert Rozman, ed., *East Asian National Identities: Common Roots and Chinese Exceptionalism*, Washington, DC and Stanford, CA: Woodrow Wilson Center Press and Stanford University Press, 147–168.

Uchida, Tatsuru (2009), *Nihon Henkyōron* [*A Frontier Theory of Japan*], Tokyo: Shichosha.

Underwood, William (2006), "The Japanese Court, Mitsubishi and Corporate Resistance to Chinese Forced Labor Redress," *Japan Focus*, March 29, available online at http:www.japanfocus.org/products/topdf/1636 (accessed December 7, 2007).

Underwood, William and Kang Jian (2007), "Japan's Top Court Poised to Kill Lawsuits by Chinese War Victims," *Japan Focus*, March 2, available online at http:www.japanfocus.org/products/topdf/2369 (accessed December 1, 2007).

Vogel, Ezra F., Yuan Ming and Tanaka Akihiko, eds. (2002), *The Golden Age of the U.S.–China–Japan Triangle, 1972–1989*, Cambridge, MA: Harvard University Asia Center.

Wakabayashi, Masahiro (1992), *Taiwan: Bunretsu Kokka to Minshuka* [*Taiwan: Democratization in a Divided Country*], Tokyo: Tokyo daigaku shuppankai.

Wakabayashi, Masahiro (2000), "'Taiwan mondai' no atarashii naijitsu [The new content of the "Taiwan issue"]," in Takagi Seiichiro, ed., *Datsu Reisenki No Chūgoku Gaikō to Ajia Taiheiyō* [*Chinese Foreign Policy and Asia Pacific in the Post-Cold War Period*], Tokyo: Japan Institute of International Affairs, 297–317.

Wan, Ming (2001a), *Human Rights in Chinese Foreign Relations: Defining and Defending National Interests*, Philadelphia: University of Pennsylvania Press.

Wan, Ming (2001b), *Japan between Asia and the West: Economic Power and Strategic Balance*, Armonk, NY: M.E. Sharpe.

Wan, Ming (2003), "Economic Interdependence and Economic Cooperation: Mitigating Conflict and Transforming Security Order in the Asia-Pacific," in Muthiah Alagappa, ed., *Asian Security Order: Instrumental and Normative Features*, Stanford: Stanford University Press, 280–310.

Wan, Ming (2006), *Sino-Japanese Relations: Interaction, Logic and transformation*, Washington, DC and Stanford: Woodrow Wilson Center Press and Stanford University Press.

Wan, Ming (2007), "Japanese Strategic Thinking toward Taiwan," in Gilbert Rozman, Kazuhiko Togo and Joseph P. Ferguson, eds., *Japanese Strategic Thinking toward Asia*, New York: Palgrave Macmillan, 159–181.

Wan, Ming (2010), "The Great Recession and China's Policy toward Asian Regionalism," *Asian Survey* 50 (3), 520–538.

Wan, Ming (2011), "The Domestic Political Economy of China's Preferential Trade Agreements," in Vinod K. Aggarwal and Seungjoo Lee, eds., *Trade Policy in the Asia-Pacific: The Role of Ideas, Interests, and Domestic Institutions*, New York: Springer, 29–48.

Wan, Ming (2013a), "Xi Jinping's 'China Dream': Same Bed, Different Dreams?" *The Asan Forum* 1 (1), available online at http://www.theasan-forum.org/xi-jinpings-china-dream-same-bed-different-dreams/ (accessed August 2, 2013).

Wan, Ming (2013b), "Back to Nature: An Achievement-based structural Assessment of the Modern International System," *The Chinese Journal of International Politics* 6 (4), 401–428.

Wan, Ming (2014), *The China Model and Global Political Economy: Comparison, Impact, and Interaction*, New York: Routledge.

Wan, Ming (2015), "Rejoinder to Bill Callahan's "China Dream" Essay," *The Asan Forum*, January, available online at http:// http://www.theasanforum.org/what-can-the-china-dream-do-in-the-prc/?t_page=1#rejoinder (accessed January 17, 2015).

Wang, Shihua (2008), *Riwei Tongzhi Shiqi De Huabei Nongcun* [*North China Rural Areas under the Reign of Japan and the Puppet Regime*], Beijing: Shehui kexue wenxian chubanshe.

Washington Post (2006), "Japan's Future — and Past," September 25, A20.

Watanabe, Shōichi and Tamogami Toshio (2008), *Nippon Wa Shinryaku Kokka Dewanai!* [*Japan is Not an Aggressor!*], Tokyo: Kairūsha.

Watanabe, Toshio and Miwara Shūmon (2009), *Nippon No Katsuro* [*Japan's Way Out*], Tokyo: Karyūsha.

Watanabe, Yurizumi (2011), *Teipipi Sanka to Iu Ketsudan* [*The Decision to Join TPP*], Tokyo: Wedge.

Wigen, Kären (1999), "Culture, Power and Place: The New Landscapes of East Asian Regionalism," *American Historical Review* 104 (4), 1183–1201.

Wodnik, Bob (2003), *Captured Honor: POW Survival in the Philippines and Japan*, Pullman, Washington: Washington State University.

World Trade Organization (2014), "China — Measures Related to the Exportation of Rare Earths, Tungsten and Molybdenum," August 10, available online at http://www.wto.org/english/tratop_e/dispu_e/cases_e/ds431_e.htm (accessed December 26, 2014).

Wu, Guanghui (2010), *Riben De Zhongguo Xingxiang* [*China's Image in Japan*], Beijing: Renmin chubanshe.

Wu, Xu (2007), *Chinese Cyber Nationalism: Evolution, Characteristics, and Implication*, Lanham, Md.: Lexington Books.

Yachi, Shōtarō (2011a), "Ajia Taiheiyō Chiiki No Kokusai Kōkyōzai Toshite No Teipipi" [TPP as an International Public Good for the Asia Pacific region], November 28, available online at http://nippon.com/ja/currents/d00009/ (accessed February 11, 2012).

Yachi, Shōtarō (2011b), "TPP Sanka Wa Tsuyoi Anbo Keizai He No Bunsuirei [TPP Membership as a Watershed Toward Strong Defense and Economics], *Wedge* 1, available online at http://wedge.ismedia.jp/articles/-/1169 (accessed February 11, 2012).

Yahuda, Michael (2013), *Sino-Japanese Relations after the Cold War: Two Tigers Sharing a Mountain: Two Tigers Sharing a Mountain*, London: Routledge.

Yamaguchi, Noboru (2013), "A Japanese Perspective on U.S. Rebalancing toward the Asia-Pacific Region," *Asia Policy* 15, 7–12.

Yasutomo, Dennis T. (1986), *The Manner of Giving: Strategic Aid and Japanese Foreign Policy*, Lexington, Mass.: Lexington Books.

Yomiuri shimbun War Responsibilities Examining Committee (2009), *Kensho Senso Sekinin* [*Examining War Responsibilities*], vol. 1, Tokyo: Chūōkōronsha.

Yonaba, Jun (2011), *Chūgokuka Suru Nihon* [*Japan's Sinicization*], Tokyo: *Bungei shunjū.*

Yoshida, Akiji (2001), "Anzen hoshō senryaku wo kangaeru kihon yōken" [The basic consideration for Japanese security strategy], Defense Research Center (DRC) (Japan), *DRC Annual Report 2001*, available online at http://www.drc-jpn.org/AR-5J/yoshida-j.htm (accessed April 18, 2005).

Yoshida, Akiji (2004), "Senryakuchiseigakuteki ni mita wagakuni no bōei tokuchō" [Our country's defense characteristics from a strategic geopolitical perspective], Defense Research Center (DRC) (Japan), *DRC Annual Report 2004*, October 15, available online at http://www.drc-jpn.org/AR-8/yoshida-04j.htm (accessed April 18, 2005).

Yoshimatsu, Hidetaka and Dennis D. Trinidad (2010), "Development Assistance, Strategic Interests, and the China Factor in Japan's Role in ASEAN Integration," *Japanese Journal of Political Science* 11 (2), 199–219.

Yū, Tatsuun (Hsiung Ta-yun) (1998), *Kindai Chūgoku Kanmin no Nihon Shisatsu* [*Observation of Japan by Chinese Officials and People in Modern Era*], Tokyo: Seibundō.

Zachmann, Urs Matthias (2007), "Blowing Up a Double Portrait in Black and White: The Concept of Asia in the Writings of Fukuzawa Yukichi at Okakura Tenshin," *East Asia Cultures Critique* 15 (2), 345–368.

Zhang, Yun (2014), "Multilateral Means for Bilateral Ends: Japan, Regionalism, and China–Japan–US Trilateral Dynamism," *Pacific Review* 27 (1), 5–25.

Zhou, Hong (2008), "Zhongguo Duiwai Yuanzhu Yu Gaige Kaifang" [China's Foreign Aid and Opening and Reform], *Shijie Jingji Yu Zhengzhi* [*World Economics and Politics*] 11, 33–43.

Zhu, Jianrong, ed. (2009), *Riben Biantian Minzhudang Zhengquan Dansheng Jinjuli Guancha* [*Change of Heaven in Japan: A Close Observation of the Birth of the Democratic Party of Japan Government*], Beijing: Xinshijie chubanshe.

Index

CPSIA information can be obtained at www.ICGtesting.com
Printed in the USA
BVOW06*0339201015

423145BV00005B/8/P